SUSTAINABLE PRACTICES FOR WASTE MANAGEMENT

SUSTAINABLE PRACTICES FOR WASTE MANAGEMENT

By

Dr. Ashok K. Rathoure
M/s Akone Services
Paschim Vihar Colony
Mohan Road, Lucknow (UP)
(India)

Dr. Shashwat Katiyar
Director, Institute of Bioscience & Biotechnology
In-charge, Department of Biochemistry
Institute of Bioscience & Biotechnology
C.S.J.M. University, Kanpur (India)

Dr. Harish Chandra
Assistant Professor
Department of Microbiology
Gurukula Kangri (Deemed to be University)
Haridwar - 249404 (India)
&

Dr. Rupesh Kumar Luhariya
Assistant Professor
Dept. of Botany, Govt. PG College
Tikamgarh, M.P. (India)

DPH

DISCOVERY PUBLISHING HOUSE PVT. LTD.
INDIA

Published by:
Namit Wasan
DISCOVERY PUBLISHING HOUSE PVT. LTD.
4383/4B, Ansari Road, Darya Ganj
New Delhi-110 002 (India)
Phone : +91-11-23279245; 23253475; 43596065
E-mail : discoverybooksindia@gmail.com
discoverypublishinghouse@gmail.com
namitwasan9@gmail.com
web : www.discoverypublishinggroup.com

***First Edition:* 2021**

ISBN: 978-93-88854-66-5

Sustainable Practices for Waste Management

Printed at:
Infinity Imaging Systems
Delhi

Foreword

Continuous degradation of earth's environment mainly due to industrial pollution is one of the major concerns of many environmental regulators. In addition to this, public attitude towards environmental protection has led governments to control industries disposing high load waste in to the environment. Pollution control standards defined first for ambient air and water and soil quality standards were mostly derived from public health considerations and ecological justifications. Public concern over industrial wastes led the application of more stringent regulations, authorization, and procedures. Based on the effects of pollutants in the environment, pollutants can be classified either as threshold or non-threshold pollutants. Waste generated from industries is nonhomogeneous, with differing characteristics and composition. Similarly, these wastes are multimedia in nature with wastes disposed in all three media namely air, water, and soil. Effect of mixed pollutants of different characteristics can be synergistic and antagonistic depending upon the resultant effects. For example, the combined effects of sulfur dioxide in the air could produce acid rain. On the other hand, it is advantageous to have wastes with two different pH ranges (acidic and alkaline) which could eliminate the neutralization unit completely.

Waste reduction at source entails limiting the amount of waste that is generated, thereby helping to eliminate the production of persistent and harmful wastes, effectively supporting efforts that promote a society that is sustainable. Thus, waste minimization involves a change of societal patterns that relate to production and consumption as well as redesigning products to eliminate the generation of waste. Reuse of waste means any operation by which products or components that are not waste are used again for the same purpose for which they were conceived. There are 7Rs viz. Refuse, Reduce, Repurpose, Reuse, Recycle, Rot, Rethink. Every year, millions of tons of waste are generated from both households and building construction, most of which end up in landfills with a small percentage being recycled. Thus, there is a great need for waste minimization as this will not only have a huge environmental impact but also present substantial economic and social benefits.

Here, in the current book, Dr. Ashok K. Rathoure and his team has done a great job for the same in the area of waste management for sustainable practices. This will be a milestone in the current era where the waste is a major global problem.

Dr. Vishnu D. Rajput

Leading Researcher, Southern Federal University,
Rostov-on-Don, Russia

Preface

Rapid industrialization and urbanization are the major cause of rapid environmental destruction. Use of nature's freely available resources in an uncontrolled manner and throwing of waste into the environment has caused more stress to the assimilative capacity to dilute and disperse the wastes and recover the used natural resources. The depletion of resources has threatened the life of future generations. Increasing numbers of industries and production of various categories of wastes cause major environmental pollution. These problems have forced governments to control the industrial activities of waste discharge directly into natural environments. Formation of effluent and emission standards and regulation for wastes to be discharged into natural bodies of water, air and soil has forced industries to establish waste treatment facilities in their own industrial premises. This was the concept of end-of-pipe treatment, in which the basic production process was the same with addition of waste treatment facilities. The basic concept of the installation of treatment units was to bring down the concentration and load of the effluent within the allowed limits before discharging into natural resources.

Living standards and quality of life in most of the developed countries have increased since the Second World War, due to rapid industrialization and urbanization. This growth and development, however, have involved a nearly thirty-fold increase in use of fossil fuels over the past century and an over fifty-fold increase in industrial production for the same period. Most of the consumption of fossil fuel and production has taken place since 1950. It is estimated that between 1955 to 1988 world industrial output increased approximately six times, the World's population only doubled. The result of rapid industrialization is the rapid depletion of resources, and environmental impacts due to production of enormous waste exceeding assimilation capacity of the environment. At the beginning of this industrialization process, not enough attention was given about the state of the environment; assumptions were made that the nature has the capacity to restore the resources we extract and accept what we throw into it. These wastes have now become pollutants due to their enormous volume and multiple characteristics.

The current scenario where we are reaching to next level of increased population (8 billion) and due to increased demand of supplies the waste generation is so high. Hence, we need to adopt zero waste policy everywhere. In this connection, the current waste minimization practices required to modify and adopt some new techniques for waste management and reduction at source for better environment and future sustainability. Here in this book, we have presented carbon footprint of coal-based power plants; application of environmental biotechnological tools; bioremediation and biodegradation technologies; coal consumption, ash generation and its utilization; e-waste and its management; environment friendly technologies; penalty and incentive mechanisms for coal-based power plants; plastic waste disposal and role of microorganisms; safe use of wastewater in agriculture; solid wastes and their sustainable management practices; agro-residue generation and availability for power sector.

–Dr. Ashok K. Rathoure

Contents

1

An Overview on Carbon Footprint of Coal-based Power Plants and Sustainability

INTRODUCTION

There has been a rapid rise in CO_2 levels in the atmosphere due to anthropogenic activities in the last two centuries. Being a greenhouse gas (GHG), increasing levels of CO_2 are resulting in rise in global temperature. The global average annual concentration of CO_2 in the atmosphere averaged 407.4 ppm in 2018, a substantial increase from pre-industrial levels, when it ranged between 180 and 280 ppm (Anon, 2020a). The world has already witnessed a temperature rise of 0.8°C, which is further set to increase up to 2°C if stringent action to curb GHG emissions is not taken. Global CO_2 emissions stand at 46 Gt, in which the energy sector contributes 36 Gt (78%). Coal is the single biggest contributor to anthropogenic climate change. Coal-based electricity contributes nearly 15 Gt (30%) of global GHG emissions and contributes 41% of GHG emissions from energy-related activities (Mengpin and Johannes, 2020). A major portion of these emissions occur in Asia, where the average plant is only 12 years old and can still look forward to many years of economical feasibility. In 2016, India generated 3.1 Gt of annual CO_2 eq. emissions, which contributed nearly 6.5% to total global GHG emissions. India's annual fuel related CO_2 emission are 2.16 Gt. Coal, being the primary fuel of the Indian economy, contributes 70% to the overall fuel-related CO_2 emissions. Power sector contributes nearly 50% of the sector-wise CO_2 emissions. Coal-based power generation contributes nearly 1.1 Gt, which is about 50% of the total fuel-related emissions.

Requisite for India's energy security More than two-thirds of India's coal consumption happens in coal-based power generation (around 600 million tonnes). Coal-based power generation sector contributes around 50% of India's fuel-related CO_2 emissions. The sector has played a vital role in meeting India's growing energy needs. During the last two decades, India has witnessed a rapid expansion in its coal-based power generation. During the period 2010-2017, India's coal capacity almost doubled from 95 GW in 2010 to 195 GW in 2017. Electricity deficit has also gone down from 7% to 0.8%. Between 2012-2017, coal power's contribution in total installed capacity and total generation have been around 60% and 73% respectively. In 2017, it was 56% and 74% respectively. By 2030, even with rapid increase in renewable energy as per India's INDC under the Paris Agreement, 60% of installed capacity will remain fossil fuel-based, 90% of which will be coal-based and the rest (10%) oil- and gas-based. Installed capacity of coal-based power generation is expected to increase to 266 GW by 2030. It will contribute 32% to the total installed capacity and 50% to electricity generation.

In recent decades, with the rapid expansion in coal-based power generation, coal consumption has increased from 300 million tonnes in 2006-2007 to 600 million tonnes in 2017-2018. Simultaneously, CO_2 emissions related to coal-based power have almost doubled, from 500 million tonnes in 2005 to almost 1,000 million tonnes in 2015. To keep global warming to less than 2°C from pre-industrial levels, countries agreed to INDCs to reduce GHG emissions. India, being the world's third largest emitter of GHGs after China and the US, promised to reduce its GHG emissions intensity by 33-35% by 2030 from 2005 levels (UNFCC, 2020).

India needs to retire around 40-50 GW of its existing capacity by 2030. These units are subcritical with a design efficiency of 35%. When they are replaced by ultra-supercritical plants of 43% efficiency, CO_2 footprints of the sector will be reduced by 14-21%. Renovation and modernization (R&M) and life extension of coal power plants can contribute substantially to reduction in India's overall CO_2 emissions. Under the new policy, the primary focus will be on 500 MW units that are more than 15 years old. Introduction of efficient coal technology will need larger investment and has limited CO_2 reduction scope whereas R&M is cost effective. If old power plants are shifted to biomass co-firing or waste-to-energy plants through life extension projects, significant reduction can be achieved in coal-based power's CO_2 footprints.

CURRENT CO_2 EMISSIONS

Specific CO_2 emissions from a coal power plant are a function of its size, vintage and the technology it employs. These parameters determine the efficiency of operation. Overall, India has a relatively young fleet around

64% (132 GW) of the capacity is less than a decade old. About 73% (150 GW) is less than 15 years old. About 16% (33 GW) is older than 25 years. Of the 33 GW of older capacity units, a major share (~76%) belongs to small units of up to 250 MW and less. Till 2009, all installed capacity was subcritical. In 2010, India installed its first supercritical plant, which has 3-4% higher design efficiency than subcritical plants. In 2012, under the 12th five-year plan, it was decided that 50% of subsequent coal capacity will be supercritical and from the 13 five-year plans onwards, 100% capacity will be supercritical. There was no clear roadmap for ultra-supercritical plants or advanced ultra-supercritical plants. By 2019, less than one-third of India's coal capacity was supercritical, the rest was subcritical. In that year, NTPC installed the first ultra-supercritical plant in Khargone, Madhya Pradesh, with a capacity of 1,320 MW. NTPC is also planning to install ten such plants in the near future.

India's power plant fleet has remained among the least efficient in the world. In 2005, the average net efficiency of the entire fleet was merely 29% (Chikkatur *et al.*, 2007). Chandra *et al.* (2015) highlighted critical issues with India's coal-based power plants and the fleet's poor efficiency was one of the them. As per the International Energy Agency (IEA), there has been a dramatic increase in India's average fleet efficiency, which has risen to 37.2% in 2016, from 32% in 2014 (Qian, 2020). An Ecofys (2018) analysis yielded similar numbers.10 India is now only the third-lowest performer. This change is likely due to significant supercritical capacity being installed and inefficient older plants being retired. Due to higher GHG emissions intensity with respect to the world's best, there is significant scope of improvement in India's coal-based power sector. The country can potentially achieve a 26% reduction in specific emissions from thermal power plants.

POTENTIAL PATHWAYS TO REDUCE CO_2 EMISSIONS

Design efficiency of a thermal power plant—its coal consumption and CO_2 emissions—is mainly determined by the technology it utilizes. The main difference between subcritical, supercritical, ultra-supercritical and advanced ultra-supercritical technologies are the temperature and pressure at which they operate, which affect the heat carrying capacity of the steam and its efficiency can be measured in terms of heat rate. Heat rate is the energy required to produce one unit of electricity and is measured in kcal/kWh. Lower the heat rate, more efficient the plant and lesser will be the coal consumption at and CO_2 emissions from the plant. Estimates of CO_2 emissions for a plant are primarily based on coal consumption. However, if we want to correlate CO_2 emissions directly with a plant's efficiency, about 1% rise in efficiency reduces CO_2 emissions by 2-3%. So, if a subcritical plant of 35% efficiency is replaced by an ultra-supercritical plant of 43% efficiency, the CO_2 footprints will be reduced in the range of 16-24%.

India's average fleet efficiency rose to 37.2% in 2016, from 32% in 2014. The 5 percentage points increase in efficiency means India achieved 10-15% reduction in CO_2 emissions. Under the 12th five-year plan (2012-2017), half of the new capacity planned was supercritical and from 13th plan (2017-2022) onwards, all new capacity was to be supercritical. In 2018, supercritical technology contributed about 26% to India's total capacity. All new planned capacity (660-800 MW) is supercritical. No official roadmap or projection for the coal-power fleet by 2030 is available.

The 2018 National Electricity Plan (NEP) included plans to build 94 GW of new coal-fired capacity (mainly supercritical) between 2017-2018 and 2026-2027. CEA has outlined a large potential investment in new coal plants up to 2030 (105 GW of pithead plants and 44 GW of load-centered plants). In its draft report Optimal Generation Capacity Mix, 2029-2030 the authority has projected that India will have 266 GW coal capacity in 2030, which roughly translates into 100 GW of capacity addition, considering NEP retirement plans. NITI Aayog, in its generation mix projection for 2030-2047, has considered significant contribution from ultra-supercritical technology or IGCC. As per NITI Aayog's clean coal technology (CCT) projections for 2032, the share of supercritical, ultra-supercritical and Integrated Gasification Combined Cycle (IGCC) plants will be 35%, 45% and 10% respectively in total electricity generation. All subcritical coal-based power capacity is projected to retire by 2032. These projections seem to be unreliable as they require nearly 100 GW of subcritical capacity to retire by 2032. On the other hand, as coal capacity has been continuously missing installation targets since 2017, it is extremely difficult to predict future installations of coal power in India.

In 2018, the NEP included a new target for the closure of 48.3 GW of end of-life coal plants. Coal-based capacity of 22,716 MW is under consideration for retirement during 2017-2022. This is based upon an assessment made by CEA and consists of 5,927 MW of capacity assuming that the normal trend of past retirement process would continue along with a coal-based capacity of 16,789 MW which doesn't have space for installation of flue gas desulphurization (FGD) systems to curb SO_2 emissions. Additionally, a coal-based capacity of 25,572 MW has been considered for retirement during 2022-2027, which will be completing 25 years of operation by March 2022.

India is missing out on the benefits it could obtain by timely retirement of old capacity. Only 4.67 GW capacity has been retired between 2018-20 (March 2020). This is a far cry from the 22.72 GW retirement plan under the NEP. Along with this capacity, an additional 20 GW capacity will be ready for retirement during 2022-2027 and can be retired by 2030. Overall, this capacity, when replaced by supercritical capacity, can reduce coal consumption by 30 million tonnes and CO_2 emissions by 55-60 million tonnes. The retirement of old and inefficient units of thermal generating stations and their replacement with new and more efficient units is one of the major initiatives required to improve average efficiency of the fleet and reduce its CO_2 emissions footprints.

The rationale for renovation and modernization (R&M) has been:

- New installation is capital-intensive; it is considered prudent to maximize generation from existing power stations to ensure optimal utilization.
- Thermal power stations were designed for a given quality of coal which has deteriorated over a period of time. These power plants need to augment systems such as coal feeding and ash handling systems to burn coal of worse quality while maintaining the rated capacity.
- To bring down the cost of energy to consumers, Merit Order Dispatch is being adopted at the plant level, which may require renovation and modernization for improving operating performance.

Renovation and modernization have played a limited role in improving efficiency as the larger focus has remained on maximizing generation with improved availability, especially in smaller units. No estimates have been compiled by the government on how much renovation and modernization projects have helped in reducing CO_2 emissions and pollution in general from coal power plants. As per the new 2019 draft policy for renovation and modernization, there is significant scope of improvement if renovation and modernization projects are utilized efficiently to move the sector towards use of biomass. Biomass co-firing consists of combusting biomass and fossil fuels together at thermal power plants. In most cases, biomass co-firing in coal power plants takes place by mixing biomass with coal before burning, but biomass can also be gasified and burned in separate burners, after which the gaseous fuel or steam is mixed with the boiler streams of the coal-fired power plant. It has been generally accepted that co-firing biomass with coal can offer a quick, cost-effective way to partially decarbonize power generation in the short-to medium term. Biomass co-firing has an enormous potential to reduce CO_2 emissions with minuscule investment. The substitution of only 10% of coal in the current globally installed coal-fired electrical capacity would result in installation of about 160–180 GW biomass power capacity, which is 2.5 times more than the current globally installed biomass power capacity.

Co-firing is the process of utilization of a certain portion of biomass with the existing base fuel. Currently, three co-firing technologies are widely used in coal plants: direct, indirect and parallel. The purpose of co-firing is to maximize the use of biomass within the existing system without impacting efficiency. Net electric efficiency of dedicated state-of-the-art biomass power plants is 25-36%, whereas conventional subcritical coal-fired power plants in Organization for Economic Cooperation and Development (OECD) countries operate at efficiencies of around 36% and modern ultra-supercritical units can exceed 45% lower heating value. Thus, co-firing enables power generation from biomass with the high efficiency achieved in modern large-sized coal-fired power plants, which is much higher than the efficiency of dedicated 100% biomass power plants. At present, co-firing projects in coal-fired power plants exceed the biomass capacity of dedicated biomass plants. The total energy efficiency can be increased even further if biomass co-firing takes place in combined heat and power plants. The other advantage of biomass co-firing is that the incremental investment required for burning biomass in coal-fired plants is significantly lower than the cost of dedicated biomass power. Co-firing also helps to extend the life of the plant. Co-firing has played an important transitional role in the decarbonization of the coal fleet and has extended the lives of power plants in Europe (Anon, 2013).

Co-firing offers an advantage to developing countries since the use of agricultural residue will increase the economic value of this sector. Instead of being burned on the fields, as is commonly done, agricultural waste could be used profitably in co-firing power plants. International cooperation is needed to ensure the environmental and social sustainability of biomass exploitation, especially in the case of wood or forestry-based biomass usage. As per Ministry of Power's (MoP) policy on biomass utilization, for every 1 GW capacity at 7% co-firing, nearly 0.25-0.3 million tonnes of biomass pellets are required (Anon, 2017). Thus, for 100 GW capacity, nearly 25-30 million tonnes of biomass pellets will be required. The problem of climate change cannot be dealt with through a single strategy. Thus, along with increasing overall efficiency of the coal power fleet, adoption of carbon capture and storage (CCS) will play a crucial role in combating global warming. CCS technology is designed to capture CO_2 emissions from fossil fuel combustion. It has the capacity of absorbing 85-95% of CO_2 emissions. The process starts with the capture of generated CO_2, which then undergoes a compression process to form a dense fluid. This eases the transport and storage of the captured CO_2. The dense fluid is transported via pipelines and then injected into an underground storage facility (Tabbi *et al.*, 2019). Captured CO_2 can also be used as a raw material in other industrial processes such as urea making or methanol production. NTPC has signed a memorandum of understanding with Larson and Turbo Hydrocarbon Engineering (L&THE) to build a CO_2-to-methanol demonstration plant at an NTPC power station. Under this agreement, L&THE and NTPC will also collaborate on accelerated development and commercialization of CO_2 to methanol plants Anon, 2020b). Since CO_2 storage is a major bottleneck, the success of the project will be a positive sign for adoption of CCS technology.

PAT SCHEME

Perform Achieve and Trade (PAT) scheme of Bureau of Energy Efficiency (BEE) is a market-based mechanism announced under the National Mission on Enhanced Energy Efficiency (NMEEE), designed to accelerate energy savings in energy-intensive sectors by incentivizing them. Under PAT cycle I, the scheme identified nine energy-intensive sectors and set targets for reduction in energy intensity for each of them. One of nine sectors was thermal power. Of the 144 thermal power plants covered under the PAT cycle I, 97 were coal or lignite-fired plants. In spite of immense potential of efficiency improvements in the thermal power sector, BEE PAT cycle I was criticized for setting easily achievable targets, particularly in the thermal power sector, the stakeholders felt that the targets for heat rate reduction are quite low which are possible merely through process optimization and improved operation and maintenance (Nihar *et al.*, 2020).

In PAT cycle I, the thermal power sector alone contributed about 50% of CO_2 emissions reduction (3.1 million metric tonnes of oil equivalent of the reduction which is equivalent to around 7 million tonnes of coal and 12 million tonnes of CO_2). The results of PAT cycle II were scheduled to be declared in December 2019 but have been delayed. The average heat rate reduction target given to the plants was 2%. Thus, efficiency improvements will be similar to those under the PAT I cycle, i.e. 0.6 percentage points. Hence, CO_2 emissions reduction of around 1-2% (10-15 million tonnes of CO_2) can be expected. Similar CO_2 emissions reduction can be assumed for the upcoming PAT cycles in 2020-2030.

But the sector needs more:

- Stringent target setting for aligning PAT cycles with CERCs norms on heat rate. PAT targets should either be at par with or more stringent than CERC norms.
- Deeper analysis of the sector for a better rationale for target setting under PAT.
- Clarity on enforcement or timelines for defaulters on energy targets.
- Transparency and clarity in the trading mechanism and regulations that will build confidence among industries and control liquidity interactions and balance in the system.

EMISSION TRADING SYSTEMS

Carbon pricing and trading systems play an important role in limiting the consumption of fossil fuels and generating funds for cleaner energy. There are two types of initiatives that put explicit monetary cost on greenhouse gases: Emission Trading System (ETS) and carbon taxes. An Emission Trading System (ETS) sometimes referred to as a cap-and trade system, caps the total level of GHG emissions, allowing industries with lower emissions to sell their extra allowances to larger emitters. By creating supply and demand for emissions allowances, an ETS establishes a market price for GHG emissions. The cap ensures that required emissions reductions takes place to keep emitters within their pre-allocated carbon budget (Anon 2020c). A carbon tax sets a price on carbon by defining a tax rate on greenhouse gas emissions or the carbon content of fossil fuels. It is different from an ETS in that the emissions reduction outcome of a carbon tax is not pre-defined but the carbon price is. The choice of the two most important carbon pricing mechanisms (carbon emission trading and carbon tax) should be based on the specific environment and should be consistent with the national economic focus. In fact, carbon emissions trading and carbon tax can play a complementary role in different areas of emissions reduction.

Carbon pricing is much easier and there are more indirect ways of pricing carbon, such as through fuel taxes, the removal of fossil fuel subsidies and regulations that may incorporate a 'social cost of carbon. Of the 185 countries that have submitted their INDCs to the UN, 96 have stated that they are planning or considering to use a carbon pricing mechanism as a tool to achieve their INDC commitments. The total carbon emissions of these countries account for 55% of global emissions. As of 1 April 2020, there were 58 different carbon pricing mechanisms worldwide, of which 28 were carbon emissions trading markets and 30 were carbon tax mechanisms. These carbon pricing mechanisms cover nearly 9 Gt of CO_2 eq. in 46 countries and 28 regions around the world, accounting for about 16% of the world's GHG emissions. Three more carbon trading systems are scheduled to operate in China, Germany and the US covering 4 Gt of CO_2 eq. representing 7.2% of global GHG emissions.

There has been a rapid increase in carbon pricing regimes; still, most of them are in the developed countries. A unified international emissions trading market is yet to be formed. A nationwide Clean Energy Tax on coal (or coal cess) was adopted in 2010. It was levied on coal production and imports. The tax was initially set at Rs 50 (US $0.72) per tonne of domestic and imported coal, but was quadrupled to Rs 200 (US $2.88) per tonne of coal in 2015 and doubled again to Rs 400 (US $5.75) per tonne in 2016. The revenue was initially allocated to the National Clean Energy and Environment Fund (NCEEF) to invest in clean energy projects and technologies. A total of US $4.2 billion accrued to the NCEEF until it was subsumed under the Goods and Services Tax (GST) reform in 2017. Earlier known as the Clean Energy Cess, it was renamed GST Compensation Cess in 2017, changing the ambit of the tax towards compensating states for losses incurred due to the GST rather than allocating it for clean energy. However, the Ministry of Finance expressed confidence that financing of clean energy and environment projects should not suffer due to the GST reforms (Anon 2020d).

In late 2019, the Central government proposed to cancel the coal cess altogether. The savings from removing the carbon tax would improve the financial health of utilities and distribution companies, besides helping power producers install 'pollution-curbing equipment', the government reasoned (Anon, 2020e).

CONCLUSION

India's reliance on coal will continue for its energy security. Coal capacity is scheduled to increase to 266 GW by 2030 from 205 GW in 2020 and will contribute 50% to the generation mix by 2030. Global pressure is already building up to phase out coal. Many developed countries have vowed to phase out coal plants and have already set deadlines in this regard. Nineteen countries have planned to stop coal power use by 2030 and some by 2040. Under such circumstances, even for developing countries, a BAU approach will not work. Thus, if developing countries want to continue to use coal for their energy security, the onus is on them to ensure it is burnt in a highly efficient and clean manner. India has the opportunity to eliminate more than 250 million tonnes of CO_2 emissions annually by 2030 in comparison with a BAU approach. To achieve this, the country will require a robust, concrete and comprehensive plan. Some of the major initiatives may work for sustainability *viz.* Clear roadmap for new technology; Renovating old plants; Renovation and modernization and life extension; Biomass co-firing; Carbon capture and Storage; Carbon tax and emissions trading mechanisms; Coal washing; Merit Order; PAT scheme etc.

REFERENCES

Anon, (2013). Technology: Policy Brief E21, IEA-ETSAP and IRENA 2013.

Anon, (2017). Biomass Utilization for Power Generation through Co-Firing in Pulverized Coal Fired Boiler, Ministry of Power.

Anon, (2020a). Emissions–Global Energy & CO2 Status Report 2019– Analysis, International Energy Agency. Available at https://www. iea.org/reports/global-energy-CO_2-status-report-2019/emissions, as accessed on 2 June 2020

Anon, (2020b). LET Hydrocarbon Engineering Signs Pact with NTPC for CO2-to-Methanol Plants-ET Energy World. ETEnergyworld.com, 20 August 2020. Available at https://energy.economictimes.indiatimes. com/news/power/let-hydrocarbon-engineering-signs-pact-with-ntpc-forco2-to-methanol-plants/77649687, as accessed on 20 August 2020

Anon, (2020c). What Does It Mean to Put a Price on Carbon? World Bank. Available at https://www.worldbank.org/en/news/feature/2014/06/11/what-does-it-mean-to-put-a-price-on-carbon, as accessed on 14 July 2020

Anon, (2020d). India 2020, Energy Policy Review, International Energy Agency.

Anon, (2020e). Government Proposes Waiving Carbon Tax on Coal, Business Today, 31 December 2019. Available at https://www. businesstoday.in/current/economy-politics/big-win-coal-industry-pmoproposes-waiving-carbon-tax/story/392877.html., as accessed on 5 May 2020

Chandra Bhushan, Priyavrat Bhati, Sanjeev Kumar Kanchan, Angeline Sangeetha, Sai Siddhartha, Soundaram Ramanathan and Abhishek Rudra (2015). Heat on Power: Green Rating of Coal-based Power Plants, Centre for Science and Environment, New Delhi

Chikkatur, Ananth P., Ambuj D. Sagar, Nikit Abhyankar and N. Sreekumar (2007). Tariff-based incentives for improving coal-powerplant efficiencies in India, Energy Policy 35, no. 3,744 :7-3,758.

Mengpin Ge and Johannes Friedrich (2020). 4 Charts Explain Greenhouse Gas Emissions by Countries and Sectors, World Resources Institute. Available at https://www.wri.org/blog/2020/02/greenhousegas-emissions-by-country-sector, as accessed on 5 May 2020

Nihar R. Sahoo, Pratap K.J. Mohapatra, Biresh K. Sahoo and Biswajit Mahanty (2017). Rationality of Energy Efficiency Improvement Targets under the PAT Scheme in India—A Case of Thermal Power Plants, Energy Economics. Available at doi:10.1016/j.eneco.2017.06.004, as accessed on 5 May 2020

Qian Zhu (2020). Historic Efficiency Improvement of the Coal Power Fleet, International Energy Agency CCC/300 978-92-9029-623-2

Tabbi Wilberforce, Ahmad Baroutaji, Bassel Soudan, Abdul Hai Al-Alami and Abdul Ghani Olabi (2019). Outlook of Carbon Capture Technology and Challenges, Science of the Total Environment 657: 56-72.

UNFCC, (2020). India's Intended Nationally Determined Contribution to UNFCC. Available at https://www4.unfccc.int/sites/ndcstaging/ Published Documents/India%20First/INDIA%20INDC%20TO%20 UNFCCC.pdf, as accessed on 5 May 2020

2

Application of Environmental Biotechnological Tools for Organic Waste Management

INTRODUCTION

Organic wastes are generated through natural and anthropogenic processes. The generation of organic wastes through anthropogenic activities is of serious concern as they have the potential to uncontrollably supplying greenhouse gases, spreading pathogens, stimulating eutrophication, odor generation and influencing many other environmental issues. Landfill and incineration are not environment friendly considerations as they have individual limitations in control all of such adversities, may generate their own set of adverse effects and also such activities remove most of the scopes to recover economic benefits from recycling and reusing the organic wastes. Landfills can be responsible for high release of greenhouse gases like methane and carbon dioxide (Manfrendi *et.al.* 2009), while incinerators can be the source of greenhouse gases and carbon monoxide (Yang *et.al.* 2012). Landfills leachate can be the sources of available nitrogen to water bodies which can be highly responsible for eutrophication (Jokela *et.al.* 2002). Bioremediation have their certain merits to reduce or reuse organic wastes with least impact on environment. Hence discussing some sources of organic wastes and the remediation through biological and biotechnological approach has been the key objective of this review. The mentioned literatures are used as evidences from the works of the researches to support the possible diverse ways to manage organic wastes efficiently, but the number of literatures and the applications are huge regarding the issues, and all of them display certain merits and limitations of bioremediation of organic wastes, which compels to perform further research initiatives and strategic developments to attain higher efficiency in organic waste management and recovering from the limitations.

CONCERN-MAJOR SOURCES OF ORGANIC WASTES

Domestic Wastes from Households

Domestic wastes constitute a significant amount of organic components which are mostly biodegradable. They consist of unused food raw material, wasted food, fecal matters, gardening and many other such noticed and unnoticed processes. Aryal *et.al* (2013) showed the domestic wastes of Bhaktapur village in Nepal contains 81.4% biodegradable materials. In South West China the average production of domestic waste is around 178 g per day per capita (Han *et.al*, 2015) of which 40.64% was biodegradable. Surendra *et.al*. (2016) mentioned that around one third of produced food is wasted around the world. The domestic soil and liquid wastes can be stressful to several biotic components in the environment. Huma *et.al* (2012), showed that domestic waste water can reduce germination of *Brassica juncea* by 18%, 20% in *Trigonella foenum-graecum*, and 23% in *Hordeum vulgare*, whereas it reduced the germination of *Coriandrum sativum* to as low as 7% and for *Nigella sativa* they found 0% germination. From the outcomes of the study by Agrawal *et.al* (2014) it can be seen direct application of domestic water may sharply increase the nitrogen and phosphorus initially but later decreases the N and P below the natural levels. If not treated properly domestic sewage can supply heavy metals like Ni, Cd, Pb to the crops and NO_3 to drinkable freshwater resources (Yadav *et.al.* 2002). These literatures indicates that domestic organic wastes constitute a large part of the urban, rural and municipal wastes, and can impact several wastes of the environment, along with the possibility of uncontrolled conversion of carbon to greenhouse gases, hence it is required to take measures to control the accumulation of domestic organic wastes of different sources. Domestic wastes has the ability to lead to eutrophication of water bodies, as well as contaminating with fecal coliform and fecal streptococci (Finley *et.al.* 2009) to water bodies through excreta, which makes them to be urgent to be controlled to preserve fresh water resources.

Hospitals and Biomedical Processes

Hospitals are sources of copious amount of organic waste, that too on daily basis and hospitals are present in both urban and rural setups making the wastes being generated from all parts of the world. Moreira and Günther (2012) showed that a single primary health clinic in São Paulo was about to generate 1.8 kg of organic waste per day in 2009. Khajuria and Kumar (2007) in a study on three hospitals of Agra showed that of the total wastes produced per day 5% was body parts of human and animal, 9% cotton and cotton based products. The human organs and the animal wastes have been categorized as infectious by Mohankumar and Kottaiveeran (2011).Phenols, oil, grease, organic pesticides along with pathogenic bacteria are found in waste water from hospitals and bioremediation can significantly decrease the BOD and COD and total count of pathogens from organic waste water from hospitals leading to regaining the utility standards of the water, as shown by El-Gawad and Aly (2011). Sawalem *et.al.* (2008) found that 38% of the general wastes from hospitals in Libya are organic in nature. Adama *et.al* (2016) mentions that even after incineration of hospital wastes, the remnants may carry organic compounds like polychlorinated biphenyls (PCBs), dioxins, polycyclic aromatic hydrocarbons (PAHs) and benzene, which can be detrimental to biodiversity and environment and can spread if the ash is dumped in open, and incineration can emit Volatile Organic Carbons (VOCs) in air (Walker and Cooper, 1992).

Opportunistic pathogenic bacteria like *Micrococcus leteus, Staphylococcus epidermidis, Micrococcus roseus, Bacillus subtilis, Bacillus licheniformis, Actinomycetes istraelii* and pathogenic fungi like *Aspergillus niger,Aspergillus flavus, Microsporum canis* were found in abundance at dumping sites of hospital wastes and adjacent soil by Oyeleke and Istifanus (2009). Tahiri *et.al.* (2012) showed that wastewater from Al Ghassani hospital is able to supply pathogens like *Escherichia coli, Klebsiella, Salmonella, Shigella, Enterococcus* and identified deposition of blood, spit and urine and remnants of analytical processes as major sources of organic component in hospital effluent. Emmanuel *et.al.* (2009) indicated possible contamination of groundwater by discharge of fecal matter from septic tank of hospitals carrying *Cryptosporidium spp.*, fecal enterococcus and the enteroviruses. These studies indicate the abundance of pathogenic and opportunistic pathogenic microbial population in hospital organic wastes and waste water. Hence careful strategies are required for decontamination and eco-friendly measures to reduce the wastes to control outbreak of diseases, reduce greenhouse gas emission and increase the possible economic benefits through harvesting the useful components through recycling from these waste.

Agriculture, Animal Husbandry and Agro-industries

The agricultural wastes, livestock wastes and food processing wastes have various areas of accumulation. They can come from household kitchen, urban and rural subsistence agriculture, intensive farming, organic farming, urban and rural markets, tannery and slaughter house, and many other such places that are related to food production and food consumptions. Mane and Raskar (2012) found that ample amount of agricultural wastes from the market at Baramati, Maharastra contains several organic wastes like- residue of sorghum, jowar, pigeon pea, groundnut, soybean, onion and vegetable, and fiber from coconut and sugarcane. Manios (2014) showed agricultural wastes of Crete Island included the leaves and branches of olive tree the pressed cake of olive, vine branches and pig manure. In the study on composting of animal waste in Japan, Haga (1999) mentioned about high availability of organic waste for composting cattle, pig and poultry rearing farms. Poultry farming and slaughterhouse can generate organic wastes like- carcass, blood, anatomic waste, fecal matter and these can be carrying microbial pathogens, veterinary drugs and even heavy metals (Salminen and Rintala, 2002). Szuster and Flaherty (2002) showed through a study on shrimp aquaculture in Thailand that shrimp cultivation in saline environment can produce high amount of sludge that carries high amount of organic wastes as well as nutrients like nitrogen and phosphorus. Hussein and Sawan (2010) mentions about the production of 30-35 million tons of agricultural waste per year in Palm cultivation and palm oil processing can generate tons of organic wastes in solid forms like branches, kernel cakes, decanter cakes and fluid wastes like palm oil mill sludge (Singh *et.al*, 2010). According to Voæa *et.al.* (2010) around 12000 tons of organic waste is produced each year in Croatia in form of olive cake after harvest of oil. Around 13 tons of organic waste is generate per hectare of pineapple cultivation during the cropping season (Ch'ng *et.al*, 2014). Omar (2007) mentions of a yearly yield of around 15 million tons of biomass wastes from cotton stalk, groundnut shell and bagasse production and 17 million tons of animal dung in Sudan. Agro-industrial wastes in Italy contains high quantity of wheat straw, maize stalk, rice chaff, dry bread, kiwi, onion and dairy products (Menardo and Balsari, 2012). According to a study by Forster-Carneiro *et.al.*(2013) in Brazil high amount of biodegradable waste are generated from production of sugarcane, soybean, maize, rice, cotton, orange, wheat, cassava and tobacco, among which the sugarcane production wastes consist around 80% of the wastes, and maximum animal waste is generated from poultry and other sources are pig and cattle management. These can be taken as examples of the amount of organic waste that is generated around the world as agricultural procedures, livestock management and agro-based industries, which needs higher attention for bioremediation to reduce associated environmental stresses as well as recycling economically important products, that will strengthen the society, reducing the dependence on nature or destructive processes that are required to harvest them from natural sources.

BIO-REMEDIATION OF ORGANIC WATSTES

Phytoremediation

Using macrophytes can be a sustainable and economic option to manage organic wastes. Cultivating duckweed such as *Lemna minor* can significantly reduce the BOD and orthophosphate from domestic waste water (Priya *et.al.*, 2011). Rahman *et.al* (2012) discussed that using micro algae can be an environment friendly and economically beneficial method to treat domestic waste water in open pond as they have been found in studies to remove excess of nitrogen, phosphorus and heavy metals, and later the grown microalgae can be used as raw material for biofuel industry. Willow can be cultivated to remove nitrogen from the wastewater as they can reduce nitrogen by uptaking and increasing denitirification (Arronson and Perttu, 2001), and also can be utilized for removal of phosphorus (Kiedrzyñska *et.al*, 2008). Bulrush and cattail marshes can also be used for removal of high amount of nitrogen from water (Bachand and Horne, 1999). The combination of anaerobic digestion treatment coupled with cultivation of *Cyperus alternifolius* and *Canna indica* were found to useful in removal of COD and nitrate from livestock wastewater in a study by Zhu *et.al.*(2012). Thus several species or macrophytes can be utilized to treat organic wastes in waste waters and also at the same time developing biomass.

Microbial Degradation

Many of the microbial organisms have the ability to consume organic wastes as a source of nutrition, along with their ability to produce economically important metabolic products. Sánchez-Andrea *et.al.* (2012) showed in anaerobic bioreactor based study that domestic waste water can act as a carbon source for successful reduction of COD, concentration of sulfate and heavy metals like Fe, Co, Ni, Cu and Zn from acid mine drainage through promoting the growth several species of fermentive and sulfate reducing bacteria. With the help of *Clostridium sp.* important products like acetone, butanol and ethanol can be produced through fermentation of domestic organic wastes glucose, xylose monosaccharides, however for economically successful production feedstock with high susceptibility to anaerobic digestion will be required (Classe *et.al.* 1999). Namsivayam *et.al.* (2011) showed that using consortia of bacteria *Lactobacillus planetarium*, yeast *Candida utilis*, actinomycetes *Streptomyces albus* and fungi *Aspergillus oryzae*, in treatment of domestic sewage waste water, was able to bring pH from highly alkaline to near neutral, reduce BOD (Biological Oxygen Demand), COD and could dissolve solids and increase dissolved oxygen (DO). *Brevibacillus agri*, *Bacillus cereus*, *Bacillus licheniformis*, and *Brevibacillus parabrevis* have been found to fermenting fish wastes into liquid fertilizer in a study by Kim (2011). Organic wastes produced from hospitals and medical treatments have certain limitations due to the possibility of containing infectious pathogens among them. Pasupathi *et.al* (2011) has described the importance of segregation and separate procedures should be implied to tackling the infectious and non-infectious wastes from hospitals. Using microbial consortium on hospital generated organic waste can also be a viable option in future. Ethica *et.al* (2018) indicates that hydrolytic bacteria producing protease, lipase, amylase and cellulase enzymes can be incorporated for biodegradation of the organic wastes from the hospital as in their study they found these microbes to be growing successfully and showing efficient enzymatic activity in untreated waste water of hospitals. Akpinar *et.al.* (2009) showed that xylanase from *Aspergillus niger* can be used to produce xylose from xylan of cotton stalk, tobacco stalk and sun flower, while xylanase from *Trichoderma longi bacterium* works efficiently on xylan of wheat straw, and xylanase also can be produced using *Penicillium janthinellum* from moderate to high quantity from sugarcane bagasse, corn husk, oat husk and corn cob (Olivera *et.al.*, 2006).

Biogas Production

Biogas is a product of anaerobic digestion of organic matter and the major component of biogas is methane. Organic wastes from different sources are suitable as feed stocks for biogas production. Weiland (2010) gives a clear outline of methane production for biogas by the anaerobic digestion by the microbes, where the production is optimum between pH 7.0-8.0 and completely stopping at pH below 6.5 and above 8.5 from feed stocks that contain carbohydrates, proteins, fats, cellulose and hemicelluloses. Yang *et.al.* (2015) mentions that two third of the agricultural residue are suitable for second generation bioenergy feedstock due to high presence of lignino-cellulose, while the food industry waste being suitable for both first and second generation biofuel production due to higher concentration of cellulose. In a comparative study on co-digestion of agricultural waste with waste of biodiesel production Kacprzak (2009) found that highest amount of methane concentration is found when corn silage, cheese whey, and the glycerol waste of biodiesel is anaerobically co-digested but the total volumetric production of biogas is much lower, and the co-digestion of corn silage and carrot residue gives much higher volume of biogas, though the concentration of methane is relatively lower than the previous, indicating biogas production from agricultural wastes can be regulated by controlling the feed stock type and can be used economically for producing fuel of higher quality or higher volume as per the requirement of energy and cost for the targeted future technologies. Chiprasert (2011) mentions that it has been estimated that Thailand has the potential of producing around 1060 and 1005 million m^3 biogas per year from animal wastes and agro-industrial wastes respectively. Anaerobic digestion of composted peels of pineapple, plantain and cassava was found to be producing biogas efficiently under NaOH solution of 1-3 % concentration with and increasing trend up to 3% and falling thereafter, by Ilaboya *et.al.* (2010). According to Menardo and Balsari (2012), among the agro-industrial wastes of Italy, rice chaff has the highest potential of biogas production in terms of production efficiency, while wheat straw and maize stalk can complete as feedstock due to their very high production in the region.

Banks *et.al* (2008) showed biogas can be produced by both thermophilic and mesophilic digestion of domestic food waste, though thermophilic process show initial higher production of biogas and destruction of volatile solid while the mesophilic process tended to be more stable outputs, but in both condition accumulation of volatile fatty acids reduced the performance which they found to be controllable by addition of freshwater. In another study, Banks *et.al* (2011) showed that while using domestic food waste, segregated at the source, as the feedstock for anaerobic digestion can convert around 90% of the provided waste into biogas and other digestates, while the biogas contained a concentration of around 62% methane. Significantly higher amount of methane can be produced by co-digesting cattle slurry and card waste with domestic organic waste (Zhang *et.al*, 2012). Cheerawit *et.al* (2012) showed that mixing food waste to domestic waste water and anaerobically digesting the mixture can produce acceptable amount of methane which is the most important component of biogas, and the production increases with the higher proportion of wastewater in the mixture as the methane production was best at 10:90 ratio and lowest at 70:30 ratio of food waste to domestic water, and the same efficiency was also seen in the removal of COD from the mixture. Iqbal *et.al.* (2014) showed that co-digestion of kitchen waste with cow manure produces biogas more efficiently than anaerobic digestion of the individuals, and the production is better when the kitchen waste is treated with 1.5% NaOH. Rattanapan *et.al.* (2019) found that mixture of 10:90 ratio of food waste to domestic waste water can produce high amount of biogas through mesophilic co-digestion.

Bio-ethanol and Bio-hydrogen

Productivity and efficiency of other biofuels like- biodiesel, bioethanol etc. are also being studied and searched significantly and can be used efficiently to convert organic biomass waste into energy resources. Bioethanol can be produced from organic biomass through a series of processes, as enzymatic or thermochemical digestion as pretreatment, hydrolysis by acids, alkalis, hydrolytic enzymes or microbes like white rot fungi, detoxification and finally fermentation of the substrate by suitable microorganisms (Chandel *et.al.* 2016). According to Kand *et.al.* (2014) amyloytic yeasts like *Saccharomyces cerevisiae* and bacteria *like Zymomonas mobiles* can be used for the fermentation process in bioethanol production, and the lignin-cellulosic biomass as feed stock can be derived from agricultural crop residue, municipal solid organic wastes, sewage sludge and agro-industrial wastes. Kongkiattikajorn and Sornvoraweat (2011) showed that co-culture of *Saccharomyces sp.* and Candida sp. can produce bioethanol more efficiently than monocultures of *Saccharomyces sp.* from fermentation of cassava peel. Fermenting groundnut shells (Nyachaka *et.al.*, 2013), sorghum stalks (Pandebesie *et.al.*, 2019) by *Aspergilus niger* and *Saccharomyces cerevisiae* can efficiently produce bioethanol. Agricultural and other organic wastes can used to produce bio-hydrogen by dark fermentation by microbes, the remnant can be further utilized to produce further bio-hydrogen by photo-fermentation by photosynthetic bacteria or microbial electrolysis or microbial fuel cells or microbial fuel cells or for methane generation (Poggi-Varaldo *et.al*, 2014). Han *et.al.* (2011) showed that anaerobic digestion method can be used to produce bio-hydrogen and bioethanol simultaneously, while the production of bio-hydrogen was optimum when the concentrations of ethanol and acetic acid were nearly similar to each other. According to Wang *et.al.* (2013), waste papers, except for magazine papers, can be used as feedstock for bioethanol production. Whereas in another study by Algapani *et.al.* (2019) it was shown that bio-hydrogen and biogas can be produced from single food waste feed stock by integrated two-stage digestate recirculation system.

Biodiesel Production

Biodiesel is another source of energy which can be produced by biodegradation of organic wastes. The fatty acid rich raw materials are required for the production which can be derived by applying macro and micro-organisms on organic wastes, and the organisms on one hand reduce the organic waste load and on the other hand can store fatty acids in their body at different stages which can be utilized to produce biodiesel, an environment friendly fuel. Surendra *et.al.* (2016) showed that wasted food can be used to cultivate black soldier fly (*Hermetia illucens*) and the pre-pupae conditions were rich feedstock for biodiesel fuel due to high concentration of medium chain fatty acids and the low concentration of polyunsaturated fatty acids. Similar results can be found using manure of cattle, pig and chicken (Li *et.al.*, 2011), dairy manure (Li *et.al.* 2011), rice straw and restaurant wastes (Zheng *et.al.* 2012) as food for the black soldier fly larvae. Even the black soldier fly can also be used on the solid organic remnants after grease extraction for biodiesel production to further utilize the wastes and increase the biodiesel production feedstock (Zheng *et.al.* 2012). Larvae of other organisms like *Boettcherisca peregrine* (Yang *et.al*, 2012), *Tenebrio molitor*-the yellow mealworm beetle (Zheng *et.al.*, 2013) can also be used to derive fatty acid rich feed stock for biodiesel production. The production of biofuel feedstock yeast, *Crytococcus curvatus* also shows high productivity when the brewery wastes are used as growth medium (Ryu *et.al.*, 2013). Selvakumar and Sivashanmugam (2017) showed that lipase produced from anaerobic digestion of peels of pomegranate, orange and pineapple can be used as a catalyst in biodiesel production from palm oil. The waste material of biodiesel can be utilized for co-digestion with fish and pig wastes (Regueiro, 2012), the waste glycerin for co-digestion with waste water sludge (Razaviarani, 2013), the karanja seed cakes after removal of oil and mixing with cow dung at 50:50 ratio (Barik and Murugan, 2015) for biogas production.

Biochar Production

Biochar can be produced by pyrolysis of organic wastes in wet or dry condition at very high temperature and can be used to increase carbon sequestration in soil, control GHG emission, supply soil nutrients, increase pH of acidic soils and CEC and can reduce organic or heavy metal pollutant concentration (Parmar *et.al.*, 2014). Biochar if mixed as bulking agent with poultry manure can effectively increase the humic acids in the manure and reduce the nitrogen loss (Dias *et.al*, 2010), probably due to absorption of ammonia and dissolved ammonium by the biochar, that is usually lost during the composting of poultry wastes (Steiner *et.al*, 2010). Hass *et.al* (2012) indicated that both steam activated and non-activated biochar from chicken manure pyrolized at 350°C and 700°C can increase pH in acidic soil, however, the study showed that in both cases quantity of carbon reduced in higher temperature, while in case of steam activated biochar Ca, K, P and Mn is slightly greater in concentration in production at higher temperature pyrolysis, and in non-activated biochar the concentration of Ca, K, P, Fe, Cu, Mn, Zn and Ni is noticeably greater in products of pyrolysis at 700°C than that of 350°C. According to Al-Wabel *et.al* (2013) biochar produced by the pyrolysis of the wastes of medicinal plant Canocarpus at 400-800°C can produce biochar that is contains high amount of stable carbon, also it contains high pH that can be applied to reduce soil acidity and concentration of Ca, Mg, K and P increases in concentration with increasing temperature from 400-800°C. Alkaline content also was found to be increasing in a study by Yuan *et.al.* (2011) with increasing pyrolysis temperature from 300°C to 700°C of straw of canola, corn, soybean and peanut. Biochar produced by charring at temperatures beyond 350°C, both dairy manure and wood mixture and also biosolids and wood mixture were seen to be effective in increasing available P in soil, even greater than some phosphate rock based P fertilizers, in a study by Wang *et.al* (2012). Jindo *et.al* (2014) showed through analyzing biochar from rice straw and husk, wood of oak and apple trees, that the ability of feed stocks to produce biochar content, enrichment with nutrients and stable carbon and other quality parameters can vary differently for feedstocks in different temperature during charring, and that carries significance to performing research to perform research on individual organic wastes to find the optimum quantity or quality of produced biochar or regulating the conditions according to the special purposes of production to produce biochar of particular quality from available feed stocks. Usman *et.al* (2015) showed that biochar produced from leaves, branches and bark of date palm tree show an increasing trend of higher concentration of carbon and nutrients like Ca, Mg, K and Na, with increase of the pyrolysis temperature from 300°C to 800°C and Ghani *et.al.* (2013) also found similar pattern of trend of increase in carbon content in biochar by co-pyrolysis of rubber, wood and saw dust. Jia *et.al* (2015) mentioned about the possible effectiveness of biochar in reducing N_2O emission from composting processes.

Kulkarni (2013) showed that activated carbon column produced from coconut coir can successfully reduce the COD (chemical oxygen demand) and organic matter, by 75-80% from domestic waste water through adsorption. Pyrolysis of sewage sludge, saw dust and rice straw together can reduce biochar of high organic content and reduced heavy metals like Cu, Zn, Ni (Huanaga *et.al*, 2017). In a comparative study by Agrafioti *et.al.* (2014) it was shown that the ability to reduce arsenic contamination is best in the biochar produced from sewage sludge and on to remove Chromium the biochar from solid municipal organic waste is the best whereas the ability of rice based biochar was seen to be low in removing these particular contamination, those results differ in other studies performed on other types of heavy metal contamination and nutrient supply. Biochar from municipality solid wastes have also been found to be a high potential option to remove arsenic (As(V)) contamination from freshwater (Hongmei *et.al.*, 2014). Xu *et.al* (2013) described that biochar produced from dairy manure at 200°C and 350°C, both rich in phosphate and carbonates, and were highly efficient in removal of Cu, Zn and Cd from waste water by precipitating as phosphates or as carbonates. However the biochar made at 350°C was more efficient due higher abundance of carbonates.

Organic Fertilizer Production

Vermicomposting and composting can be an efficient way to reduce and recycle the domestic organic wastes leading to removal of contaminants and producing organic fertilizers with the help of earthworms. Bajsa *et.al.* (2003) discussed vermicomposting of organic waste water from domestic sources using *Eisenia fetida* can be an effective way in both arid and humid climatic region by dry and wet composting respectively to remove pathogens like- fecal coliforms, *Salmonella* sp., enteric viruses and helminthes. Aryal *et.al.* (2013) showed that's similar domestic wastes treated shows different outcomes when composted differently and the study showed that among the compost products the moisture content and C:N ratio was highest in anaerobic bin compost, pH was most near to neutrality in farm yard manure and most alkaline in pit compost, whereas bacterial and fungal population, organic matter and nitrogen was highest in vermicompost, and potassium was highest in farm yard manure. Rice straw and grass clipping can be important feed stocks for vermicomposting by *Eisenia fetida* and can be rich sources of fertilizers that are rich in N, P, K, Ca, Mg, Mn, Cu, Zn and Fe (Ramnarain *et.al.* 2019). However, Domingo *et.al* (2009) indicates that composting is always not removal potential contaminants and release of

VOCs, heavy metals, bioaerosols and pathogens must be monitored before applying compost for agriculture or other purposes. Vermicomposting of infectious organic wastes including anatomical wastes by *Eisenia fetida* and *Eudrilus Eugenia* has been found to be effective in removing pathogens like *Escherichia coli, Proteus vulgaris, Staph aureus, Pseudomonas pyocyaneae* in a study by Mathur *et.al* (2006). Pramanik and Chung (2010) showed mixing 10% cow dung with waste from hospital enables to produce high quality of vermicompost by *Eisenia fetida,* by increasing the activity of cellulase and growth of cellulolytic fungi. Bharadwaj (2010) showed that vermicomposting kitchen waste mixed with cow dung by *Eisenia fetida* can produce organic fertilizer enriched with N and P, and at the same time reduce the mass of the organic waste by around 61.94%.

Composting fish processing wastes with seaweed and pine bark has been found by López-Mosquera *et.al.* (2011) to be producing organic fertilizers that are rich in in N, P and K. According to Hussein and Sawan (2010) around 4 million tons of agricultural wastes in Egypt is used for composting and they give the acceptability ranges of quality of agricultural waste for composting are – C:N = 20:1 to 40:1, water content = 40-70%, pH= 5.5-9.0 etc. In a comparative analysis among different organic wastes from island of Crete by Manios (2004) it was shown that nitrogen, potassium and organic carbon were highest in vine branch compost, phosphorus, calcium and magnesium was highest in pig manure compost, while the study also showed co-composting sewage with green waste sewage with green residue gives highest amount of N and P and co-composting olive leaves with cucumber waste gives highest amount of K, Ca and Mg, some individually composted and co-composted manures showed pH that varied from near neutral to highly acidic and alkaline. Haga (1999) mentioned all the animal wastes in Japan can provide almost equal amount of N, P, K that is derived from all the chemical fertilizers applied in agriculture in Japan. The study also mentions of about the waste from cattle and pigs should be dried or sawdust, rice hull to be added for controlling moisture content for better composting. The study by Ch'ng *et.al* (2014) showed that biochar produced from chicken litter consisted higher pH, total carbon, N, P, K, Ca, Zn, Cu content, whereas composted pineapple residue consisted of higher Mg, Na, Fe, Al content, and application of individual or mixture of these two amendment increased total and available P in acidic soil by increasing pH and increased fixing of Al and Fe. Randhawa and Kullar (2011) mentions that utilizing cow dung slurry can be useful for composting as biodegradable biomedical wastes as it contains several decomposers including *Periconiella sp.* fungi that has particularly been mentioned to be efficiently degrading biomedical wastes. Sancom *et.al* (2006) showed that *Trichoderma viride* can fast decompose organic waste from hospital sewage sludge when co-composted with straw.

Producing biofuels is one of the economically beneficial methods for management of many of the organic wastes as discussed in the earlier parts. However, one problem still remains that is to tackle the issues related to the sludge produced by biofuel industry which is also rich in organic matter. Odlare *et.al.* (2015) found through a 16 years on continuous studies that applying biofuel sludge to agricultural field shows that the barley produced using biofuel residue show lower accumulation of cadmium, chromium, cobalt and nickel in comparison to those produced with sewage sludge and mineral fertilizer, and no accumulation of organic pollutants, while showing almost similar effect in increasing soil fertility as does the mineral and other organic fertilizers. Digestates of anaerobic treatment of poultry slaughterhouse can be an important source of nitrogen for agriculture, but at the same time can show phytotoxicity due to organic acids and ammonia that can be removed by further aerobic treatment (Salminen *et.al*, 2001). Granular municipal sludge, digestate of biogas production process and ash of biomass combustion were found by Lapiñski *et.al* (2019) to be potential to reduce soil acidity due to their alkaline nature and the study also suggested that thermal treatment can reduce the mobility of heavy metals in such products.

Animal Feed

Food wastes from hospitals can be used for animal husbandry as Martini *et.al.* (2017) mentions the use of food leftovers from Hospital de Clínicas de Porto Alegre supplies food for around 1800 pigs. Hussein and Sawan (2010) mentions that around 7 million tons of agricultural waste is utilized to supply food for livestock in Egypt, and they also give a viable solution to cultivate edible mushroom like *Pleurotus spp., Agaricus bisporus, Volvariella volvacea* on agricultural organic wastes. The study by Oribhabor and Ansa (2006) from Niger Delta suggests that properly treated excreta of poultry, cattle, pigs and goats, as well as anatomic remnants food processing from livestock or aquaculture organisms, even crop wastes, can serve as fish feed, if applied carefully. Substantial amount of food processing waste, leftover food etc. can be fermented by lactic acid bacteria or dried to produce animal food (Sugiura *et.al.* 2009). Ajila *et.al* (2012) suggests that wastes of agro-industrial processes such as wastes of banana, pineapple, citrus, sugarcane, root crops, oil seed cakes, wastes of cereal and palm oil mills, molasses etc. can be used to produce food for animal that can supply several nutrients, crude fiber, protein, polyphenols and carotinoids etc. to the food. Red grape pomace has been shown by Kumanda *et.al* (2019) as a sustainable and nutritious feed for poultry. Garcia *et.al* (2005) suggested that meat waste and fish as good protein resource and wastes of vegetable for carbohydrates in animal feed and microbial standard can be maintained by heating these feed stocks at 65°C for 20 minutes. Fermenting corn cobs with *Aspergilus niger, Saccharomyces cerevisiae* and other selected microbes has been shown by Arwinsyah *et.al* (2019) to produce sheep feed of high crude protein, low crude fiber and high digestibility.

Fish fecal matter, sludge from sugar and starch production industry have been shown by Elissen *et.al* (2015) to be successfully used to cultivate the worms *Lumbriculus variegatus* which can be used as fish feed. Acording to Adewumi (2011) guts, bones and feather can from poultry farming and food processing can also be used for the production of fish feed. Though not a livestock option, yet organisms like larvae of *Hermetia illucens* L. can be incorporated to reduce organic wastes (Manurung *et.al*. 2016) generated from market, municipality and dewatering of fecal sludge Zurbrügg (2011), and these larvae can be an important source of fish food which is especially rich as a protein source (Nyakeri *et.al*., 2017). According to Antonov *et.al*. (2019) *Hermetia illucens* larvae can be cultivated using fecal waste from poultry as nutrition source and the larvae can be fed to the poultry birds and also can be used to produce Zoogumus fertilizer that can be used to cultivate the cereals used as poultry feed.

CONCLUSION

From these studies it can be identified that organic wastes generated from different sources must be segregated according to their chemical, physical and biological properties. Such segregation can help in selecting cost effective and efficient management of organic wastes, while possibilities of utilizing the products and by products for bioenergy production, organic fertilizer production, carbon sequestration, important organic chemical synthesis, animal feed production and many other diverse set of economic process. Using phytoremediation to reduce to manage organic wastes can efficiently work for nutrient removal from fluid organic wastes to avoid eutrophication. The process increases carbon sequestration and removal of excess of such biomass can serve as a feedstock for organic fertilizer or for bioenergy production. Several types of microbial organisms can digest organic wastes under different regulatory parameters and can reduce the organic loads while producing economically profitable organic chemicals and biofuels, ensuring the efficient recycling and reducing the organic remnants to undergo uncontrolled biological processes before being finally exposed to nature. Biogas production by anaerobic digestion of organic wastes can be an effective way to reduce the organic matter from the environment and at the same time can be used to replace the fossil fuel. Bioethanol and bio-hydrogen production are the other methods to convert organic wastes into environment friendly fuels, and there are several feed stocks and applicable fermenting microorganisms that can efficiently be used to produce bioethanol and bio-hydrogen, in order to reduce and replace fossil fuel, sustain in energy scarcity condition, control the global climate change and generating economic benefits. The use of biotechnological knowledge of cultivate organisms as rich sources of animal, plant and microbial fats that are required as raw material for the production of biodiesel, using organic wastes as their nutrition sources. The studies also indicates that carefully selected different types of organic wastes can be used to be co-digested by similar microbial consortia at the same time while producing targeted biofuels efficiently and different biofuels can be and that too of different qualities can also be efficiently produced from same initial feedstock or simultaneously in systematical arranged biochemical processes. The wastes of biofuel production process have the potential to be used in fertilizing agricultural soil through proper application. Producing biofuel from organic waste will not only help in managing the quantity of organic waste but also will be helping in achieving the target to reduce the dependence on fossil fuel, thus combating the global warming and climate change.

Differently produced biochar can be used for individual purposes like pH correction, supply of particular nutrients, fertilizer production, reducing heavy metal pollution and many other economic and environment management purposes. The studies show that organic fertilizers can produced by vermicomposting, composting of the organic wastes and there is possibility to produce fertilizers in future from digestates of anaerobic digestion of organic wastes through proper strategies and monitoring at large scale. These diverse production methods show a great opportunity to treat individual types of organic wastes for specific methodologies to produce fertilizer of targeted physicochemical properties. The organic fertilizers will be effective in reducing the dependence on chemical fertilizers and the associated environmental problems. Organic wastes generated through economic activities can be utilized to feed the livestock and fishes as rich sources of nutrients through proper management and monitoring. This can reduce the costs of livestock management. While using the organic wastes to produced feed the careful monitoring is needed to find the presence of contaminants, pathogens and nutritional value so that the animals can maintain a proper health conditions and the animal products can maintain the quality for human consumption. Most of the studies, mentioned in this review and beyond, indicate that a single usage as feedstock does not limit the utility of organic waste, but their lies several steps of opportunities to utilize the products and byproducts of each step of management of organic waste for further reduction of organic waste and gaining economic benefits. Hence serious research initiative and investments should be made to properly reduce the organic wastes and to harvest the maximum of economic and environmental benefit of the management process.

REFERENCES

Adama M., Esena R., Fosu-Mensah B. & Yirenya-Tawiah D. (2016). Heavy Metal Contamination of Soils around a Hospital Waste Incinerator Bottom Ash Dumps Site.Journal of Environmental and Public Health, 2016, 6 pages. Article ID 8926453, http://dx.doi.org/10.1155/2016/8926453

Adewumi A., AdewumiI. K. & Olaleye V.F. (2011). Livestock Waste-menace: Fish wealth-solution, African Journal of Environmental Science and Technology, 5(3), 149-154. ISSN 1996-0786.

Agrafioti E., Kalderis D. & Diamadopoulos E. (2014). Arsenic and Chromium Removal from Water using Biochars Derived from Rice Husk, Organic Solid Wastes and Sewage Sludge. Journal of Environmental Management, 133, 309-314. http://dx.doi.org/10.1016/j.jenvman.2013.12.007

Agrawal V., Bhagat R. & Thikare N. (2014). Impact of Domestic Sewage for Irrigation on Properties of Soil, International Journal of Research Studies in Science. Engineering and Technology, 1(5), 60-64. ISSN 2349-4751 (Print) & ISSN 2349-476X (Online)

Ajila C.M., Brar S.K., Verma M., Tyagi R.D., Godbout S., &Valéro J.R. (2012). Bio-processing of Agro-byproducts to Animal Feed. Critical Reviews in Biotechnology, 32(4), 382-400. DOI: 10.3109/07388551.2012.659172

Akpinar O., Erdogan K. & Bostanci S. (2009). Enzymatic Production of Xylooligosaccharide from selected Agricultural Wastes, Food and Bioproducts Processing, 87, 145-151, doi:10.1016/j.fbp.2008.09.002.

Algapani D.E., Qiao W., Ricci M., Bianchi D., Wandera S.M., Adani F. & Dong R. (2019). Bio-hydrogen and Bio-methane Production from Food Waste in a Two Stage Anaerobic Digestion Process with Digestate Recirculation. Renewable Energy 130 (2019) 110-115. https://doi.org/10.1016/j.renene.2018.08.079

Al-Wabel M.I., Al-Omran A., El-Naggar A.H., Nadeem M. & Usman A.R.A. (2013). Pyrolysis Temperature induced Changes in Characteristics and Chemical Composition of Biochar Produced from Conocarpus Wastes. Bioresource Technology, 131, 374-379. http://dx.doi.org/10.1016/j.biortech.2012.12.165

Antonov A., Ivanov G. & Pastukhova N. (2019). The Poultry Waste Management System, IOP Conf. Series: Earth and Environmental Science, 272, 022050. doi:10.1088/1755-1315/272/2/022050

Aronsson P. & Perttu K. (2001). Willow Vegetation Filters for Wastewater Treatment and Soil Remediation Combined with Biomass Production. The Forest Chronicel, 77 (2), 293-299. DOI: 10.5558/tfc77293-2

Arwinsyah, Tafsin M. & Yunilas, (2019) Effect of Bio Activator use on Corn Cobs as a Complete Feed on Performance and Digestibility of Local Sheep. IOP Conf. Series: Earth and Environmental Science, 260, 012047. doi:10.1088/1755-1315/260/1/012047

Aryal J. & Tamrakar S, A. (2013) Domestic Organic Waste Composting in MadhyapurThimi, Bhaktapur. Nepal Journal of Science and Technology, 14(1), 129-136.https://doi.org/10.3126/njst.v14i1.8933

Bachand P.A.M. & Horne A.J. (1999). Dentrification in Constructed Free-water Surface Wetlands:II. Effects of Vegetation and Temperature, Ecological Engineering, 14 (1-2), 17-32.

Bajsa O., Nair J, Mathew P, K. & Ho G.E. (2003).Vermiculture as a tool for Domestic Wastewater Management.Water Science and Technology, 48(11/12), 125-132. DOI: 10.2166/wst.2004.0821

Banks C.J., Chesshire M., Heaven S. & Arnold R. (2011). Anaerobic Digestion of Source-segregated Domestic Food Waste: Performance Assessment by Mass and Energy Balance. Bioresource Technology, 102, 612-620, ISSN 0960-8524, 10.1016/j.biortech.2010.08.005.

Banks C.J., Chesshire M. & String fellow A. (2008). A Pilot-scale Comparison of Mesophilic and Thermophilic Digestion of Source Segregated Domestic Food Waste. Water Science and Technology 58(7), 1475-1481. DOI 10.2166/wst.2008.513

Barik D. & Murugan S. (2015). Assessment of Sustainable Biogas Production from De-oiled Seed Cake Seed Cake of Karanja- an Organic Industrial Waste from Biodiesel Production. Fuel, 148, 25-31. DOI: 10.1016/j.fuel.2015.01.072

Bharadwaj A. (2010), Management of Kitchen Waste Material through Vermicomposting. Asian J. Exp. Biol. Sci., 1 (1), 175-177. ISSN 0975-5845.

Ch'ng H.Y., Ahmed O.H. & Majid N.M.A. (2014). Improving Phosphorus Availability in an Acid Soil Using Organic Amendments Produced from Agroindustrial Wastes. The Scientific World Journal, Volume 2014, 6 pages, Article ID 506356, http://dx.doi.org/10.1155/2014/506356

Chaiprasert P. (2011). Biogas Production from Agricultural Wastes in Thailand. Journal of Sustainable Energy & Environment Special Issue, 63-65.

Chandel A.K., Chan ES, Rudravaram R., Narasu M.L., Rao L.V. & Ravindra P. (2013). Economics and Environmental Impact of Bioethanol Production Technologies: An Appraisal, African Journal of Environmental Economics and Management, 1 (5), 126-143.

Cheerawit R., Thunwadee T.S., Duangporn K., Tanawat R. & Wichuda K. (2012). Biogas Production from Co-digestion of Domestic Wastewater and Food Waste. Health and The Environment Journal, 3(2), 1-9.

Claassen P.A.M., Budde A.W. M. & López-Contreras A.M. (2000). Acetone, Butanol and Ethanol Production from Domestic Organic Waste by Solventogenic Clostridia. J. Mol. Microbiol. Biotechnol, 2(1), 39-44.

Dias B.O., Silva C.A., Higashikawa F.S., Roig A. & Sánchez-Monedero M.A. (2010). Use of Biochar as Bulking agent for the Composting of Poultry Manure: Effect on Organic Matter Degradation and Humification. Bioresource Technology, 101, 1239-1246, doi:10.1016/j.biortech.2009.09.024

Diener S., Zurbrügg C., Gutiérrez F.R., Nguyen D.H., Morel A., Koottatep T. & Tockner K. (2011). Black Soldier Fly Larvae for Organic Waste Treatment – Prospects and Constraints. Proceedings of the Waste Safe 2011 – 2nd International Conference on Solid Waste Management in the Developing Countries, 52 (1-8). ISBN: 978-984-33-2705-5.

Domingo J.L. & Nadal M. (2009). Domestic Waste Composting Facilities: A Review of Human Health Risks. Environment International, 35, 382-389, doi: 10.1016/j.envint.2008.07.004.

El-Gawad H.A.A, & Aly A.M. (2011). Assessment of Aquatic Environmental for Wastewater Management Quality in the Hospitals: A Case Study. Australian Journal of Basic and Applied Sciences, 5(7): 474-782. ISSN 1991-8178.

Elissen H.J.H., Hendrickx T.L.G., Temmink H., Laarhoven B. & Buisman C.J.N. (2015). Worm-it: Converting Organic Wastes into Sustainable Fish Feed by using Aquatic Worms. Journal of Insects as Food and Feed, 1(1), 67-74. ISSN 2352-4588 online, DOI 10.3920/JIFF2014.0012.

Emmanuel E., Pierre M.G. & Perrodin Y. (2009). Groundwater Contamination by Microbiological and Chemical Substances released from Hospital Wastewater: Health Risk Assessment for Drinking Water Consumers. Environment International, 35, 718-726. doi:10.1016/j.envint.2009.01.011

Ethica S.N., Muchlissin S.I., Saptaningtyas R. & Subdono A. (2018). Protease Producers Predominate Cultivable Hydrolytic Bacteria Isolated from Liquid Biomedical Wastes. Asian Journal of Chemistry, 30(9), 2035-2038.

Finley S., Barrington S. & Lyew D. (2009). Reuse of Domestic Greywater for the Irrigation of Food Crops. Water, Air and Soil Pollution, 199 (1-4), 235-245. DOI: 10.1007/s11270-008-9874-x

Forster-Carneiro T., Berni M.D., Dorileo I.L. & Rostagno M.A. (2013). Biorefinery Study of Availability of Agriculture Residues and Wastes for Integrated Biorefineries in Brazil. Resources, Conservation and Recycling, 77, 78-88. http://dx.doi.org/10.1016/j.resconrec.2013.05.007

Garci´a A.J., Esteban M.B., Ma´rquez M.C. & Ramos P. (2005). Biodegradable Municipal Solid Waste: Characterization and Potential use as Animal Feedstuffs. Waste Management, 25, 780-787, doi:10.1016/j.wasman.2005.01.006

Ghani W.A. W.A.K., Mohd A., da Silva G., Bachmann R.T., Taufiq-Yap Y.H., Rashidf U., Al-Muhtaseb A.H. (2013). Biochar Production from Waste Rubber-wood-sawdust and its Potential use in C Sequestration: Chemical and Physical Characterization. Industrial Crops and Products, 44, 18-24. http://dx.doi.org/10.1016/j.indcrop.2012.10.017

Haga K. (1999). Development of Composting Technology in Animal Waste Treatment-a Review. Asian-Aus. J. Anim. Sci., 12(4), 604-608.

Han W., Wang Z., Chen H., Yao X. & Li Y. Journal of Biomedicine and Biotechnology Volume 2011, 5 pages, Article ID 343791. doi:10.1155/2011/343791

Han Z., Liu D., Lei Y., Wu J. & Li S. (2015). Characteristics and Management of Domestic Waste in the Rural Area of Southwest China.Waste Management & Research, 33(1) 39-47, DOI: 10.1177/0734242X14558668

Hass A., Gonzalez J.M., Lima I.M., Godwin H.W., Halvorson J.J. & Boyer D.G. (2012). Chicken Manure Biochar as Liming and Nutrient Source for Acid Appalachian Soil. J. Environ. Qual, 41, 1096-1106. doi:10.2134/jeq2011.0124

Huanga H., Yanga T., Laia F. & Wu G. (2017). Co-pyrolysis of Sewage Sludge and Sawdust/rice Straw for the Production of Biochar. Journal of Analytical and Applied Pyrolysis, 125, 61-68, http://dx.doi.org/10.1016/j.jaap.2017.04.018

Huma Z., Naveed S., Rashid A., Ullah A. & Khattak I. (2012). Effects of Domestic and Industrial Waste Water on Germination and Seedling Growth of some Plants. Current Opinion in Agriculture, 1(1), 27-30.

Hussein S.D. A. & Sawan O.M. (2010).The Utilization of Agricultural Waste as One of the Environmental Issues in Egypt (A Case Study). Journal of Applied Sciences Research, 6(8), 1116-1124.

Ilaboya I.R., Asekhame F.F., Ezugwu M.O., Erameh A.A. & Omofuma F.E. (2010). Studies on Biogas Generation from Agricultural Waste; Analysis of the Effects of Alkaline on Gas Generation. World Applied Sciences Journal, 9 (5), 537-545. ISSN 1818-4952.

Iqbal S.A., Rahaman S., Rahman M. & Yousuf A. (2014). Anaerobic Digestion of Kitchen Waste to Produce Biogas. Procedia Engineering. 657-662. doi: 10.1016/j.proeng.2014.11.787

Jia X., Yuan W. & Ju X. (2015). Short Report: Effects of Biochar Addition on Manure Composting and Associated N_2O Emissions. Journal of Sustainable Bioenergy Systems, 5, 56-61. http://dx.doi.org/10.4236/jsbs.2015.52005

Jin H., Capareda S., Chang Z., Gao J., Xu Y. & Zhang J. (2014). Biocharpyrolytically produced from Municipal Solid Wastes for Aqueous As(V) removal: Adsorption Property and its Improvement with KOH Activation. Bioresource Technology, 169, 622-629. http://dx.doi.org/10.1016/j.biortech.2014.06.103

Jindo K., Mizumoto H., Sawada Y., Sanchez-Monedero M.A. & Sonoki T. (2014). Physical and Chemical Characterization of Biochars Derived from different Agricultural Residues. Biogeosciences, 11, 6613-6621. doi:10.5194/bg-11-6613-2014.

Jokela J.P.Y., Kettunen R.H., Sormunen K.M. & Rintala J.A. (2002). Biological Nitrogen removal from Municipal Landfill leachate: Low-cost Nitrification in Biofilters and Laboratory Scale *in-situ* Denitrification. Water Research, 36 (16), 4079-4087. DOI:10.1016/s0043-1354(02)00129-x

Kacprzak A., Krzystek L. & Ledakowicz S.L. (2010). Co-digestion of Agricultural and Industrial Wastes. Chemical Papers, 64 (2), 127-131. DOI: 10.2478/s11696-009-0108-5

Kang Q., Appels L., Tan T. & Dewil R. (2014). Bioethanol from Lignocellulosic Biomass: Current Findings Determine Research Priorities. The Scientific World Journal, Volume 2014, 13 pages, Article ID 298153. http://dx.doi.org/10.1155/2014/298153

Khajuria A. & Kumar A. (2007). Assessment of Healthcare Waste Generated by Government Hospital in Agra City, India. Our Nature, 5, 25-30. DOI: 10.3126/on.v5i1.794

Kiedrzyñska E., Wagner I. & Zalewski M. (2008). Quantification of phosphorus retention Efficiency by Floodplain Management Strategy for a Eutrophic Reservoir Restoration. Ecological Engineering, 1(33), 15-25. DOI: 10.1016/j.ecoleng.2007.10.010

Kim J.K. (2011). Cost-Effectiveness of Converting Fish Waste into Liquid Fertilizer. FishAquatSci 14(3), 230-233. http://dx.doi.org/10.5657/FAS.2011.0230

Kongkiattikajorn J. & Sornvoraweat B. (2011). Comparative Study of Bioethanol Production from Cassava Peels by Monoculture and Co-Culture of Yeast. Kasetsart J. (Nat. Sci.), 45, 268-274.

Kulkarni Sunil J. (2013). Removal of Organic matter from Domestic Waste Water by Adsorption/International Journal of Science, Engineering and Technology Research (IJSETR), 2(10), p 1836-1839.ISSN: 2278-7798.

Kumanda C., Mlambo V. & Mnisi C.M. (2019). From Landfills to the Dinner Table: Red Grape.

Pomace Waste as a Nutraceutical for Broiler Chickens. Sustainability, 11, 1931. doi:10.3390/su11071931

Lapiñski D., Wiater J. & Szatylowicz E. (2019). The Content of Heavy Metals in Waste as an Indicator Determining the Possibilities of Their Agricultural Use, Journal of Ecological Engineering, 20(4), 225-230. https://doi.org/10.12911/22998993/103013

Li Q., Zheng L., Cai H., Garza E., Yu Z. & Zhou S. (2011). From Organic Waste to Biodiesel: Black Soldier Fly, *Hermatiaillucens*, makes it Feasible. Fuel, 90(4), 1545-1548. https://doi.org/10.1016/j.fuel.2010.11.016

Li Q., Zheng L., Qiu N., Cai H., Tomberlin J.K. & Yu Z. (2011). Bioconversion of Dairy Manure by Black Soldier Fly (Diptera: *Stratiomyidae*) for Biodiesel and Sugar Production. Waste Management, 31(6), 1316-1320. DOI:10.1016/j.wasman.2011.01.005

López-Mosquera M.E., Fernández-Lema E., Villares R., Corral R., Alonso B. & Blanco C. (2011). Composting Fish Waste and Seaweed to produce a Fertilizer for use in Organic Agriculture, Ecological Engineering: From Concepts to Applications. Procedia Environmental Sciences, 9, 113-117. DOI: 10.1016/j.proenv.2011.11.018

Mane T.T. & Raskar S.S. (2012). Management of Agriculture Waste from Market yard through Vermicomposting. Research Journal of Recent Sciences, 1, 289-296.ISSN 2277-2502.

Manfredi S., Tonini D., Christiansen T.H. & Scharff H. (2009). Landfilling of Waste: accounting of Greenhouse Gases and Global Warming Contributions. Waste Management & Research, 27(8), 825-836. DOI:10.1177/0734242X09348529

Manios T. (2004). The Composting Potential of different Organic Solid Wastes: Experience from the Island of Crete. Environment International, 29, 1079-1089.doi:10.1016/S0160-4120(03)00119-3

Manurung R., Supriatna A., Esyanthi R.R. & Putra R.E. (2016). Bioconversion of Rice Straw Waste by Black Soldier Fly larvae (*HermetiaillucensL.*): Optimal Feed Rate for Biomass Production. JEZS, 4(4), 1036-1041.E-ISSN: 2320-7078,P-ISSN: 2349-6800.

Martini M., da Fonseca R.C., Severiano L.V., Garbin H.I., da Rosa T.F. & Klück M. (2017). Hospital Waste: Can we Reduce the Environmental Impact of a Large University Hospital? Clin Biomed Res, 37(4): 288-294. http://dx.doi.org/10.4322/2357-9730.74075

Mathur U.B, Verma L.K & Srivastava J.N. (2006). Effects of Vermicomposting on Microbiological Flora of Infected Biomedical Waste. Journal of ISHWM, 5, 21-26.

Menardo S. & Balsari P. (2012). An Analysis of the Energy Potential of Anaerobic Digestion of Agricultural By-Products and Organic Waste. Bioenerg. Res., 5, 759-767. DOI 10.1007/s12155-012-9188-0

Mohankumar S. & Kottaiveeran K. (2011). Hospital Waste Management and Environmental Problems in India. International Journal of Pharmaceutical & Biological Archives, 2(6), 1621-1626. ISSN 0976-3333.

Moreira A.M.M. & Günther W.M.R. (2013). Assessment of Medical Waste Management at a Primary Health-care Center in São Paulo, Brazil. Waste Management, 33, 162-167/http://dx.doi.org/10.1016/j.wasman.2012.09.018

Najar I.A. & Khan A.B. (2013). Management of Fresh Water Weeds (macrophytes) by Vermicomposting using *Eiseniafetida*, Environ SciPollut Res, 20, 6406-6417, DOI 10.1007/s11356-013-1687-9

Namsivayam S.K.R., Narendrakumar G. and Kumar J.A. (2011). Evaluation of Effective Microorganism (EM) for Treatment of Domestic Sewage. Journal of Experimental Sciences, 2(7), 30-32. ISSN: 2218-1768

Nyachaka C.J. Yawas D.S. & Pam G.Y. (2013). Production and Performance Evaluation Of Bioethanol Fuel From Groundnuts Shell Waste. American Journal of Engineering Research, 02(12),303-312. (AJER) e-ISSN: 2320-0847 p-ISSN : 2320-0936

Nyakeri E.M., Ogola H.J., Ayieko M.A. & Amimo F.A. (2017). An Open System for Farming Black Soldier Fly larvae as a source of Proteins forsmall Scale Poultry and Fish Production. Journal of Insects as Food and Feed, 3(1), 51-56. ISSN 2352-4588 online, DOI 10.3920/JIFF2016.0030.

Odlare M., Lindmark J., Ericsson A. & Pell M. (2015). Use of Organic Wastes in Agriculture. The 7th International Conference on Applied Energy – ICAE2015, Energy Procedia,75, 2472-2476, DOI: 10.1016/j.egypro.2015.07.225

Oliveira L.A., Porto A.L.F. & Tambourgi E.B. (2006). Production of xylanase and Protease by *Penicilliumjanthinellum* CRC 87M-115 from different Agricultural Wastes. Bioresource Technology, 97, 862-867. doi:10.1016/j.biortech.2005.04.017.

Omer A.M. (2007). Organic Waste Treatment for Power Production and Energy Supply. Journal of Cell and Animal Biology. 1 (2), 034-047.

Oribhabor B.J. & ANSA E.J. (2006). Organic Waste Reclamation, Recycling and re-use in Integrated Fish Farming in the Niger Delta. J. Appl. Sci. Environ. Mgt., 10 (3), 47-53. DOI: 10.4314/jasem.v10i3.17319

Oyeleke, S.B. & Istifanus, N. (2009). The microbiological Effects of Hospital Wastes on the Environment. African Journal of Biotechnology, 8 (22), 6253-6257. ISSN 1684-5315.

Pandebesie E.S., Kartini A.M., Wilujeng S.M. & Warmadewanthi I. (2019). Utilization of Stalks Waste of Sorghum to Produce Bioethanol by Using *Saccharomyces cerevisiae* and *S. cerevisiae-Pichia stipitis* Consortium, Journal or Ecological Engineering, 20(4), 54-60. https://doi.org/10.12911/22998993/102616

Parmar A., Nema P. K. & Agarwal T. (2014). Biochar Production from Agro-food Industry Residues: A Sustainable Approach for Soil and Environmental Management. Current Science, 107(10), 1673-1682.

Pasupathi P., Sindhu S., Ponnusha B.S. & Ambika A. (2011). Biomedical Waste Management for Health Care Industry.Int J Biol Med Res, 2(1), 472-486. ISSN: 0976:6685.

Poggi-Varaldo H.M, Munoz-Paez K.M., Escamilla-Alvarado C., Robledo-Narváez P.N., Ponce-Noyola M.T., Calva-Calva G., Ríos-Leal E., Galíndez-Mayer J., Estrada-Vázquez C., Ortega-Clemente A. & Rinderknecht-Seijas N.F. (2014). Biohydrogen, Biomethane and Bioelectricity as Crucial Components of Biorefinery of Organic Wastes: A Review. Waste Management & Research, 1-13. DOI: 10.1177/0734242X14529178.

Pramanik P. & Chung Y.R. (2010). Efficacy of Vermicomposting for Recycling Organic Portion of Hospital Wastes using *Eiseniafetida*: Standardization of Cow Manure Proportion to Increase Enzymatic Activities and Fungal Biomass. Environmentalist, 30, 267-272. DOI 10.1007/s10669-010-9273-x

Priya A., Avishek K. & Pathak G. (2012). Assessing the Potentials of *Lemna minor* in the Treatment of Domestic Wastewater at Pilot Scale. Environ Monit Assess, 184, 4301-4307. DOI 10.1007/s10661-011-2265-6.

Rahman A., Ellis J.T. & Miller C.D. (2012).Bioremediation of Domestic Wastewater and Production of Bioproducts from Microalgae Using Waste Stabilization Ponds. J Bioremed Biodeg, 3(6), http://dx.doi.org/10.4172/2155-6199.1000e113

Ramnarain Y.I., Ansari A.A. & Ori L. (2019). Vermicomposting of different Organic Materials using the Epigeic Earthworm *Eisenia foetida*. Int J Recycl Org Waste Agricult, 8, 23-36. https://doi.org/10.1007/s40093-018-0225-7

Randhawa G.K. and Kullar J.S. (2011). Bioremediation of Pharmaceuticals, Pesticides, and Petrochemicals with Gomeya/Cow Dung. International Scholarly Research Network, ISRN Pharmacology, 2011, 7 pages. Article ID 362459. doi:10.5402/2011/362459

Rattanapan C., Sinchai L., Suksaroj T.T., Kanatchote D. & Ounsaneha W. (2019). Biogas Production by Co-digestion of Canteen Food Waste and Domestic Wastewater under Organic Loading Rate and Temperature Optimization. Environments, 6, 16. doi:10.3390/environments6020016

Razaviarani V., Buchanan I.D, Malik S. & Katalambula H. (2013). Pilot Scale Anaerobic Co-digestion of Municipal Wastewater Sludge with Biodiesel Waste Glycerin. Bioresource Technology, 133, 206-212. DOI: 10.1016/j.biortech.2013.01.101

Regueiro L., Carballa M., Álvarez J.A. & Lerna J.M. (2012). Enhanced Methane Production from Pig Manure Anaerobic Digestion using Fish and Biodiesel Wastes as Co-substartes. Bioresource Technology, 123, 507-513.DOI: 10.1016/j.biortech.2012.07.109

Ryu B.G., Kim J., Kim K., Han J.I. & Yan J.W. (2013). High Cell-density Cultivation of Oleaginous Yeast Cryptococcus Curvatus for Biodiesel Production using Organic Waste from the Brewery Industry. Bioresource Technology, 135, 357-364. DOI:10.1016/j.biortech.2012.09.054

Salminen E. & Rintala J. (2002). Anaerobic Digestion of Organic Solid Poultry Slaughterhouse Waste – A Review. Bioresource Technology, 83, 13-26. DOI:10.1016/s0960-8524(01)00199-7

Salminen E., Rintala J., Härkönen J., Kuitunen M., Högmander H. & Oikar A. (2001). Anaerobically Digested Poultry Slaughterhouse Wastes as Fertiliser in Agriculture. Bioresource Technology, 78, 81-88. https://doi.org/10.1016/S0960-8524(00)00160-7

Sánchez-Andrea I., Triana D. & Sanz J.L. (2012). Bioremediation of Acid Mine Drainage Coupled with Domestic Wastewater Treatment. Water Science & Technology, 66(11), 2425-2431, doi: 10.2166/wst.2012.477.

Sancom A., Sopajaree K. & Cheunbarn T. (2006). Effect of Temperature on Total Organic Carbon Degradation Using Trichoderma Fungal in Co-composting of Straw and Hospital Sewage Sludge. The 2nd Joint International Conference on "Sustainable Energy and Environment, E-077(P), 21-23.

Sawalem M., Selic E. & Herbell J.-D. (2016). Hospital Waste Management in Libya: A Case Study. Waste Management, 29, 1370-1375. doi:10.1016/j.wasman.2008.08.028

Selvakumar P. & Sivashanmugam P. (2017). Optimization of Lipase Production from Organic Solid Waste by Anaerobic Digestion and its Application in Biodiesel Production. Fuel Processing Technology, 100 (165), 1-8. DOI: 10.1016/j.fuproc.2017.04.020

Singh R.P., Ibrahim M.H., Esa N. & Iliyana M.S. (2010). Composting of Waste from Palm Oil Mill: A Sustainable Waste Management Practice. Rev Environ SciBiotechnol, 9, 331-344. DOI 10.1007/s11157-010-9199-2

Steiner C., Das K.C., Melear N. & Lakly D. (2010). Reducing Nitrogen Loss during Poultry Litter Composting Using Biochar. J. Environ. Qual, 39(4), 1236-42.doi:10.2134/jeq2009.0337

Sugiura K, Yamatani S., Watahara M. & Onodera T. (2009). Ecofeed, animal feed produced from Recycled Food Waste. VeterinariaItaliana, 45(3), 397-404.

Surendra K.C., Olivier R., Tomberlin J.K., Jha R. & Khanal S.K. (2016). Bioconversion of Organic Wastes into Biodiesel and Animal Feed via Insect Farming. Renewable Energy 98 (2016) 197-202. http://dx.doi.org/10.1016/j.renene.2016.03.022

Szuster B. & Flaherty M. (2002). A Regional Approach to Assessing Organic Waste Production by Low Salinity Shrimp Farms. Aquaculture Asia, VII (2), 49-52.

Tahiri E.M., Benaabidate L., Nejjari C. & Benbrahim K.F. (2012). Assessment of Physicochemical and Biological Parameters of Al Ghassani Hospital Wastewaters, Fez – Morocco, J. Mater. Environ. Sci., 3 (1), 115-120. ISSN: 2028-2508 CODEN: JMESCN.

Usman A.R.A., Abduljabbar A., Vithanage M., Ok Y.S., Ahmad M., Ahmad M., Elfaki J., Abdulazeem S.S. & Al-Wabel M.I. (2015). Biochar Production from Date Palm Waste: Charring Temperature induced changes in Composition and Surface Chemistry. Journal of Analytical and Applied Pyrolysis, 115, 392-400. http://dx.doi.org/10.1016/j.jaap.2015.08.016

Voca N., Kricka T., Savic T.B., Matin A. & Jurišic V. (2010). Organic Waste after Wine and Olive Oil Production as Raw Material for Thermal Energy Generation. Journal on Processing and Energy in Agriculture,14 (2), 69-71. Biblid: 1821-4487.

Walker B.L. & Cooper C.D. (1992). Air Pollution Emission Factors for Medical Waste Incinerators.J. Air Waste Manage. Assoc., 42, 784-791. ISSN 1047-3289

Wang L., Sharifzadeh M., Templer R. & Murphy R.J. (2013). Bioethanol Production from various Waste Papers: Economic Feasibility and Sensitivity analysis. Applied Energy, 111, 1172-1182.http://dx.doi.org/10.1016/j.apenergy.2012.08.048

Wang T., Camps-Arbestain M., Hedley M. & Bishop P Predicting Phosphorus Bioavailability from High-ash Biochars, Plant and Soil, 357 (1-2), 173-187. DOI 10.1007/s11104-012-1131-9

Weiland P. (2010). Biogas Production: Current State and Perspectives. ApplMicrobiolBiotechnol, 85, 849-860. DOI 10.1007/s00253-009-2246-7

Xu X., Cao X., Zhao L., Wang H., Yu H. & Gao B. (2013). Removal of Cu, Zn, and Cd from Aqueous Solutions by the Dairy manure-derived Biochar. Environ SciPollut Res, 20, 358-368. DOI 10.1007/s11356-012-0873-5

Yadav R.K., Goyal B., Sharma R.K., Dubey S.K. & Minhas P.S. (2002). Post-irrigation Impact of Domestic Sewage Effluent on Composition of Soils, Crops and Ground Water—A Case Study/Environment International, 28, 481-486.

Yang N., Zhang H., Chen M., Shao L.M. & He P.J. (2012). Greenhouse Gas Emissions from MSW incineration in China: Impacts of Waste Characteristics and Energy Recovery. Waste Management (New York, NY), 32(12), 2552-2560. DOI:10.1016/j.wasman.2012.06.008

Yang S., Li Q., Zeng Q., Zhang J., Yu Z. & Liu Z. (2012). Conversion of Solid Organic Wastes into Oil via Boettcherisca peregrine (Diptera: *Sarcophagidae*) larvae and Optimization of Parameters for Biodiesel Production. PloS one, 7(9), e45940, https://doi.org/10.1371/journal.pone.0045940

Yang X., Choi H.S., Park C. & Kim S.W. (2015). Current States and Prospects of Organic Waste Utilization for Biorefineries. Renewable and Sustainable Energy Reviews, 49, 335-349. http://dx.doi.org/10.1016/j.rser.2015.04.114

Yuan J.H., Xu R.K. & Zhang H. (2011). The forms of alkalis in the biochar produced from Crop Residues at different Temperatures. Bioresource Technology, 102, 3488-3497/doi:10.1016/j.biortech.2010.11.018

Zhang Y., Banks C.J. & Heaven S. (2012) Co-digestion of source Segregated Domestic Food Waste to Improve Process Stability. Bioresource Technology, 114, 168-178. doi: 10.1016/j.biortech.2012.03.040

Zheng L., Hou Y., Li W., Yang S., Li Q. & Hu Z. (2013). Exploring the Potential of Grease from Yellow Mealworm Beetle (*Tenebriomolitor*) as a Novel Biodiesel Feedstock. Applied Energy 101, 618-621.http://dx.doi.org/10.1016/j.apenergy.2012.06.067

Zheng L., Hou Y., Li W., Yang S., Li Q. & Yu Z. (2012). Biodiesel Production from Rice Straw and Restaurant Waste Employing Black Soldier Fly assisted by Microbes. Energy 47(1), 225-229. https://doi.org/10.1016/j.energy.2012.09.006

Zheng L., Li Q., Zhang J. & Yu Z. (2012). Double the Biodiesel yield: Rearing Black Soldier Fly larvae, *Hermetiaillucens*, on Solid Residual Fraction of Restaurant Waste after Grease Extraction for Biodiesel Production. Renewable Energy, 41, 75-79. DOI: 10.1016/j.renene.2011.10.004

Zhu D., Sun C., Zhang H., Wu Z., Jia B. & Zhang Y. (2012). Roles of Vegetation, Flow Type and filled Depth on Livestock Wastewater Treatment through Multi-level Mineralized Refuse-based Constructed Wetlands. Ecological Engineering, 39, 7-15. DOI:10.1016/j.ecoleng.2011.11.002

3

Bioremediation and Biodegradation Technologies for Removal of Pollutants and Wastes from Environment

INTRODUCTION

Bioremediation is defined as "The use of biological mechanisms to destroy, transform, or immobilize environmental contaminants in order to protect potential sensitive receptors." In the past, thermal, chemical, and physical treatment technique have didn't eliminate the pollution drawback as a result of those technique solely shift the pollution to a replacement part like air pollution (Kleijntjens *et.al.*, 2000 and Klein 2000). Bioremediation technology, which leads to degradation of pollutants, may be a lucrative and environmentally beneficial alternative that could produce economic profit (Hlihor *et.al.*, 2017).

Bioremediation has been used at a number of sites worldwide, with varying degrees of success (Boopathy *et.al.*, 2000). Techniques are rising as larger data and knowledge are gained, and there's little doubt that bioremediation has nice potential for coping with certain kinds of website contamination. Unfortunately, the principles, techniques, advantage, and downsides of bioremediation don't seem to be wide identified or understood, particularly among those that can ought to deal directly with bioremediation proposal, like site owners and regulators. (Van Deuren *et.al.*, 2002). We have a tendency to mean to help by providing a simple, pragmatic read of the processes concerned in bioremediation, the proposal and cons of the technique, and therefore the problems to be thought of once dealing with a proposal and cons of the techniques, and therefore the problems to be thought of once dealing with a proposal for bioremediation. Some tests make an exhaustive examination of the literature of bioremediation of organic and inorganic pollutants, and another test takes a look at pertinent field application case histories.

Wastes arise from domestic and industrial activity i.e., sewage, waste waters, agriculture, food processing, wood wastes and an ever-increasing range of toxic industrial chemical products & by products. Pollutants is also within the kind of any chemical (radionuclide, organo-phosphorus compound or trace gases) or geochemical substances (dust, sediment, grit etc.), biotic component or product or physical agent (heat, sound etc.), that's free by man in to the atmosphere in such quantities that will have adverse effects. For an environmentally compatible sustainable development, the core problems such as management of wastes and other pollutants require application of clear technologies. The use of microbes in the degradation of different types of pollutants and wastes leading to bioremediation, is one such way. Microbes may be deployed as voracious scavengers, removing all types of pollutants, similarly within the world utilization of matter, since they unloose carbon, nitrogen, phosphorus and sulfur from a large range of advanced organic compounds (Iranzo *et.al.*, 2001). On the basis of their behavior in the environment, organic compounds are classified as the following:

(i) **Biodegradable:** Those organic compounds which undergo biological transformations are termed as biodegradable.

(ii) **Persistent:** Those organic compounds which do not undergo biodegradation in certain environment, are termed as persistent.

(iii) **Recalcitrant:** Those which resist biodegradation in a wide range of environments are termed as recalcitrant.

Xenobiotics are synthetic compounds not formed by natural biosynthetic processes, and can be recalcitrant. Therefore, xenobiotic compounds are foreign substrates in our ecosystem and may have toxic effects when accumulated above threshold value (Chojnacka, 2010).

BIOREMEDIATION STRATEGIES

Bioremediation can be achieved by different techniques. Bioremediation has two strategies, *In-situ* bioremediation "can be used at the site of contamination" and *Ex-situ* Bioremediation means "on contamination removed from the original site" (Shannon *et.al.*, 2000).

IN-SITU BIOREMEDIATION

In situ bioremediation is the application of biological treatment to the cleanup of hazardous chemicals present in the subsurface (Held and Don, 2000). The optimization and management of microorganism transformations of organic contaminants need the mixing of the many scientific and engineering disciplines.

BIOSCREENS

Bioscreens are a lovely treatment choice as a result of they need high longevity, no important maintenance, and no nutrient renewal. These screens are composed of organic wastes and sedimentary rock. The organic wastes not solely function a high permeableness structure, however conjointly as a supply of nutrients and bacterium. The bioscreens even have high material retentions and inflated bioactivity. The hydraulic conductivity of the material within the bioscreens is ten times over that of the encompassing formation. The thickness of the bioscreens depends on groundwater flow rates, the pollute concentrations, and therefore the degradation rates.

BIOSPARGING

Biosparging involves the injection of air harassed below the formation to extend groundwater O_2 concentrations and enhance the speed of biological degradation of contaminants by in-vivo bacterium. Biosparging will increase the blending within the saturated zone and thereby will increase the contact between soil and groundwater. The benefit and low price of putting in small-diameter air injection points permits significant flexibility within the style and construction of the system.

BIOVENTING

Bioventing could be a promising new technology that stimulates the natural unchanged biodegradation of any aerobically degradable compounds in NAPL among the soil by providing O_2 to existing soil micro-organisms. In distinction to soil-vapor extraction (SVE), bioventing uses low air-flow rates to supply simply enough O_2 to sustain micro-organism activity. O_2 is most ordinarily provided through direct air injection into residual contamination in soil by means that of wells. adsorbable fuel residuals are biodegraded, and volatile compounds are biodegraded as vapors inch through biologically active soil.

BIOAUGMENTATION

Bioaugmentation is that the introduction of a bunch of natural microorganism strains or a genetically built variant to treat contaminated soil or water (Akhtar *et.al.*, 2013). it's ordinarily employed in municipal waste treatment to restart activated sludge bioreactors. Most cultures accessible contain a research based association of micro-organism cultures, containing all necessary microorganisms At sites wherever soil and groundwater are contaminated with chlorinated ethenes, like tetrachloroethylene and trichloroethane, bioaugmentation is employed to make sure that the naturally occuring micro-organisms will fully degrade these contaminants to chloride, that are non-toxic observation of this technique is tough (Guidi *et.al.*, 2018).

BIOPILING

Biopile treatment could be a complete technology within which excavated soils are mixed with soil amendments, placed on a treatment space, and bioremediated exploitation forced aeration. The contaminants are reduced to CO_2 and water. The essential biopile system includes a treatment bed, water irrigation, nutrient management and a leach ate assortment system. Temperature, Moisture, micro and macro nutrient nutrients, O_2, and pH scale are controlled to increase biodegradation. The irrigation/nutrient system is buried below the soil to pass air and nutrients either by vacuum or positive pressure. Soil piles may be up to twenty feet high and will be lined with plastic to manage runoff, evaporation and volatilization, and to enhance solar heating system. If volatile organic compounds (VOCs) within the soil change into the air stream, the air move out the soil is also treated to get rid of or destroy the VOCs before they're discharged into the atmosphere. Treatment time is usually three to six months.

EX-SITU BIOREMEDIATION

Ex situ Bioremedy includes techniques like Composting, land-farming, biopiling, and process by bioreactors along side thermal, chemical, and physical processes. *Ex situ* bioremedy could be a lot of thorough remedy technique, however because of the prices associated not solely with the remediation processes, however conjointly can the excavation and transportation of the soil, many persons are trying towards *in situ* remediation techniques. *Ex situ* thermal Technique involves the transfer of pollutants from the soil to a gaseous part. The pollutants are free by vaporization and therefore the burned at high temperatures. Ex situ thermal remedy is completed in three phases: soil condition, temperature treatment, and exhaust gas purification. Soil condition could be a method within which broken into little grains and sieved in preparation for thermal treatment. In temperature treatment, temperature of the soil in order to convert volatile pollutants to a gas phase. Heating is completed by employing a sintering strand, fluid bed, or rotary oven plants. The heating range of the soil is typically vary between 350-550°C. Combustion of the gases occurs on the uppermost of the soil, but the volatile gases are not terminated. The gases are then burned in an after-burner chamber at more than the 1000°C dioxins are destroyed.

Ex situ thermal remediation processes are ideal for use when removing polycyclic aromatic hydrocarbons (PAH), petroleum hydrocarbons (TPH), benzene, toluene, ethylbenzene, xylenes (BTEX), phenolic compounds, cyanides, and chlorinated compounds like polychlorinated biphenyls (PCB), pentchlorphenol (PCP), chlorinated hydrocarbons, chlorinated pesticides, polychlorinated dibenzodioxins (PCDD), and polychlorinated dibenzofurans (PCDF) (Alegbeleye *et.al.*, 2017, Gogoi *et.al.*, 2002).

Ex situ biological processes include; composting, landfarming, Heap Technique and the use of bioreactors which are given below:

COMPOSTING

Composting could be a method by which organic wastes are degraded by microorganisms, generally at elevated temperatures. Typical compost temperatures are within the range of 55° to 65° C. The inflated temperatures result from heat created by microorganisms throughout the degradation of the organic material within the waste.

LAND FARMING

Land farming could be a method by which the soil is excavated and mechanically separated via sieving. The impure soil is then place in layers no quite 0.4 meters thick. An artificial, concrete, or clay membrane is then used the contaminated soil layer. O2 is supply and mixing occurs via harrowing, or milling. Nutrients and wetness also be used to assist the remedy method. The pH scale of the soil is additionally regulated (keeping it approximately 7.0) using crushed sedimentary rock or agricultural lime. Land farming is most felicitous in removing PAH and PCP. It illustrates the land farming technique. (Schnoor *et.al.*, 2000).

HEAP TECHNIQUE

Biopiling is an *In situ* process that is also known as the heap technique (Schulz-Berendt, 2000). The primary step in the biopiling method is to perform qualitative tests that may confirm the biological degradation capabilities of the soil sample. The next step involves the mechanical separation of the soil, which which is able to homogenize the sample and remove any disruptive material such as plastics, metals, and stones (Brooks *et.al.*, 1998 and pandey *et.al.*, 2011). The stones can then be crushed into smaller particle and then based on the degree of impurities can either be additional to a pile or sent out for utilize. The soil is then homogenized, meaning that the pollution concentration is averaged out across the entire soil sample (Congeevaram *et.al.*, 2007). Homogenization allows for biopiling to be more effective. As soon as the soil is piled, micro and macro nutrients, microbes, O_2, and substrate are introduced to begin the biological degradation of the contaminants. The results of the initial laboratory exams illustrate to the operators which substrates consisting of bark, lime, or composts desires to be delivered to the soil. nutrients such as mineral fertilizers will also be delivered. Moreover, microorganisms along with fungi, bacteria, or enzymes might be added.

Static piles are normally within the form of pyramids or trapezoids. Their heights vary between 0.6 and 1.8m depending at the form of aeration used (either passive or active). Dynamic biopiles are always plowed and grew to become to maximize their exposure to growth the bioavailability of the contaminants via continuously exposing them to O_2, water and microbes. Regardless of which varieties of lots are used, the region under every heap should be protected in asphalt or concrete to save you the seepage of contaminants and the place above the thousands need to be included with the intention to manipulate temperature and moisture content material conditions.

BIOREACTORS

Slurry reactors or aqueous reactors are used for *Ex situ* remedy of contaminated soil and water pumped up from a contaminated plume (Khan *et.al.*, 2009). Bioremediation in reactors includes the processing of infected strong material (soil, sediment, sludge) or water through an engineered containment device. A slurry bioreactor may be described as a containment vessel and apparatus used to create a 3-segment (stable, liquid, and fuel) mixing situation to growth the bioremediation fee of soil sure and water-soluble pollution as a water slurry of the tainted soil and biomass (commonly indigenous microorganisms) capable of degrading goal contaminants (Faryal *et.al.*, 2007). In well known, the fee and volume of biodegradation are extra in a bioreactor system than in situ or in strong-phase systems because the contained environment is greater manageable and for this reason greater controllable and predictable. despite the blessings of reactor systems, there are a few hazards. the tainted soil calls for pre-treatment (e.g., excavation) or rather the contaminant can be stripped from the soil thru soil washing or physical extraction (e.g., vacuum extraction) earlier than being positioned in a bioreactor (Jain *et.al.*, 2012). Bioremediation techniques and its utility shown in Table 3.1.

Table 1: Bioremediation techniques, benefits and its application

Techniques	Examples	Benefits	Applications
(1)	(2)	(3)	(4)
In situ	Biosparging	Most efficient & Non Invasive	• Biodegradative abilities of indigenous microorganisms presence of metals and inorganic compounds
	Bioventing	Relative Passive	• Environmental Parameters • Biodegradability of pollutants
	Bioaugmentation	Naturally attenuated process, treat soil and water	• Chemical solubility geological factors • Distribution of pollutants
Ex-situ	• Land farming (solid –phase treatment system)	• Cost efficient, Simple, Inexpensive, self heating	• Surface application, aerobic process, application of organic materials to natural soils followed by irrigation and tilling

(Table Contd...)

(1)	(2)	(3)	(4)
	• Composting (Anaerob ic, converts solid organic wastes into humus – like material) • Biopiles	• Low cost rapid reaction rate, Inexpensive, self heating • Can be done on site	• To make plants healthier good alternative to land filling or incinerating practical and convenient. • Surface application, agricultural
Bioreactors	• Slurry reactors • Aqueous reactor	• Rapid degradation kinetic Optimized environmental parameters • Enhances mass transfer effective use of inoculants and surfactant	• Bioaugmentat Toxicity of amendments • Toxic concentration of contaminants
Precipitation or flocculation	• Non-directed physic-chemical complexation reaction between dissolved contaminants and charged cellular components (dead Biomass)	• Cost effective	• Removal of heavy Metals
Microfiltration *Electrodialysis*	• Microfiltration membranes are used at a constant pressure • Use cation and anion exchange membrane pairs	• Remove dissolved solids rapidly • Withstand high temperature and can be reused	• Waste water treatment: recovery and reused of more than 90% of original waste water • Removal of dissolved solid efficiently

MECHANISM OF BIOREMEDIATION

Microbes are the play the key role in bioremediation as they generate the enzymes that catalyze the degradative reactions. Why the microbes carry out degradative reactions? It is because the microbes use organic substances as a source of carbon and energy. Thus while transforming the contaminant microbes gain energy and raw material for their multiplication and maintenance.

Based totally on the mechanism by using which microbes gain energetically, they're extensively labeled into three classes (Table 3.2). But, numerous xenobiotic contaminants won't be amenable to one of the above described categories and other mechanisms are hired by way of the microorganisms for degradation of such compounds.

Table 3.2: Mechanisms of energy generation by the microbes

Mechanism	Electron donor	Electron acceptor	Product
Aerobic respiration	Organic compound	Oxygen	CO_2, H_2O
Anaerobic respiration	Organic compound	NO_3, SO_4, Fe^{+3}, Mn^{+4}, CO_2	N_2, H_2S, CH_4, Reduced metal
Fermentation	Organic compound	Organic compound	Organic acids, alcohols, H_2 & CO_2

REDUCTIVE DEHALOGENATION

It plays very important role in the detoxification of halogenated organic contaminants. Microorganisms catalyze a reaction in which halogen atom of contaminant is replaced by hydrogen atom. Thus the reaction adds 2 electrons to contaminant and reduces it. It yields no energy but seems to be detoxification mechanism as dehalogenated derivatives are less toxic and susceptible to further microbial decay.

COMETABOLISM

In this example additionally the conversion response yields no benefit to the cell. This non-useful transformation is regularly termed as secondary utilization, cometabolism or gratuitous metabolism. Co-metabolism is one form of secondary substrate transformation wherein enzymes produced for number one substrate oxidation are capable of degrading the secondary substrate happily, even though the secondary substrates do not have enough money enough strength to maintain the microbial populace. it's miles consequently defined as degradation of a compound most effective in presence of other natural compound that serves as a primary energy source. numerous contaminants such as Poly-nuclear Aromatic Hydrocarbons (PAHs) and pesticides are degraded through this mechanism. A rising application entails the injection of water containing dissolved primary substrate (e.g. methane, toluene) and oxygen into ground water to guide the co-metabolic breakdown of targeted natural contaminants (Chen *et.al.*, 2015). The addition of methane or methanol helps methanotrophic pastime, which has been validated powerful to degrade chlorinated solvents, along with vinyl chloride and Trichloroethane (TCE), via co-metabolism.

CONTAMINANT STRUCTURE V/S BIODEGRADABILITY RELATION

Biodegradability is important for bioremediation of organic pollution. Chemical shape of pollutant governs the ability of microorganisms to metabolize them, specially the rate and quantity of biodegradation. As we mentioned above, some compounds are conveniently biodegradable while others are not. let us study the general rules that determine this.

- Low to mid molecular weight hydrocarbons and alcohols constitute easily biodegradable chemicals.

- Branched and polynuclear compounds are greater tough to degrade that the instantly-chain and easy non-fragrant compounds.
- Halocarbons are immune to biodegradation and are often termed as xenobiotic compounds. Dioxns are very tough to degrade. Increasing degree of halogenation decreases the charge of biodegradation. as an example Dichloromethane as well as Monochloro biphenyls are degraded fast as these are used as carbon and power supply via the microbes. On the other hand Trichloroethane or TCE (widely used solvent) and Polychlorinated biphenyls (widely used in transformers/insecticides) aren't used as carbon/energy source and are degraded slowly through cometabolic direction.

Such rules have been more clearly defined for broad structural categories of the pollutants as below:

PETROLEUM HYDROCARBONS

- quick chain alkanes are more poisonous and comparatively tough to biodegrade
- N-alkanes of intermediate chain length (C_{10}-C_{24}) degraded most unexpectedly
- Very lengthy chain alkanes are increasingly proof against degradation
- whilst molecular weight is greater than 500, such long chain alkanes are not viable as carbon source
- fragrant hydrocarbons (in particular condensed polynuclear aromatic compounds) degrade extra slowly than alkanes
- a few fragrant compounds (benzene, toluene) metabolized beneath anaerobic situations but the charges are slower than cardio reactions
- Alicyclic compounds can't serve as carbon supply until they've long aliphatic aspect chains, consequently often degraded by means of cometabolism

HALOCARBONS

- Most common mechanism is stepwise reductive dehalogenation under anerobic conditions.

  e.g.

$$\text{TCE} \xrightarrow[\textit{step wise dechlorination}]{} \text{Vinyl Chloride} \rightarrow \text{Ethane}$$

- Cometabolic degradation by using methanogenic consortium additionally said.
- cardio degradation of TCE by way of methane making use of consortium is also possible.
- Microcosm research record both cardio/anaerobic ameliorations.
- In case of haloaromatics including chlorobenzenes, cardio biodegradability decreases with wide variety of halosubstituents.
- substantially chlorinated haloaromatics degraded by way of stepwise anaerobic dechlorination. The consecutive dechlorination steps are greater hard, sluggish and often incomplete but the mono and dichloro substitutes can be aerobically degraded.

NITRO-AROMATICS

- Nitro-substitution makes the compounds less biodegradable
- Excessively nitro-substituted aromatics transformed under anaerobic conditions by stepwise conversion of nitro groups to amino groups

BIOREMEDIATION MICROORGANISMS/AGENTS

Distinctive microorganisms are capable of degrade unique contaminants relying upon the nature and coencentration of contaminant and the metabolic needs of the microorganisms. Scientists round the sector are constantly operating to find out novel and more efficient biodegraders. allow us to discuss the crucial bioremediation microorganisms underneath the following;

PURE CULTURES

For the reason that conventional techniques of microbiology are designed for natural lifestyle studies and also it is easy to exercise session the efficiency of microbes in such systems, maximum of the laboratory research recognition on biodegradative capability of pure cultures. desk three indicates the famous bioremediation microorganisms. Pseudomonas species are most extensively detected microbes inside the contaminated website online due to their sizeable biodegradation capacities (Naz, 2015). most of the fugal groups, phanerochaete has been proposed for the biodegradation of numerous pollution including DDT, TNT, excessive molecular weight polynuclear aromatics like benzo (a) pyrene and plastics which includes polyethylene (Benson *et.al.*, 1990).

ACCLIMATIZED MICROORGANISMS AND MOLECULAR BREEDING

The metabolic variety of obviously going on microbiota won't be capable of degrading certain compounds or sure training of compounds. There it could be necessary to complement with the specialised microbes

Table 3.3. One way of developing such specialised microbes is via repeatedly exposing them to better attention of contaminants. Frequently the microorganisms with specialized degradation capability also can be enriched from the tainted site.

Table 3.3: Micro-organisms (Pure culture) helpful in bioremediation

S.No.	Pollutant	Microorganism (s)
1.	Atrazine	*Pseudomonas* sp. strain ADP, Acinetobacter species
2.	Chlorpyrifos	*Aspergillus niger,Trichoderma viride, Bacterium strain* B-14
3.	2,4,6-Trichlorophenol	*Alcaligenes eutrophus* TCP
4.	2,4-Dichlorophenoxyacetic acid	*Ralstonia eutropha* (pJP4), *Ralstonia eutropha* JMP134
5.	Carbon tetrachloride	*Pseudomonas stutzeri* KC
6.	Methyl *tert*-butyl ether	*Hydrogenophaga flava* ENV735, β-proteobacterium strain PM1
7.	BTEX	B. sp. Strain JS150 B. Cepacia G4 R. Pickettii PKO1 S. yanoikuyae B1
8.	Orange 3, 4-(4-nitrophenylazo) aniline	Pleurotus ostreatus

MICROBIOLOGY OF BIODEGRADATION

Microbial degradation technologies aim to render harmless those substances which cannot be utilizes profitably and includes both natural and chemically synthesized substrates. This decomposition of substance is brought about by microbial activities either by single organisms or more often by microbial consortia. All natural organic compounds should be degraded under suitable environmental conditions. Microorganisms found in soil and water utilize the organic substance encountered as sources of energy and carbon by enzymatically breaking them downinto somple molecules which can be absorbed and utilized. If alteration is brought about by a single reation, it is referred to as primary biodegradation, and if more extensive chemical changes are involved, then partial biodegradation. When these is complete degradation to end products of CO_2, water and other inorganic compounds, it is refereed to as mineralization.

Natural microbial communities are in the form of com.plex assemblages in which various microorganisms are highly interdependent thought interactions like commensalism and mutualism. Commensalism may take different forms; eg,many soil microorganism require aminos acids or vitamins for growth, which many other such organisms produce these compounds. This cross feeding is a general feature of natural microbial communities. Similarly, the ability of anaerobes to survive in surface layer of soil depends on the efficient consumption of oxygen by aerobes. Ethanol, which produced by yeast from sugars in fruit is oxidized to acetic acid by *Acetobacter* species. Methane, the product of anaerobic breakdown of various organic compounds by methane producing methanogens, is oxidized aerobically by methane oxidizing bacteria. Similarly, mutualistic interactions are diverse; eg. Where nitrogen fixers and cellulose decomposer coexist, each organism utilizes compounds produced by h other. *Lactobacillus arabinosus* and *Strepococcus faecalis* depend on each other to satisfy nutntional requirements; L. arabinosus makes the folic acid required *by S. faecalis* and *S. faecalis* makes the *phenlalanine* that *L. arabinosus needs.*

Organic compounds as a rule, are more effectively degraded in environments containing many microorganisms that in a pure culture of a single organism. This is because the range of degradative capabilities represented in a complex community of many bacteria and fungi is far greater than the capabilities of any single organism. The concerted action of several different organisms may lead to complete mineralization of the xenobiotic. Furthermore, a microbial community is likely to be more resistant than a solitary species to a toxic product of biodegradation, since one of its members may be able to detoxify it.

Several physical, chemical and biological factors may determine the fate of organic compounds introduced into the soil. Particular molecules may be removed by volatilization or leaching, or adsorption. The molecules may be degraded photo chemically, or undergo biodegradation though the action or bacteria and fungi. Sometime the products of nonbiological ad biological degradation may be same or otherwise nonbiological degradation may be very slow compared to biotransformation.

In nature, microbial communities are likely to be exposed to mixture of organic compounds and heavy metals (Abbas *et.al.*, 2014). Many strains are unable to grow in the presence of heavy metals (Zhiqi *et.al.*,1999). The order of resistance to heavy metals in generally, fungi > acticomycetes > Gram – negative bacteria > Gram – positive bacteria. Therefore, the bacteria which can degrade certain persistent organic chemicals, such as polycyclic aromatic hydrocarbons or chlorinated organic compounds, may disappear from the environment, when heavy metals are also present. Consequently those organic chemicals may persist much longer in such an environment.

FORTUITOUS BIODEGRADATION AND CO-METABOLISM

These are two key factors influencing the degradation of *xenobiotics.* Since the stereo specificity of enzymes may not always be exact, biodegradation of *xenobiotic* compounds can be possible by naturally occurring enzymes (Koning *et.al.*, 2000). If the functional groups of these enzymes do not greatly alter the charge make up of active site, then it is possible for the enzyme to catalyze its specific reaction on the *xenobiotic* compound. This appropriation of an existing enzyme toward a novel substrate is called fortuitous or gratuitous biodegradation, i.e., when an enzyme is able to transform a compound other than its natural substrate. Since bacteria and fungi are so diverse in their metabolic capabilities, they produce enzymes able to act on a wide range of organic molecules. If these organisms use the energy released and can utilize the resulting carbon skeletons for growth, the degradation will proceed as in natural substrates.

If bacteria are unable to extract energy from the reactions, they can effect degradation of xenobiotic compound only through the use of additional carbon and energy sources provided in the environment. The ability of an organism to transform a nongrowth substrate as long as a growth substrate or other transformable compound, called co-substrate, is also present, is defined as Co-metabolism. A non growth substrate is one that cannot serve as the sole source of carbon and energy for a pure culture of a bacterium and therefore cannot support cell division (Santini *et.al.*, 2002).

A single reaction step catalyzed by an enzyme is called transformation, and the transformation product may be transformed by a second species until, finally, a product results which is a normal metabolite and can be completely utilized as an energy and carbon source. Therefore complete pathways of degradation are more likely to be operational through the combined effects of different types of organisms within a community, than a single species. Biodegradable analogues of the pollutant, may be even the pollutant itself, may induce the enzymes needed and may enrich microorganisms capable of metabolic degradation of the organic pollutant. An attempt to estimate the role of co-metabolism in biological oxidation of synthetic compounds was made by Venkataramani and Ahlert (1985) using high strength complex industrial wastewater, and a model was developed with couples co-metabolism countributes substantially to over degradation. Also bacteria growing on mixed substrates have the ability to select for a specific substrate, which is preferentially utilized for the energy and carbon requirement of the cell.

Bioremediation is defined as the spontaneous or managed process in which biological catalysis acts on pollutants and thereby remedies or eliminates environmental contamination.

BIODEGRADATION OF WASTES

The most important and challenging practical application of microbes is in the treatment of different types of waste materials, since they occur in highly diversified and time variable composition. By weight and volume, the solid wastes (urban garbage, crops and food processing wastes and manures) are the most significant (Rani *et.al.*, 2010). These are either burnt for energy, normally decomposed, anaerobically digested, dumped in landfills or bio converted into diverse products.

Some examples of groups of organisms capable of degrading different solids are given in Table 3.4. However, compared to solid and gaseous wastes, liquid wastes are the most troublesome because of their unusual contents of non retractable substances. The amounts of waste materials discharged around the world are rising steadily as population increases and dependence of agriculture on fertilizer and pestidcides increases. Also, the expansion of food industry and growth of other industrial processes contribute to volume of sewage and waste water. Thre treatment processes involve primary, secondary and tertiary treatment operations, of which the secondary and tertiary are multistage biological system.

The secondary treatment exploits the degradative capabilities of various bacteria and fungi, whereas tertiary treatment is necessary to prevent eutrophication (i.e., reduction of dissolved oxygen in the water, resulting from bacterial and algal growth promoted by discharge of phosphate and nitrate), and to render the treated water potable (Jones *et.al.*, 2000).

Table 3.4: Degradation of Solids by Microorganisms

Compounds	Microorganisms
Cellulose	*Trichoderma, Mucor*
Cotton	*Aspergillus species, Mucor*
Animal fibers	*B. mesentericus*
Oil paints	*Altermaria dianthicola*
Kerosine	*Claudosporium resinae*
Picric acid	*Corynebacteria*
Wood	*Fungi*
Glass	*Aspergillus, Penicillim*
Concrete	*Thiobacillus*

Purification of Effluents: The Purification process may involve aerobic and anaerobic condition.

PURIFICATION OF EFFLUENTS WITH AEROBIC PROCESSES

In the aerobic phase of the treatment process, a mixed microbial population degrades the complex mixture of organic compounds in liquid waste of carbonate, nitrate, ammonia, phosphate and sulphate. For this purpose, either **A.** activated sludge processes, **B.** fixed film processes are used.

Activated Sludge: The principle of activated sludge is that in a reactor a community of microorganisms is constantly supplied with organic matter and oxygen. The microorganisms consume the organic matter and transform it by means of aerobic metabolism, partly into new microbial biomass and partly into carbon dioxide, water minerals (Dixit *et.al.*, 2015). The reactions involved are:

(a) Sorption of soluble colloidal and suspended organic in and on the sludge flocs.

(b) Biodegradation of the organics resulting in end products (i.e., carbondioxide, water, minerals) and synthesis of new microbial biomass.

(c) Ingestion of bacteria and possibly of other suspended matter b protozoa and other predators

(d) Oxidation of ammonium to nitrite and further to nitrate by nitrifying bacteria.

(e) When there is insufficient supply of energy (or waste) – oxidation of cell reserves resulting in sludge mineralization and lysis.

There are several process types in which three fundamental aspects can be varied independently i.e.

(i) The layout (convential completely mixed or gradient in substrate or aeration supply)

(ii) Loading rate (high rate, conventional and low rate or very low i.e. extended aeration)

(iii) The aeration system (surface aeration or submerged aeration.)

MICROBIAL COMMUNITY OF ACTIVATED SLUDGE

The incoming water contains a multitude or organic and inorganic substrates. A diverse assemblage of bacteria, fungi, protozoa and rotifers, living directly on the incoming substrates using metabolites thus produced, or preying on primary users, come into existence. The activated sludge community is normally dominated by organotrophic bacteria. The major part is aggregated in sludge flocs, but some are freely dispersed in the liquor. The bacteria, together with some saprobic protozoa, from the lowest trophic level, on which holozoic protozoa and rotifers feed.

Some, commonly encountered bacterial genera in activated sludge, and their niche specialities are:

(a) *Pseudomonas* - Removal of carbohydrates, and denitrificaiton.

(b) *Arthrobacter* – Removal of carbohydrates

(c) *Baccillus* – Breakdown of Protein

(d) *Cytophaga* – Breakdown of Polymericsubstrates

(e) *Zoogloea* – Formation of slime matrices

(f) *Acinetobacter* – Storage of Polyphosphate

(g) *Nitrosomonas* and *Nitrobacter* – Nitrification

(h) *Sphaerotolus* – Filamentous growth

Fungi and yeasts are usually present, but are not capable of dominating, except in unusual conditions, eg. High levels of sugars or constant influx of recralicitrant organo chemicals. Some commonly found protozoa are; *Aspidisca costata* (crawling), *Vorticella convallaria* (sessile), *Trachelophyllum pusillum* (free swimming).

Fixed Film Processes: These attached growth or fixed film treatment systems are amongst the oldest of the currently used waste water treatment processes i.e., those in which microorganisms for waste treatment are attached to stationary media or rotating media, eg. Trickling filters, rotating biological contractors, activated biofilters, biological towers, submerged filters and biological fluidized beds. The objective of all these processes is the removal of dissolved and suspended organic matter. Some processes may be capable of providing nitrification or denitrification and also removal of phosphorus and may be used in association with tertiary treatment. The organisms responsible for treatment are present in the form of a biofilm, attached to a solid support surface. Waste water either flows over the film or the support surface moves through waste water. Organics are transported to microorganisms in the biofilm and subsequently biodegraded.

The biological slime layer or biofilm contains bacteria, protozoa and fungi and may also contain algae, sludge worms, filter fly larvae, rotifers or other metazoan. As waste water passes over biofilm, soluble organic diffuse into the film and are sorbed on to the microorganisms and metabolized. Colloidal organics adsorb onto the biofilm surface and can be solubilized by extracellular enzymes. Molecular oxygen also diffuses into the film, providing a terminal electron acceptor for aerobic metabolism. Heterotrophic organisms in upper part of film, obtain energy and nutrients by oxidizing organic matter and therefore multiply and new film is formed.

Purification of Effluents with Anaerobic Processes: After aerobic digestion, sewage sludge is generally digested under anaerobic condition. Materials with high content of insoluble organic matter eg. Cellulose, concentrated industrial wastes e.g. those from food processing industry, are commonly treated by anaerobic digestion. The capacity of anaerobic bacteria for degrading organic substances to methane and carbon dioxide has been utilized since a very long time. The other products produced during anaerobic degradation (sludge and effluent) can be reused and nutrients recovered. Because of increasing energy costs, methane fermentation or *Biomethanation* with high loads of organic matter has attracted great interest. It was assumed for a long time that only two groups of bacteria are involved in the anaerobic conversion of organic substances into methane and carbon dioxide. It is well known now that at least three different groups of bacteria are involved i.e., (i) Hydrolytic and Acid forming, (ii) Acetogenic (acetic acid and hydrogen forming), (iii)

Methanogenic (Methane Forming). In the degradational chain, the various organic compounds are degraded to acids, alcohols, hydrogen, and carbon dioxide in the first step by the first group of microorganisms.

The second group of bacteria then converts these alcohols, acids etc., into acetic acid, hydrogen and carbon dioxide, which are in turn used as substrate by the last group, i.e. methane bacteria, and are converted into methane and carbon dioxide. Some examples of fermentative, hydrolytic bacteria are *Clostridia, Bacteroides, Bifidobacteria, Enterobacteria and Streptococci. Syntrophomonas* and *Desulphovibrio* belong to the second group i.e. the Acetogenic bacteria and the third group include *Methanabacterium, Methanobrevibacter, methanococcus, Methanomicrobium, Methanospirillu*. This last group is the most oxygen sensitive and require a redox potential of about – 300 mV and some get killed very rapidly by oxygen. They have a very limited substrate spectrum – most species assimilate hydrogen as the sole source of energy. For anaerobic degradation of butyric acid and propionic acid, very low pH_2 values ($< 2 \times 10^{-3}$ and $< 9 \times 10^{-3}$) are necessary. Therefore the hydrogen produced must be consumed immediately at the position where it arises, for which an intimate contact between cells of acetogenic and methanogenic bacteria is necessary.

Thus maintenance of pH and constant temperature are important requirements for the processes. An important practical aspect of anaerobic digestion is that most of the free energy present in the substrate is conserved in the methane that is produced. Using the methane for energy generation offsets the cost of the sewage treatment process. The other advantages are that higher organic loadings are possible, a smaller volume of sludge is produced, and the energy consuming aeration is unnecessary.

CONCLUSION

The outcome of consumption and production activities is the generation of large amounts of waste and release of pollutants. For an environmentally compatible sustainable development, application of clean technologies such as, use of microbes in degradation and bioremediation, is urgently required. For understanding these knowledges of their microbiological processes and the microbiological communities involved in different types of waste treatment processes aerobic and anaerobic, is very important. Recent development in the bioremediation strategies and the use of specialized microbial strains for degradation of recalcitrant compounds are important aspects to be looked into.

Microbial degradation technologies render harmless substances which cannot be utilized profitably and include both natural and chemically synthesized substrates. Primary or particle biodegradation may be possible depending on interactions such as communalism and mutualism. Understanding of fortuitous biodegradation and co- metabolism, is required for the degradation of xenobiotics. By weight and volume solid wastes are significant and are either burnt for energy, decomposed naturally or are anaerobically digested, dumped in landfills or bioconverted into diverse products by a variety of organisms. Liquid wastes are the most troublesome because of their non retraitable substance content. Their treatment involves primary, secondary and teriary operations of which secondary and tertiary are multistage biological systems. Secondary treatment processes may be aerobic and anaerobic and accordingly different processes are possible by different microbial communities. Tertiary processing of waste water is required for removal of phosphate and nitrate in facultative waste stabilization ponds or by recent use of fish periphyton system.

REFERENCES

Abbas, S., Ismail, I., Mostafa, T., Abbas, S. (2014). Biosorption of Heavy Metals: Review. J ChemSciTechnol 3: 74-102.

Akhtar, M.S., Chali, B., & Azam, T. (2013). Bioremediation of Arsenic and Lead by Plants and Microbes from Contaminated Soil. Res. Plant Sciences. 1(3): 68-73.

Alegbeleye, O.O., Opeolu, B.O., & Jackson, V.A. (2017) Polycyclic Aromatic Hydrocarbons: A Critical Review of Environmental Occurrence and Bioremediation. Environ Manag 60: 758-783.

Benson HJ. (1990) Microbiological Application – A Laboratory Manual in General Microbiology. C. Brown Publishers, USA. 15-21.

Boopathy, R., (2000) Factors Limiting Bioremediation Technologies, Bioresources Technology, 74, 1, 63-67.

Brooks, R.R. (1998). Plants that Hyperaccumulate Heavy Metals. Cambridge University Press, London, UK. 92-96.

Chen, M., Xu, P., Zeng, G., Yang, C., Huang, D., Zhang,J. (2015) Bioremediation of Soils Contaminated with Polycyclic Aromatic Hydrocarbons, Petroleum, Pesticides, Chlorophenols and Heavy Metals by Composting: Applications, Microbes and Future Research needs. Biotechnology Adv 33: 745-755.

Chojnacka, K., (2010). Biosorption and Bioaccumulation – the Prospects for Practical. Appl. Environ. 36: 299-307.

Congeevaram, S., Dhanarani, S., Park, J., Dexilin, M., Thamaraiselvi, K. (2007). Biosorption of Chromium and Nickel by Heavy Metal Resistant Fungal and Bacterial Isolates. J. Hazard Mater.146: 270-277.

Dixit, R., Wasiullah Malaviya, D., Pandiyan, K., Singh, U.B., Sahu, A., Shukla, R., Singh B.P., Rai, J.P., Sharma, P.K., Lade, H., Paul, D. (2015) Bioremediation of Heavy Metals from Soil and Aquatic Environment: An overview of Principles and Criteria of Fundamental Processes. Sustainability 7: 2189-2212.

Faryal, R., Sultan, A., Tahir, F., Ahmed, S., Hameed, A.(2007). Biosorption of Lead by Indigenous Fungal Strains. Pak. J. of Bot. 2007; 39: 615-622.

Gogoi, B.K., Dutta, N.N., Goswami, P., Krishna Mohen, T.R., (2002) A Case Study of Petroleum Hydrocarbon Contaminated Soil at a Crude Oil Site, Advances in Environmental Research, 7,4, 767-782.

Guidi, W., Palm, E., Mancuso, S., & Azzarello, E. (2018). "Trace Element Phytoextraction from Contaminated Soil. A Case Study under Mediterranean Climate". Environmental Science and Pollution Research. 18: 1197-1205.

Held, T. and Don, H. (2000). *In Situ* Remediation. Biotechnology. 11b: 350-370.

Hlihor RM, Gavrilescu M, Tavares T, Fvier L, Olivieri G (2017) Editorial Bioremediation: An Overview of Current Practices, Advances, and New Perspectives in Environmental Pollution Treatment Hindawi. Biomed Res Int 2: 3-5.

Iranzo, M., Sainz-Padro, I., Boluda, R., Sanchez, J., and Mormeneo, S., (2001) The Use of Microorganisms in Environmental Engineering, Annals of Microbiology, 51, 135-143.

Jain, R., Ahmad, P., Gadgil, K., Sarma, S.(2012). Heavy Metal Toxicity: Effect of Plant Growth, Biochemical Parameters and Metal Accumulation by Brasica juncea, L. Int.J. Plant Production. 3(3): 65-75.

Jones, C.A., Langer, H.W., Anderson, K., McDermott, T.R., Inskeep, W.P.(2000). Rates of Microbially Mediated Arsenate Reduction and Solubilization. Soil Science Soc.Am. J. 64: 600-608.

Khan, M.S., Zaidi, A.A., Wani, A.P,A., & Mohammad, A. (2009). Role of Plant Growth Promoting Rhizobacteria in the Remediation of Metal Contaminated Soils. Environ Chem Lett. 2009; 7: 1-19.

Kleijntjens, R.H., and Luyben, K.C.A.M. (2000) Bioremediation, Biotechnology, 11b, 329-347.

Klein, J. (2000). Possibilities, Limits and Future Developments of Soil Bioremediation, Biotechnology, 11b, 466-476.

Koning, M., Hupe, K., & Stegmann, R. (2000) Thermal Processes, Scrubbing/Extraction, Bioremediation and Disposal. Biotechnology, 11b, 306-317.

Konopka, A., Zakharova, T., Bischoff, M., Oliver, L., Nakatsu, C., Turco, R.F. (1999). Microbial Biomass and Activity in Lead-contaminated Soil. Appl Environ Microbiol. 65: 2256-2259.

Naz, T., Khan, M.D., Ahmed, I., Rehman, S.U., Rha, E.S., Malook, I. (2015). Biosorption of Heavy Metals by Pseudomonas species Isolated from Sugar Industry. Toxicol. Ind. Health. 10: 525-534.

Pandey, S., Saha, P., Biswas, S., Maiti, T.K. (2011). Characterization of Two Heavy Metal Resistant Strains Isolated from Slag Disposal site at Burnpur. Indian J. Environ Biol.; 32: 773-779.

Rani, A., Ray, K., & Goel, R. (2010). Stratiges for Crop Improvement in Contaminated Soils using Metaltolerant Bioinoculants. Springer. 2010; 11: 105-132.

Santini, J.M., Stolz, J.F., Macy, J.M. (2002). "Isolation of a New Arsenate Respiring Bacterium – Physiological and Phylogenetic Studies," Geomicrobiol. J. 19: 41-52.

Schnoor, J.L. (2000) Degradation by Plants-Phytoremediation, Biotechnology, 11b, 372-384.

Schulz-Berendt, V. (2000) Bioremediation with Heap Technique. Biotechnology, 11b, 320-328.

Shannon, M.J.R. & Unterman, R. (2000). Evaluation Bioremediation: Distinguishing Fact from Fiction. Annual Review of Microbiology. 47: 715-738.

Van Deuren, J., Lloyd, T., Chhetry, S., Raycharn, L., & Peck, J. (2002). Remediation Technologies Screening Matrix and Reference Guide. Federal Remediation Technologies Roundtable.5: 1-4.

Zhiqi, H., Reiske, H.R., & Wilson, D.B. (1999). Chatacterization of Cadmium uptake in Lacto Plantarum and Isolation of Cadmium and manganese uptake System. Applied and Environmental Microbiology. 65: 4741-4745.

4

Coal Consumption, Ash Generation and its Utilization for Sustainability

INTRODUCTION

Coal-based power is one of the most resource-intensive and polluting industries, and contributes significantly to ambient air pollution in India. Currently, coal- and lignite-based utility power plants account for 77% of the country's total electricity generation (Soundaram *et.al.*, 2020). The sector consumes about 65% of the total coal consumed in India. In order to meet the growing electricity demand, a huge capacity addition has occurred to the Indian coal-based power sector in the past 10 years. Around 64% (132 GW) capacity was added in the last 10 years, which has also led to a surge in coal consumption in the sector. Between 2009-10 and 2018-19, annual coal consumption rose from 367 million tonnes to about 629 million tonnes, an increase of almost 71%. Fly ash is the by-product or unburnt residue formed during combustion of coal in a furnace. It is emitted along with the flue gases and collected either by mechanical separators or electrostatic precipitators in the dry form. The collected fly ash is normally stored in silos. Heavier unburnt ash, collected at the bottom of the furnace, is called bottom ash and constitutes around 20% of the total ash generated at a power plant. Unused fly ash and bottom ash from plants is generally transferred in the wet slurry form to ash ponds with the help of ash slurry supply lines.

A rise in coal consumption naturally increases the production of fly ash as a by-product or residue, which not only requires large tracts of land for disposal but also leads to significant pollution. This problem is particularly severe in India, because Indian coal is low-grade, with high ash content (of the order of 30-45 per cent) and low calorific value (3,500-4,000 kcal/kg). Annual fly ash generation from Indian coal power plants rose from 123 million tonnes in 2009-10 to 217 million tonnes in 2018-19, an increase of almost 76% (Anon, 2019). Fly ash is ultra-fine, prone to becoming air borne in the dry state. This significantly affects air quality near coal-based plants. Long-term exposure to fly ash in the air can lead to serious pulmonary illnesses like bronchitis, silicosis, fibrosis, pneumonitis, etc. The ash contains toxic heavy metals that are known carcinogens. Ash disposed of in the wet form in ash ponds can be equally harmful if not handled in an environmentally sound manner. Several cases of contamination of nearby surface water bodies and groundwater due to ash pond overflows or leakages have been reported. This may even lead to accumulation of heavy metals beyond permissible limits in the contaminated water bodies. Naturally, fly ash has been under the regulatory scanner for quite some time now. The effort has been to convert potentially harmful waste into a resource. The notification on fly ash utilization first came into force in 1999. Over the years, it has gone through several amendments in 2003, 04, 09 and 16, in order to move towards the goal of 100% utilization of fly ash produced by all coal- and lignite-based plants. As the quantity of coal consumed in India increased, and fly ash generated increased proportionally, Ministry of Environment, Forest and Climate Change (MoEF&CC) brought in several other policy measures and reforms to increase utilization of residual ash. Currently, fly ash is utilized in India in cement, brick and tiles manufacturing, filling up abandoned mines, reclamation of low-lying areas and construction of roads and flyovers. The ministry has also set certain limits, in terms of geographical area, within which fly ash is to be compulsorily used for manufacturing bricks or in the construction industry. Yet, 21 years after the notification first came into force, many plants have still not been able to achieve the target. As per a December 2019 report submitted to the National Green Tribunal (NGT), the quantity of unused ash from the coal power sector is 1,647 million tonnes (as on 31 March 2019). This is almost eight times the current annual ash generation. Ash is piling up in the wet form as slurry in ash ponds and in the dry form in open fields. Fugitive emissions and leakages have increased substantially. The severity of the problem was exemplified by the major coal ash pond accidents that occurred between 2010 and 2020 (Anon, 2020a). This risk of overabundance of ash has been further aggravated with the recent government orders of doing away with mandatory coal washing and opening the coal sector for commercial mining by private players, which will lead to increase in ash generation. Improper maintenance and lining of ash ponds continues to be a problem. This particular area does not have any regulatory oversight. In recent years, National Green Tribunal (NGT) has passed several orders pertaining to non-compliant plants for depositing environmental compensation towards damage caused by ash accidents. However, after pleas filed by power producers stating that NGT had not analysed the situation on a plant-to-plant basis and end users like cement plants and other agencies that can utilize ash should also be made accountable for it, Supreme Court put a stay on a few such orders. This has been continuing, derailing the regulations and the enforcement system. While end users like cement and construction agencies should be made accountable to some extent, it is primarily the responsibility of the power producers to make efforts for effective utilization of waste generated by them, whether it be coal ash or any other hazardous waste. Power producers must ensure disposal of ash in an environmentally sound manner that does not cause harm to the surrounding areas. With so many ash breach incidents, it is clear that power plants have been negligent on their part and must be dealt with strictly by regulatory bodies. Therefore, in order to tackle the growing concerns and impacts associated with overabundance of ash, and to clear the huge stockpile of legacy ash, urgent interventions—in terms of policy measures, technologies and practices—are needed to enhance fly ash utilization.

India's total power generation capacity (as on 31 March 2020) stood at 370 gigawatts (GW), 4 of which thermal power capacity alone is about 230 GW. Coal-and lignite-based power stations continue to be the bulk energy providers, making up 205 GW (89 per cent) of the total thermal power capacity. Significant coal-based capacity has been added in the last 15 years. Around 64% (132 GW) of the capacity is less than a decade old. About 74% (152 GW) is less than 15 years old. Huge capacity additions have led to a gradual increase in coal consumption over the years, thereby also leading to an increase in fly ash generation. Moreover, Indian coal has high ash content (about 30-45 per cent), which leads to generation of large quantities of fly ash at coal- and lignite-based thermal power stations. Trends in coal consumption and ash generation in a span of ten years (i.e. from 2009-10 to 2018-19), coal consumption in the power sector increased by almost 71% and the corresponding ash generation increased by almost 76 per cent. At present, the power sector currently consumes about 623 million tonnes of coal and generates about 217 million tonnes of ash, 94 million tonnes up from the 2009 ash generation figures. This is a significant increase.

TRENDS IN ASH UTILIZATION AND RESIDUAL ASH GENERATION

Tremendous increase in coal consumption by the power sector in the past decade has ballooned fly ash generation and resulted in large quantities of unused ash. As per Central Electricity Authority's (CEA) 2018-19 annual report on fly ash, 103 thermal power stations were able to achieve the target of 100% ash utilization. However, 83 power stations have not been able to achieve this target. Though the all India average fly ash utilization percentage from TPPs has jumped from 63% (77 million tonnes) in 2009 to 78% (168 million tonnes) now, the major cause of concern is the amount of residual or unutilized ash that has gradually accumulated over the past many years due to the low utilization percentage. For about five years (between 2012-13 and 2016-17), the quantity of fly ash utilized has remained stagnant at around 100 million tonnes; however, during the same period, annual generation has been above the 150 million tonne mark, which indicates a huge pile up. Only in the last two years (i.e., 2017-18 and 2019-19) has there been an additional 30 million tonnes increase in utilization each year.

Average ash utilization percentage between 2009 and 2019 has been about 62 per cent. During the period, on an average, almost 60 million tonnes of fly ash has remained unutilized annually.

State-wise ash utilization and residual ash generation Coal-based power plants are spread over 17 states in India. They are heavily concentrated in Andhra Pradesh, Chhattisgarh, Madhya Pradesh, Maharashtra, Odisha, Uttar Pradesh and West Bengal. Substantial quantities of coal are consumed in these states, generating humongous quantities of ash. Uttar Pradesh and Chhattisgarh have had the highest ash generation, followed by West Bengal, Maharashtra, Andhra Pradesh, Madhya Pradesh and Odisha. All these states have large coal-based power capacity. High generation and low utilization percentage in many states indicate pile up of unused ash in those states. Chhattisgarh and Uttar Pradesh have accumulated the most ash in this decade. Madhya Pradesh, Andhra Pradesh, Maharashtra and Odisha also have a huge ash backlog. States with large coal-based capacity and limited ash demand in nearby areas have low ash utilization rates.

West Bengal is the only state that produces a sizeable quantity of ash but manages to clear the stock. It has utilized 131 million tonnes out of the total of 157 million tonnes of ash it produced in the past decade. Fly ash is used extensively in cement manufacturing in the state. It is also used in construction of roads and highways. Some fly ash is even exported to Bangladesh for manufacturing Pozzolana Portland Cement (PPC) cement. Ash is transported pneumatically through pipelines to silos located on jetties by the riverside. Ash from the silos is loaded into covered barges and exported to Bangladesh (Anon, 2020b).

A few states, notably Haryana, Gujarat, Punjab and Rajasthan, utilized as much ash in 2018-19 as they produced in that year, but no state has been able to completely utilize its accumulated stock of legacy ash. Jharkhand, Punjab and Rajasthan are the only states that have achieved an average fly ash utilization rate of 90-100 per cent. In fact, Gujarat, Haryana, Punjab and Rajasthan do not have any plants with a poor ash utilization rate.

CONCENTRATION OF LARGE CAPACITY COAL POWER PLANTS IN A REGION

Regions where many power plants are in close proximity tend to have lower utilization rates as there is overabundance of ash and the demand cannot keep up with it, due to limited number of cements, brick or construction agencies present within a 300 km radius of such regions. Singrauli–Sonebhadra, spread across parts of Uttar Pradesh and Madhya Pradesh, is one such region. The two states together account for about 51 GW of power generation capacity in India, half of which is generated in the Singrauli–Sonebhadra region. Nine major power plants operate in this region, with a combined capacity of around 21,270 MW. More than half of the capacity (11,180 MW) is less than 10 years old and was added by construction of either new power plants or addition of stages to existing plants in the region. Due to a skewed demand–supply ratio, the two states are in the top four in terms of fly ash generation and in the bottom four in terms of utilization rates.

DISTANCE FROM CEMENT AND BRICK MANUFACTURING AND CONSTRUCTION UNITS

Transportation and settlement play an important role in determining the ash utilization rate. States with more cement or brick manufacturing units, that are in proximity to power plants, tend to have higher utilization rates. Andhra Pradesh, Haryana, Karnataka, Punjab, Rajasthan and Tamil Nadu together account for about 60% of total cement production capacity in India. These are also the states with the highest ash utilization percentages. On the other hand, in states like Chhattisgarh, demand for ash is limited due to minimal presence of businesses that utilize ash.

NOTIFICATION ON FLY ASH UTILIZATION

In order to minimize environmental pollution caused due to fly ash, Ministry of Environment, Forest and Climate Change (MoEF&CC) has come up with several notifications in the past. These notifications have sought to promote utilization of fly ash produced by coal- or lignite-based thermal power plants, including captive power plants and co-generation plants. They have also sought to restrict excavation of top soil for manufacture of bricks.

- The notification on fly ash utilization came into force in September 1999. It stipulated targets for utilization of fly ash produced at thermal power plants by construction companies falling within the prescribed radius. The notification was subsequently amended in 2003, 2009, 2016 and 2019. With each subsequent amendment, the radius around coal- and lignite-based thermal power plants for which the said norm is applicable was increased to enhance use of fly ash.

- The August 2003 amendment mandated the use of 100% fly ash by construction agencies in a phased manner in five years (by August 2007).
- Following this, the November 2009 amendment revised and extended the timelines and the period of implementation for achieving 100% utilization in a phased manner to 2014.
- In January 2016, another amendment extended the area within which fly ash was to be utilized from 100 km to 300 km. The time period to comply with the requirements of 100% utilization of fly ash was extended to 31 December 2017.
- In September 2020, a draft fly ash amendment has for the first time introduced a penalty framework based on polluter pays principle. The draft specifies a fine of Rs 1,500 per tonne of unused ash if the plant does not achieve at least 80% ash utilization annually or is unable to utilize, on an average, 100% of ash in a three-year cycle. There is also a fine of Rs 2,000 per tonne for non-utilization of legacy ash. User agencies within 300 km radius of a power plant have also been made accountable through imposition of a fine of Rs 2,000 per tonne of nonutilized ash. The draft amendment is out for comments, and is likely to face criticism and objections, especially from the power sector, because, if notified, it will definitely lead to huge penalties on the large number of non-compliant plants, and especially those with poor ash utilization rates.

The deadline for complying with the notification has already passed. However, even after 21 years since the first notification came into force, many power plants are still not able achieve the target of 100% utilization. As per CEA's latest report, the number of such power plants is 83.

Management of fly ash has been a matter of concern for coal- and lignite-based power plants due to the requirement of a large area for its disposal and its adverse impact on the environment and health of the people living nearby due to its hazardous nature. Non-utilization and improper disposal of fly ash leads to severe air and water pollution. Apart from lime, silica and alumina, fly ash contains toxic heavy metals like lead, mercury, arsenic and hexavalent chromium, all of which are known carcinogens. Several health studies conducted in communities living near thermal power plants have clearly established health problems associated with fly ash. Several major coal ash pond accidents have been reported across the country in the last ten years, from utility thermal plants as well as captive power plants. Minor fly ash incidents which occur on a regular basis are not even reported. At times, these incidents have led to loss of life and property in nearby settlements. Since many power plants are located close to surface water bodies serving as a source of freshwater for the plant, leaking or overflowing slurry from ash ponds often finds its way into these surface water bodies leading to their contamination.

NGT has recently come down harshly on non-compliant power plants and those facing litigation due to ash dyke breaches or ash leakages, by way of imposing penalties on them. However, penalties imposed on plants in the last two-three years have not been an effective deterrent as many of them are far from meeting the 100% utilization rate and continue to pollute their immediate surroundings with ash. A good illustrative example of continuous non-compliance is the North Chennai Thermal Power Station (NCTPS), where fly ash leaked from a busted pipeline in August 2020 and flooded the nearby village. The residents of the village have been battling against this issue (and the plant) for many years. At times, ash slurry enters their houses and there are high levels of ash in the air and nearby waterbodies which affect the health of residents. River and borewell samples show high rates of contamination with heavy metals. Back in 2017, NGT had warned that the plant would be completely shut down if discharge of fly ash was not contained. Later, a committee was appointed to observe the plant for violations. In January 2020, NGT even imposed a penalty of Rs 8.34 crore on the plant. Despite all these measures, the plant continues to pollute the area. Over the last few years, such incidents have increased. To ensure better compliance, stricter penalties, shutting down non-complying plants and stricter monitoring are the need of the hour.

There have been cases where power plants have expanded without obtaining land for additional ash ponds and continue to dump huge quantities of ash in the existing ponds. At times, ash overflows in these ponds or the boundary walls are breached. A major fly ash breach incident occurred on 10 April 2020 at the Sasan ultra-mega power plant (owned by Reliance Power in Singrauli– Sonebhadra region). It resulted in human causalities and spread of toxic slurry in the surrounding areas (up to six kilometres), destroying agricultural fields. In 2019, similar incidences of ash dyke breaches had occurred at the Essar Mahan Power plant and NTPC Vindhyachal plant located in the same region. Three instances of fly ash breach within a year have raised concerns regarding the management of fly ash at coal power plants. A committee appointed by NGT to look into the breaches at ESSAR thermal power plant and NTPC, Vindhyachal found that no sincere efforts had been made for ash disposal by these plants since their commissioning in the early 1980s.

There are also issues with improper maintenance and lining of ash ponds. Environmental clearances granted to thermal power plants set up after 2006 made it mandatory for plants to have impervious lining at the bottom of ash ponds. This requirement was to avoid any leaching of toxic heavy metals present in ash slurry into the groundwater. No monitoring agency exists to ensure that plants put in place impervious lining before disposing of ash slurry into the ponds. There is gross mismanagement and unsafe disposal, evident from the high levels of contaminants and heavy metals found in groundwater samples taken from the vicinity of ash ponds.

The following section covers recent NGT orders and committees formed on fly ash utilization:

(i) **January 2018:** NGT passed an order directing states to submit action plans for fly ash use (Anon, 2020c).

- States and Union territories were directed to furnish their action plans for 100% utilization of fly ash generated by thermal power plants in accordance with the 2009 amendment to the notification.
- Following this order, in August 2018, 20 states submitted their action plans—13 of them were incomplete and not unsatisfactory. MoEF&CC was directed to monitor compliance and submit a status report on them.
- Thereafter, MoEF&CC submitted a status report to NGT in September 2018 wherein it was noted that the states had sought further extension of time by two to five years, i.e. upto 2023, for 100% fly ash utilization. Moreover, a few plants had not even submitted action plans for 100% utilization.

(ii) **November 2018:** NGT passed an order on forming a joint committee and imposing penalty on defaulters.

- NGT directed MoEF&CC to constitute a committee comprising of representatives from MoEF&CC, CPCB, IIT Roorkee and any other members considered necessary for implementation of the action plan to achieve 100% fly ash utilization by power plants in an environmentally sound manner. The committee was also required to assess the amount of damages to be paid for non-compliance with the notification. Following this order, MoEF&CC constituted a joint committee comprising of member secretary, CPCB and representatives from IIT Roorkee, Ministry of Power, Ministry of Coal, Ministry of Housing and Urban Affairs, National Highway Authority of India (NHAI) and Odisha SPCB.
- Until the committee can assess the damages, thermal power plants that failed to utilize 100% fly ash by the end of 2017 have to deposit specified environmental penalty.

  If the penalty was not deposited with CPCB within one month, an interest of 12% per annum would be payable
- Following the November 2018 NGT order, the joint committee filed its report on December 2019 on the progress made on action

plans and compensation assessment. The report states that the quantity of unused ash was as high as 1,647 million tonnes as on 31 March 2019. The committee recommended a maximum of two years' time for 100% utilization. It also recommended that compensation should be obtained only from non-pit-head power plants. Construction of fly ash dykes and their maintenance was not found technically sound at many plants.

(iii) **February 2019:** Supreme Court stayed environmental compensation imposed by NGT on non-compliant plants of NTPC and MPPGCL.

The Supreme Court stayed NGT's November 2018 order of imposing fines on NTPC and MPPGCL plants. These fines ranged from Rs 1-5 crore, depending on the power plant's capacity. NTPC mentioned in its plea that NGT did not take into consideration the reluctance of end use industries, like cement and brick manufacturing plants, for taking fly ash from power plants as the 2016 notification had made it obligatory for user industries to uptake fly ash. The plea further mentioned that power plants only have to facilitate transportation of fly ash but cannot force user agencies to uptake fly ash.

(iv) **February 2020:** NGT passed an order on directing all power plants to take steps for scientific disposal of fly ash (Anon, 2020c).

- Following three fly ash breach incidents in Singrauli region in 2019-20, in February 2020 NGT directed thermal power plants to take prompt steps for scientific disposal of fly ash, warning that failure to do so would lead to penalty. The tribunal stated that non-compliant plants will have to pay environmental compensation which would be determined from the cut-off date of 31 December 2017 as stipulated in the notification issued by the Union environment ministry (Anon, 2020d).
- In the same order, NGT asked CPCB to compute and levy environmental compensation with respect to individual plants in accordance with the law and submit a compliance report to the tribunal.

  Supreme Court issues a stay order on recovery of environmental compensation imposed by NGT on non-compliant plants.
- On 14 September 2020, Supreme Court stayed the recovery of fines imposed by NGT through its February 2020 order against noncompliant thermal power plants (that have not achieved the target of 100% fly ash utilization and disposal). CPCB had issued notices to various non-compliant power plants after NGT's February order.
- The plea was filed by power producers stating that due to COVID-19 pandemic, there has been disruptions in fly ash

utilization and disposal. The plea also mentioned that no case-by-case analysis was done while determining the environmental compensation for each plant.

Thus, it is clear that proper enforcement of regulations is lacking, both at the level of power plants and at the level of end users. The blame game has been continuing with NGT passing orders for environmental compensation against non-compliant plants and Supreme Court staying those orders after hearing pleas from power plants.

UTILIZATION OF FLY ASH FROM THE POWER SECTOR

Andhra Pradesh, Haryana, Karnataka, Punjab, Rajasthan and Tamil Nadu together account for about 60% of the cement production capacity of India. These are also the states utilizing the most fly ash, especially Haryana, Punjab, Rajasthan and Tamil Nadu, all of which have ash utilization percentages between 70-99 per cent. Though fly ash utilization in the cement sector has increased over the last few years due to several government interventions and policy measures mandating its use, the uptake has not been commiserate with the tremendous growth in the production of cement. Between 2009 and 2019, cement production in India increased from 187 million tonnes to 334 million tonnes, an increase of almost 78 per cent. Currently, India produces about 334 million tonnes of cement annually and the production is expected to reach 400 million tonnes by 2025, owing to continuously rising demand. In 2017, MoEF&CC formed a committee, with representatives from the Ministry of Mines, Ministry of Power, CEA, Department of Industrial Policy and Promotion (DIPP) and Ministry of Coal, to examine the possibility of building cement plants near power plants to enhance utilization of fly ash. But utilization of fly ash in the cement manufacturing industry is hindered by several factors, chief among them being lack of or costly transportation, lack of awareness among cement manufacturers, and poor implementation and monitoring by government agencies.

Fly ash bricks are made from fly ash, lime, gypsum and cement. Use of fly ash in the manufacture of fly ash bricks is a technically well-established practice. However, average ash utilization percentage in the brick manufacturing sector has only been a low 7 per cent. Bureau of Indian Standards (BIS) has formulated standards for fly ash bricks. IS 12894: 2002 establishes specifications for fly ash-lime bricks. Fly ash can be easily used as a building material in place of red clay bricks and save precious top soil as well. Moreover, producing fly ash bricks is a relatively cleaner process as it does not require firing. India is currently the second largest producer of bricks in the world and with the rising demand for bricks, there is immense potential for utilization of fly ash in the brick sector. The major fly ash brick producing states are Andhra Pradesh, Bihar, Delhi, Maharashtra, Odisha, Tamil Nadu and West Bengal.

To enhance utilization in this sector, MoEF&CC had issued the following directions through its 2016 notification:

- Mandatory use of fly ash-based products for construction activity within a radius of 300 km from coal- and lignite-based power plants.
- Power plants to bear transportation cost of fly ash up to a radius of 100 km. Beyond the radius of 100 km (up to 300 km), transportation cost shall be borne equally by fly ash users and power plants.
- MoEF&CC also issued a draft amendment to the notification in February 2019 inviting public comments, wherein the following proposals were made:
  - ❖ No new red clay brick kiln shall be established within a radius of 300 km of a thermal power plant.
  - ❖ Existing red clay brick kilns within a radius of 300 km of thermal power plants shall be converted to fly ash brick, block or tile manufacturing units.

To enhance utilization, a few state governments have started providing incentives to fly ash start-ups, made use of fly ash bricks compulsory in construction near coal power plants, and mandated use of fly ash bricks in construction of government buildings. Despite government policies, fly ash utilization in the brick manufacturing sector remains poor in many states because:

- Brick kiln contractors still prefer clay bricks over fly ash bricks.
- There is no quality control system in place to ensure that fly ash production units comply with BIS standards.
- Lack of incentives to fly ash start-ups in many states.
- The process of making fly ash bricks requires more training and knowhow in the hands of the workers, which is missing.
- There is also an absence of an existing market for fly ash bricks as adequate initiatives have not been taken by Central and state governments in this direction.
- Transportation of fly ash from power plants to brick units and costs involved in transportation also act as a hindrance to its utilization.
- A robust monitoring system in missing.

USE OF FLY ASH

- *Reclamation of low-lying areas:* Soil or sand can be substituted with fly ash in reclamation of low-lying areas. This helps save precious top soil. Average ash utilization from power plants for reclamation activities is only around 8.45 per cent. About 21 million tonnes (out of 217 million tonnes) of fly ash generated was utilized in 2018-19 in reclamation of low-lying areas.

- *Backfilling of mines:* Traditionally, river sand has been used as mine backfilling material, but its continued availability is suspect. Fly ash offers a viable alternative. Average ash utilization rate as mine filling has been around 6 per cent. About 0.65 million tonne of fly ash was used in backfilling and stowing of open cast and underground mines during 1998-99, which increased to 10 million tonnes by 2018-19.
- *Construction of roads and fly overs*: Road networks are expanding in India. New roads, highways and flyovers are coming up and existing ones are being widened. Fly ash can be used in this sector as well. Fly ash is pozzolanic and can enhance the strength of road structures. However, average ash utilization in this sector has only been 3.6%.
- *Manufacturing blocks and tiles for walls and floors*: Fly ash is also used to manufacture floor and wall tiles (with fly ash content not exceeding 50%). Fly ash-based blocks and tiles are as good as conventional clay-based building tiles.
- *Agriculture*: Several studies proclaim the benefits of using fly ash in agriculture. However, there are risks associated due to presence of toxic heavy metals in the ash which can find their way into the food chain.

MEASURES TO BE ADOPTED

It is clear that coal will remain the mainstay of energy generation in India in the near future, which will further aggravate the problem of fly ash management. A proper disposal and utilization framework are vital in view of the growing environmental concerns associated with its generation. Along with the current emphasis on meeting emissions standards, ash utilization must also be made a priority area as its improper disposal significantly contributes to air pollution. Although there is a well-defined policy and regulatory framework for 100% fly ash utilization, thermal power plants have failed to achieve the targets due to one or the reason discussed in this report. Ash lying around will always be a hazard despite the best disposal measures. Ensuring its 100% utilization by converting it into a variety of useful products or using it in construction activities is the only way forward. Concerted efforts are required at the plant level as well as by agencies that utilize ash to make this possible. Only if all thermal power plants consistently utilize 100% of the ash they generate in the coming years, while also clearing the ash backlog from previous years, will the adverse environmental impacts created due to ash be minimized. Instead of utilizing ash in batches, its continuous utilization should be made possible. User agencies within a stipulated radius of thermal power plants must be made accountable and should be strictly monitored for use of ash in their products. Thermal power capacity additions should work in tandem with the capability in any region to ensure 100% utilization of ash in an environmentally sound manner. Coal power plants should explore avenues to ensure 100% utilization, and the government can regulate this with stricter monitoring and stringent penalties, and by creating a conducive fly ash-product market. Thus, power plants, regulatory bodies as well as the government need to take definite measures to improve fly ash utilization. Following are the suggestions:

1. Discourage expansion or installation of coal capacity in regions where it is already heavily concentrated. Doing so will ensure that there is no overabundance of fly ash in such regions and reduce the chances of serious fly ash pollution.
2. Capacity addition should not be allowed in plants with limited ash pond capacity. There have been several instances where plants have undertaken capacity addition without assessing the carrying capacity of their ash ponds. This should be strictly discouraged.
3. Power plants not utilizing 100% of their ash should not be given approval to expand capacity.
4. It must be made mandatory for non-compliant power plants to set up fly ash depots in regions with high ash demand. In particular, plants with capacities exceeding 2,000 MW and also those with low ash utilization rates must set up such depots in urban areas.
5. Monitor periodically and take strict action against plants not meeting the 100% utilization target. Government must come up with strict policy measures in the form of penalties and disincentives against such plants. Power stations should be asked to determine their availability only after accounting for their ability to utilize 100% of the ash they produce, before committing to scheduling their stations to state load dispatch centres.
6. Make disclosure of fly ash data by power plants mandatory to ensure better transparency. It must be made mandatory for each power plant to put its annual ash generation and utilization (including of legacy ash) data on its official website for better transparency. Power plants must also disclose their fly ash procurers along with the amount utilized by each.
7. Reduce plant load factor (PLF) of plants not meeting the 100% target. A low PLF will lead to lesser coal consumption and fly ash generation. The reduced amount can then be easily utilized to the extent of 100 per cent, solving the problem of its disposal.
8. Provide guidelines on proper construction of ash dykes and appoint dedicated government- or SPCB-appointed authorities or officials in each state for periodic monitoring. Capacity building of such officials is also needed.

9. Provide adequate transport infrastructure for bulk transfer of ash through roads, railways or waterways from power plants to utilizing agencies.
10. Ensure strict monitoring of the mandated use of fly ash. State governments must come up with stricter regulations and enforcement systems to ensure mandatory use of fly ash in the making of cement, bricks and roads. Noncompliance with such a mandate should be dealt with strictly.
11. Encourage setting up of new cement and fly ash-based brick manufacturing units in close proximity to power plants. State governments must provide suitable incentives and support to start-ups, agencies or power plants willing to establish fly ash-based units in the vicinity of power plants.
12. Establish a market for fly ash-based products. States should make use of fly ash products compulsory in construction activities near power plants. Use of fly ash bricks and cement should be made mandatory in construction of all government buildings.
13. Strict enforcement of already existing policies. MoEF&CC had mandated 100% utilization of fly ash by power plants by end of December 2017. Regulations were passed on transportation cost bearing and mandatory use of fly ash by user agencies located within 300 km radius of power plants. However, on ground enforcement and monitoring has been poor. Stricter enforcement is required.
14. Replication of success stories for higher ash utilization rate. Success stories (whether intra-country of global) must be replicated.

MEASURES TO BE TAKEN BY COAL- AND LIGNITE-BASED POWER PLANTS

1. Ensure dry extraction of ash to the maximum extent possible by building sufficient storage silos. Dry ash is more suitable for making cement, bricks and for other uses. After a proper assessment of monthly fly ash generation, plants should ensure that they have at least one month's fly ash storage capacity within their premises. Power plants should also create facilities for faster loading of ash onto vehicles.
2. Every power plant must have a dedicated ash management cell working for proper management, safe disposal and utilization of ash. The cell must ensure the quality of fly ash supplied to user agencies. It must also inspect ash ponds periodically for leakages and other maintenance issues.

3. For bringing in more transparency, power plants must disclose their annual ash generation and utilization figures, including of legacy ash, on their official website and also in the annual environment statements they submit to pollution control boards.
4. Every power plant with a low ash utilization rate must install fly ash depots in regions with high demand for fly ash.
5. Power plants must explore the possibility of building fly ash-based brick or cement units adjacent to the plant or selling fly ash for nearby construction activities.

MEASURES TO BE TAKEN BY REGULATORY BODIES AND POLLUTION CONTROL BOARDS

1. Regulatory bodies must devise a clear penalty mechanism as environmental compensation for damage and should impose strict penalties on plants mismanaging fly ash. The collected money should be spent on restoration of the environment and in compensating the people affected by such incidents.
2. Closure notices should be issued and heavy penalty must be imposed on plants with poor ash utilization rates.
3. Pollution control boards should renew 'consent to operate' only for stations that demonstrate adequate fly ash management and submit proper action plans for its 100% utilization.
4. State and regional pollution control boards must periodically inspect and assess the condition of ash dykes. Ash ponds must be monitored for leaks or overflow. Appropriate action should be taken against power plants through show cause notices, closure notices or by imposing penalty on defaulters, in case of mismanagement and unsafe disposal of ash in dykes or overflow of ash dykes.

REFERENCES

Anon (2019). Executive Summary on Power Sector, Central Electricity Authority. Available at http://cea.nic.in/reports/monthly/ executivesummary/2019/exe_summary-10.pdf, as accessed on 21 September 2020

Anon (2020a). Coal Ash in India—A Compendium of Disasters, Environmental and Health Risks, Health Energy Initiative & Community Environmental Monitoring.

Anon (2020b). Environment Management and Pollution Control, Limited, CESC. n.d. Retrieved from https://www.cesc.co.in/ as accessed on 21 September 2020

Anon (2020c). Order of the National Green Tribunal, February. Retrieved from https://greentribunal.gov.in/ as accessed on 21 September 2020

Anon (2020d). NGT Directs Thermal Power Plants to take Prompt Steps for Scientific Disposal of Fly Ash, ET Energy World, February 2020.

Soundaram Ramanathan, Sugandha Arora and Vinay Trivedi (2020). Coal-based Power norms—Where do we stand today? Centre for Science and Environment.

5

Earlier, Current and Forecasts of E-Waste and its Management

INTRODUCTION

The electronic industry has been raised as one of the world's leading and inventive sector as one of its kind. This is attributed to the profound privilege of the contemporary generation, which enjoys their entire social and economic life surrounded by electronics. This has led to an exceptional expansion of electronics, making them cheaper and more available. Unfortunately, the waste management system has not improved at a similar pace (Masud *et.al.*, 2019). All these reasons and others have contributed to the unprecedented accumulation of electronic waste. Other reasons for e-waste present the anthropocentric view of humans since most of the reasons do not have a requirement to dispose of e-waste, and some are merely for personal satisfaction. These include very less lifespan of electronic items since the consumer would like to upgrade technologically (even when the old or previous item is in good condition) and technological advancements that are being released into the market every day. For instance, in 2008, the users of computers are increased and surpassed 1 billion, and these goods are obsoleted in the next five years. For these and many other petty known reasons, e-waste ends up in dump yards resulting in environmental pollution. Components of e-waste yet times enter the food chain and affect humans also.

Pollution from e-waste is a global problem. According to the UN, global e-waste is projected to exceed 40 million tons per year. Recycling end of product life results in enhanced pollution, economically unviable, and is unregulated in most countries. Severe health concerns are caused by e-waste in millions of people, precisely in developing countries like Europe, Africa, and Asia. It is reported that more than 200 million people around the world are at threat from exposure to toxic waste. Recycling of valuable elements in e-waste like copper and gold has been a source of income typically in the informal sector from emerging industrialized countries. However, some of the recycling techniques employed like cable burning for retention of inherent copper leads to hazardous substances exposure to both adult and child workers and their families (Lakshmi and Raj, 2017; Li *et.al.*, 2020).

The objective of this chapter is to present an overview of electronic waste, the current status of electronic waste management, and recycling technologies for the recovery of metals from end-of-life electronic equipment.

DEFINITION OF E-WASTE

Some known definitions of E-waste are as follows:

- According to the Sinha-Khetriwal, 2002, the power-driven electronic appliances that have reached its End of life (EOL) is called E-Waste.
- Puckett *et.al.*, 2002, described that Electronic devices were ranging from individual household items to personal computers that have been discarded after EOL.
- The APME, 1995, defined as it is a combination of Ferrous, Non-ferrous, Ceramic, and Plastic Materials.

The term E-Waste and WEE (Waste Electronic Equipment's) is repeatedly used in the present scenario as the usage of electronic devices in our day to day life are increasing. Discarded electronic appliances belong to E-waste Category, whereas WEE additionally refers to EOL appliances. The European Commission Defined WEE as Wide-Ranging EOL is the raw material that can be utilized to produce, measure, and transfer electromagnetic current (EU RoHS Directive 2002/95/EC, 2003).

CLASSES OF E-WASTE BASED ON THEIR APPLICATION AND SIZE

Since much difference is not made between E-waste and WEEE, Indian legislation has considered e-waste for E-waste management (E-Waste Rules, 2011; Rodrigues *et.al.*, 2020). In this chapter, we use the term "E-waste" to refer to all the discarded/broken/surplus/obsolete electrical and electronic devices, as stated by Pathak *et.al.*, 2017. More specifically, E-waste can be divided into six categories Balde *et.al.*, 2015, as shown in Table 5.1.

Table 5.1: E-waste categories

Illustrations	Examples	Illustrations	Examples
Equipment's that Exchange heat and temperature comprises heat pumps, Air Conditioners, Refrigerators		Large size equipment, Comprises Xerox machines, Washing Machines, Electronic Stoves.	
Computers, televisions, laptops, notebooks, and tablets		Electric lamps comprise Fluorescent lamps & LED Bulbs	
Small size equipment Comprises household items such as toasters, microwaves, electric kettles, vacuum cleaner, calculators, electrical toys, video cameras, and small medical devices		Small ICT equipment Comprises landline telephones, mobile phones, and routers, printers, GPS (global positioning systems)	

CHARACTERISTICS OF ELECTRONIC WASTE

Hazardous Components in e-Waste

E-waste consists of components like ferrous, non-ferrous, ceramic, and plastic in large quantities with different size and shapes; some of these materials contain hazardous components which need separate and precise treatment for their removal shown in Table 5.2 (Cooper, 2000).

Table 5.2: Hazardous components in WEE

Materials	Elucidation
(1)	(2)
Batteries	Batteries consist of heavy metals like Pb (Lead), Hg (Mercury), and Cd (Cadmium).
CRTs (Cathode ray tubes)	Lead is present in the cone glass and Fluorescent coatings inside the glass panel.
Switches and its components containing mercury	Thermostats, sensors, and relay Switches generally consist of mercury. In addition, it is also used in mobile phones, data transmission devices, and medical equipment.
Asbestos left-over	Separate treatment is required for treating these left-overs.
Cartridge tonners and colors	Toners and Colours consist of Toxic Chemical and Hazardous Substances, and these are abstemiously toxic if acute exposure occurs.
Printed Circuit Boards	In these boards, cadmium and lead are common and present in solder; SMD chip resistors, Semiconductors, and Infrared detectors contain cadmium.

(Table Contd...)

(1)	(2)
Capacitors containing PCBs (Polychlorinated biphenyl)	Capacitors containing PCBs have to be removed for Safe Obliteration.
LCDs (Liquid Crystal Displays)	LCDs with older versions and Designs consist of Lead and Mercury in larger quantities, But the Surface area greater than 100 Cm^2 is removed from WEE.
Plastics with halogenated flame retardants.	Toxic substances will be released during the combustion and incineration of these types of plastics.
Equipment containing CFC HCFC or HFCs.	The CFC, HFC, or CFCs present in the foam and the refrigerating circuit must be properly extracted and destroyed or recycled.
Gas discharge lamps	Mercury has to be removed before discarding.

COMPOSITION OF E-WASTE

With reference to material composition, electronic waste can be defined as a mixture of various metals, particularly copper, aluminum, and steel, which are either attached to or covered with or mixed with various types of plastics and ceramics (Hoffmann, 1992). Precious metals have wide application in the manufacture of electronic appliances (Table 5.3), serving as contact materials due to their high chemical stability and their good conducting properties. Platinum group metals are used, among other things, in switching contacts (relays, switches) or as sensors to ascertain the electrical measure and as a function of the temperature (Teller, 2006).

Table 5.3: Composition of metals of Different Electronic Scrap

E-Waste (Scrap)	Mass (%)					Mass (mg kg^{-1})			Reference
	Fe	Cu	Al	Pb	Ni	Ag	Au	Pd	Hageluken, 2006
TV boards	28	10	10	1.0	0.3	280	20	10	Hageluken, 2006
PC boards	7	20	5	1.5	1	1000	250	110	Hageluken, 2006
Mobile phone	5	13	1	0.3	0.1	1380	350	210	Hageluken, 2006
Portable audio	23	21	1	0.14	0.03	150	10	4	Hageluken, 2006
DVD player	62	5	2	0.3	0.05	115	15	4	Hageluken, 2006
Calculator	4	3	5	0.1	0.5	260	50	5	Hageluken, 2006
PC mainboard	4.5	14.3	2.8	2.2	1.1	639	566	124	Legarth *et.al.*, 1995
Printed circuit boards	12	10	7	1.2	0.85	280	110	-	Zang and Forssberg, 1997
TV scrap (CRTs removed)	-	3.4	1.2	0.2	0.038	20	<10	<10	Cui & Forssberg, 2007
Electronic	8.3	8.5	0.71	3.15	2.0	29	12	-	Ilyas *et.al.*, 2007
PC	20	7	14	6	0.85	189	16	3	Patil and Sharma, 2017

(Table Contd...)

E-Waste (Scrap)	Mass (%)					Mass (mg kg^{-1})			Reference
	Fe	Cu	Al	Pb	Ni	Ag	Au	Pd	Hageluken, 2006
Typical electronic	8	20	2	2	2	2000	1000	50	Sum, 1991
E-scrap sample 1	37.4	18.2	19	1.6	-	6	12	-	Busselle *et.al.*, 1991
E-scrap sample 2	27.3	16.4	11.0	1.4	-	210	150	20	Busselle *et.al.*, 1991
Printed circuit boards	5.3	26.8	1.9	-	0.47	3300	80	-	Theo, 1998
E-scrap (1972 sample)	26.2	18.6	-	-	-	1800	220	30	Bhuie *et.al.*, 2004
Nokia Cellular phones	8	19	9	0.9	1	9000	-	-	Bhuie *et.al.*, 2004

GLOBAL GENERATION OF E-WASTE

The Global development of electronic items has overstated modes of communication, transportation, entertainment, edification, and healthcare resulting in a mammoth amount of E-waste, which is discarded periodically and frequently. The global E-waste Monitor Report 2017 revealed that 44.7 Million Metric Tons of electronic waste had been produced in 2016 (Balde *et.al.*, 2017), which might surge beyond 50 MMT in the years to come. Fuelling is the major concern of sustainable management of E-waste, and it contributes a share of 5% of the entire solid waste generated in the world-wide (Kiddee *et.al.*, 2013). Developed countries like the United States and the leading countries of Europe are considered to be the main manufacturers and generators of the E-Waste (Robinson, 2009).

E-waste generation statistics change rapidly in the present scenario. Nations like China are leading in the generation of E-Waste (7.2 MMT/ year), leaving the United States in second place. The share of another fast-developing country, India, is also increasing and expected to overtake the japan by 2020 for the third rank in global E-waste generation. During the year 2016, 44.7 MMT of E-waste was generated, out of which, small types of equipment has a major share with 16.8 MMT, large types of equipment with 9.1 MMT, temperature exchange equipment like freezing and cooling contributing 7.6 MMT, screens and monitors with 6.6 MMT, small ICT with 3.9 MMT and electric lamps with 0.7 MMT (E-Waste Recycling Facts and Figures, 2018). It was understood that the annual growth rate generated (E-waste) per category differs, but the overall amount will be increased in the coming years (Kumar *et.al.*, 2020).

CHALLENGES TO THE ENVIRONMENT

E-Waste is a protuberant environmental management problem that is alarmingly increasing with the pace of the global population and consumption. It has become an environmental curse to be battled. Owing to the stringent rules on the disposal of E-waste, the need for effective management has become mandatory, thus attracting researchers towards finding solutions. Apart from being the biggest contributors to E-waste, nations like China and India are also acting as dumping grounds for world-wide E-waste trade (Pathak *et.al.*, 2017; Zeng *et.al.*, 2017). Major reasons governing E-waste movement into these countries are deficiency of treatment facilities, valuable secondary materials recycling, and inexpensive operating costs for the transfer of waste.

DIRECT AND INDIRECT IMPACTS ON ENVIRONMENT AND HUMAN HEALTH

Human health and the environment are adversely affected by the improper management of E-waste, either directly or indirectly. In order to reduce the cost of recycling, methods that are unsafe and informal are being used for recycling E-waste; these methods being unscientific, have a direct impact on humans and the environment. To illustrate these direct impacts, some cases in the different parts of India where the informal recycling taking place are accounted for here. A study conducted by Pathak *et.al.*, 2017; Pradhan *et.al.*, 2017 reported severe environmental problems causing serious threats to human health at Mandoli industrial area in New Delhi. Kumar, 2014 analyzed soil and water around E-waste recycling areas revealed that heavy metal concentrations and hazardous materials are beyond the acceptable levels (Cadmium – 1.29mg/kg; Copper – 115.50mg/kg; Arsenic – 17.08mg/kg; Zinc – 776.84mg/kg; Selenium – 12.67mg/kg and Lead – 2,645.31mg/kg) which is attributed to the leaching of metals from E-waste into soil and groundwater. Additionally, Ha *et.al.*, 2009, found that the soils near the recycling areas consist of hazardous substances like organochlorine compounds (7mg/kg soil).

In Moradabad, Uttar Pradesh, severe pollution was observed due to the burning of PCBs (Printed Circuit Board) containing dioxins and furan and practicing improper disposable methods like dumping the burnt ashes in a subsidiary of Ganga, i.e., Ramganga river created severe acute water pollution as these ashes generally contain a high amount of heavy metals and poly-carbonaceous materials (Centre for Science and Environment, 2015).

Furthermore, during the attempts to recover valuable metals from the E-Waste, cyanide leaching into the soil and water was observed in the slum areas of Bangalore (Ha *et.al.*, 2009). In the process of extracting gold from the E-Waste, cyanidation is the most effective process for complete recovery; however, this cyanidation process should maintain alkaline conditions throughout the leaching as its pKa value is 9.5. Maintaining other than these conditions will form HCN gas, which is highly toxic in nature; if these exposures are greater than 500ppb, it causes severe impacts on human health. Discharging effluents generated from the cyanidation process will contaminate soil and groundwater. Sepulveda *et.al.*, 2010, observed from his study that nearly 247-fold higher content of lead leached into groundwater attributed to the burning of E-waste in the open. The presence of Higher concentrations of copper (Cu), Antimony (Sb), Bismuth (Bi), Cadmium (Cd), and Silver (Ag) in the blood and hair samples of workers is strong evidence of the adversity caused by improper recycling of E-waste.

Additionally, the elements in E-waste may vary according to the produced goods/devices and contain more than 1000 diverse substances, many of which fall under the hazardous and radioactive waste category (see Table 5.4).

Table 5.4: Hazardous and radioactive waste category

E-waste Components	Toxic Metals	Limit (ppm)	Disease Caused by the Exposure to Above Permissible Limit
(1)	(2)	(3)	(4)
Batteries and Capacitors made up of Ceramics	Ag^x	5.0	It Causes blue pigmentation on the body, damages the liver, kidney, and brain.
Light-emitting devices	As^y	5.0	Skin disease, cancer, and impaired nerve signaling.
A fluorescent lamp, CRT gun	Ba^y	<100	Brain swelling, weakness in the muscle.
Motherboards	Be^y	0.75	Causes lung cancer, skin disease, beryllioisis.
PVC Cables, PCB casings	Br^y	0.1	Hormonal issues, hearing loss, DNA damages.
Printer ink, toners	Cd^y	1.0	Irreversible effects on the kidney.
Printed circuit boards	CN^y	< 0.5	Cyanide poisoning, >2.5 ppm cause to coma.
Computer hosing, cabling, hard discs.	Cr $(VI)^y$	5.0	DNA damage and permanent eye impairment.
LCD, switches, backlight bulbs	Hg^y	0.2	Damages brain, kidney, and fetuses.
Mobile batteries	Li^x	$< 10^a$	Diarrhea, vomiting, drowsiness,
CRT, PCB	Ni^x	20.0	Allergic reaction, bronchitis, lung cancers.
LED lead-acid battery, solder, fluorescent tubes	Pb^z	5.0	Damages the nervous system and reproductive system.
CRT glass and a solder alloy	Sb^y	< 0.5	Carcinogen, diarrhea, and stomach ulcer.
A fax machine, photoelectric cells	Se^y	1.0	High concentration causes selenosis.
CRT, batteries	Sr^y	1.5	Somatic as well the genetic changes due to this cancer in the bone.

(Table Contd...)

(1)	(2)	(3)	(4)
Luminous substances	Zn[y]	250.0	Nausea, vomiting, pain, cramps, and diarrhea.
Cooling units and insulation foam	CFCs[y]	<1.0	Depletes the ozone layer and leads to the incidence of skin cancer.
Transformer, capacitor	PCBs[y]	5.0	PCB causes cancer in animals
Computer input units	PVC[y]	0.03	Hazardous and toxic air contaminants.

[x] Critical, [y] hazardous and toxic, [z] radioactive waste, [a] limit in serum/blood.

The penalties due to these substances are primarily physical health outcomes, for example, dysfunction of lungs, thyroid, the nervous system, and fertility in mammals (Agrawal *et.al.*, 2012; Sepulveda *et.al.*, 2010). It has been observed that local refurbishes in India are not practicing eco-friendly disposable techniques as these methods are expensive, and locals follow the rudimentary techniques to reduce the cost of disposing of to gain more profits. Dumping of E-Waste in landfilling sites releases a huge amount of heavy metals and toxic substances that can eventually drain to pollute the groundwater (Kiddee *et.al.*, 2013).

Up to 600 m^3 of the water can be polluted by the cadmium content present in one mobile phone. Awasthi *et.al.*, 2017 and Wang *et.al.*, 2005 stated that electronic appliances containing PCB and other plastic components are highly inflammable in nature, releasing acute toxic gases like dioxins and furans on burning and these cause severe threat to the ecosystem. The Physico-chemical parameters of the soil are altered by the heavy metals after leaching of these substances from the landfill. During the process of dismantling and shredding, the suspended particles released into the atmosphere causes atmospheric pollution. The atmospheric pollution increases the particulate matter in the ambient air and causes severe adverse respiratory and non-respiratory problems like the enhanced concentration of particulate matter in the ambient air causing breathing difficulties, eye and respiratory irritation, coughing, choking, pneumonitis, tremors, and neuropsychiatric problems for humans.

Air pollution is caused by practicing unscientific incineration practices for E-waste, and this results in the release of hazardous substances and has indirect impacts on human health. For instance, the crops grown in contaminated soils with heavy metals can easily absorb the pollutants. Post-harvesting, the contaminants enter the human body through an indirect route, but they have the same effect as direct pollution (Vara *et.al.*, 2019, Varghese *et.al.*, 2016). Furthermore, valuable metals might be lost by improper management/recycling of E-waste, therein, and hence virgin materials are required from the primary source. Thus, the mining-to-metal retrieval process will be required again.

For instance, every year globally, 100% of In (indium), 72% of Ru (ruthenium), 50% of Sn (tin), 44% of Cu (Copper), 34% of Ag (Silver), and 22% of Hg (mercury) are mined resulting in severe environmental pollution (Zeng *et.al.*, 2017). The recovery of metals from primary sources during mining can approximately save 41% of the energy cost of mining and water consumption up to 391.5 m^3/kg in ore milling, and this process will help in reducing the environmental pollution generated by the energy-intensive process. Remarkably, on an average of 10 million cellular phones contain approximately 160 tons of Cu(copper), 3500 kg of Ag(silver), 340 kg Au(gold), and 150 kg of Pd (palladium).

DISASSEMBLY OF E-WASTE

Disassembly is a selective process, involves segregating valuable or singling of hazardous components, and it is a vital process in the recycling of E-Waste. Moreover, it is a systematic approach that allows the removal of components or sub-assembly from a product for a particular purpose. Researchers are focussed on innovation in disassembly facilities and the disassembly planning process (DPP). The main motto behind the DPP is to advance software and procedures in disassembly strategies.

Gupta *et.al.*, 1996 proposed the following phases for the DPP plan:

- In the phase of input and output product analysis, valuable, reusable, and hazardous components are defined after the identification of optimal disassembly and preliminary cost analysis.
- In the following phase (Assembly analysis), component hierarchy, joining elements, and former assembly sequences are analyzed.
- Uncertainty issues analysis: originates from defective parts or joints in the products while upgrading or downgrading the quality of the product for consumer satisfaction.
- Determination of dismantling strategy: this a final phase for deciding whether to use destructive or non-destructive disassembly. Highly flexible tools are required for a process plan and implementation of good disassembly. Even though the electronic equipment used for assembly is well advanced, the automation for disassembly of E-waste is too complicated and not developed.

The automated disassembly is being prevented from becoming commercially successful due to the following reasons:

(1) Similar type of products; (2) the number of products that are similar is too small; (3) un-friendly product design for general disassembly; (4) problem in logistics during returns; and (5) dissimilarities in giving back products that to be disassembled.

Dismantling of electronic equipment in the recycling process in indispensable because; (1) the first priority is to reuse the components; (2) Hazardous components dismantling is essential; (3) High valuable and high-grade materials used in printed circuit boards, cables, and engineering plastics are common and simple to recover. In general, the manual dismantling process is practiced by recycling plants. Ragn-Sells Elektronika tervinning AB in Sweden is a typical electronics-recycling corporation (Cui & Forssberg, 2003). Wide – a variety of tools are involved in the process of dismantling for the removal of hazardous components and for the recovery of valuable and reusable materials.

RECYCLING TECHNOLOGY OF ELECTRONIC WASTE

Magnetic Separation

Magnetic separators, i.e., low-intensity drum separators, are mostly used for separating the ferromagnetic metals from non-ferrous metals. The high-intensity magnetic separators design has been modified after the introduction of rare earth alloy permanent magnets capable of providing very high-field strengths and gradients.

Eddy Current Separation

Introducing eddy current separators in recycling industries is one of the most significant development. Eddy currents can be actuated in an electrically conductive particle by a time-dependent attractive magnetic field (magnet rotor in the figure). Further, the eddy currents will, in return, result in magnetic fields that oppose the inducing fields, giving rise to a so-called Lorentz force, a repulsive force.

Density-Based Separation

Gravity concentration separates materials of different specific gravity by their relative movement in response to the force of gravity and one or more other forces, the latter often being the resistance to motion offered by a fluid, such as water or air (Wills & Finch, 2015). The motion of a particle in a fluid is dependent not only on the density of the particle but also on its size and shape; large particles will be affected more than smaller ones. In practice, close size control of feeds to gravity processes is required to reduce the effect on the size and make the relative motion of the particle specific gravity-dependent.

OPTICAL SORTING

With the fast development of the Charge- Coupled Device (CCD) sensor, computing, and software technology, optical sorting processes have been developed in both the recycling and mineral processing industry. In addition, recording more and better data with sensors improves the

Table 5.5: Metals recovery from various process

Techniques	Metals recovered	Main process features	Main results	References
(1)	(2)	(3)	(4)	(5)
Noranda process	Cu, Au, Ag, Pt, Pd, Se, Te, Ni	Copper smelter is feeding with 14% of copper for total throughput; Converter upgrading; Metal recovery by electrorefining	Copper and precious metals are recovered in huge amounts	Veldhuizen & Sippel, 1994
Boliden Ro¨nnska¨r Smelter	Cu, Ag, Au, Pd, Ni, Se, Zn, Pb	Kaldo reactor is feeding with high concentrations of lead; Coper converter up-gradation and refining process	Copper and precious metals are recovered in huge amounts	Theo, 1998; Lehner, 2003
Test at Ro¨nnska¨r Smelter	Copper and precious metals	Computer component scrap feeding to Zinc fuming process in 1:1 ratio with revert slag; Plastics were used as fuel and reducing agents; Copper smelter recovers the precious metals and Copper that are following the copper collector	Complete recovery of precious metals and copper in the Zinc fuming process	Mark & Lehner, 1999
Umicore's Precious metal refining process	Base metals, Precious metals, Platinum group metals and Selenium, Tellurium, Indium	Electrowinning, IsaSmelt copper leaching and precious metal recovery for precious metal operation; E-waste cover up to 10% of the feed; Plastics substitute coke, which acts a reducing and fuel to the IsaSmelt; Off gas emission control system is installed at the IsaSmelt furnace	Special metals like Sb, Bi, Sn, Se, Te, In are recovered along with base metals and precious metals.	Hagelüken, 2006; Hageluken & Art, 2007

(Table Contd…)

(1)	(2)	(3)	(4)	(5)
Full-scale trial at Umicore's smelter	Metals in electronic scrap	Coke is replaced by plastic rich materials from WEEE, and these substances act as a reducing agent as well as an energy source for the IsaSmelt	Using WEEE (6%) and coke (1%) doesn't negatively affect the metal recovery process (instead of using only coke (4.5%))	Brusselaers *et.al.*, 2005
Dunn's patent for gold refining	Gold	Gold scrap subjected to chlorine at 300°C to 700°C; Impurity-Metal chlorides are washed with Hydrochloric acid; Silver chloride is dissolved by ammonium hydroxide and nitric acid washing; Samples should contain more than 80% of gold	Gold with 99.9% purity was recovered from gold scraps	Dunn *et.al.*, 1991
Day's patent for refractory ceramic precious metals scraps	Platinum and palladium	In the plasma arc furnace, scrap was subjected to heat (at least 1400 C); Precious metals in molten metallic phase and collector metals were produced; Ceramic residues went into a slag phase.	Recoveries of 80.3% and 94.2% were obtained for platinum and palladium, respectively	Day, 1984
Aleksandrovich's Patent for recovery of platinum group metal and gold from electronic scraps	Platinum group metal and gold	Fusing together scraps based on chalcogenides of base metals with carbon reducer; After the settling and cooling of melted materials, solidification and separation of solidified products are facilitated by formed phase boundaries	Platinum group metal and gold was recovered	Aleksandrovich *et.al.*, 1998

separation performance of automated sorting equipment. The measuring of particle properties such as color, texture, morphology, conductivity, and others allows high-quality sorting of mixed materials into almost pure fractions. Hence, multisensory systems involving the use of two or more different sensors have been developed over the past few years.

PYROMETALLURGICAL PROCESS

Pyrometallurgical processing is a traditional method for recovering precious and non-ferrous materials from electronic waste. The pyrometallurgical process includes incineration, smelting in the blast furnace, sintering, melting, dross formation, and reactions in a gas phase at high temperatures. In this process, the scrap that is crushed was subjected to heating in a furnace or in a molten bath to remove plastics and the refractory oxides from the slag phase together with some metals.

Table 5.5 gives a summary of typical pyrometallurgical methods for the recovery of metals from electronic waste. The traditional technology of pyrometallurgy has been used for the recovery of copper and precious metals from electronic waste equipment for years. However, most methods involving the pyrometallurgical processing of electronic waste has the following limitations (Hageluken, 2006; Sum, 1991):

- Integrated smelters cannot recover aluminum and iron as metals; they are transferred into the slag component. Unfortunately, aluminum has an influence on the slag properties that are undesirable in most cases.
- The presence of halogenated flame retardants in the smelter feed can lead to the formation of dioxins unless special installations and measures are present. Traditional smelters designed for the treatment of mining concentrates or simple copper scrap encounter some challenges for electronic waste treatment. However, state-of-the-art smelters are highly dependent on investments.
- Ceramic components and glass in the e-waste increase the amount of slag from blast furnaces, which results in a loss of precious metals and base metals from the scrap.
- Energy recovery and the use of organic constituents as reducing agents are beginning to be used only now.
- Only partial separation of metals can be achieved using pyrometallurgy, resulting in a limited upgrading of the metal value. Subsequent hydrometallurgical techniques and/or electrochemical processing are therefore necessary.
- Precious metals take a long time to separate in pyrometallurgical processes and are thus only obtained at the very end of the process.

HYDROMETALLURGICAL PROCESS

Precious metals contribute the highest value to electronic scrap. From an economic point of view, the recovery of precious metals from e-waste is most attractive. In the past two decades, the most active research area on the recovery of metals from electronic scraps is recovering precious metals by hydrometallurgical techniques (Quinet *et.al.*, 2005; Macaskie *et.al.*, 2007; Ogata & Nakano, 2005). Compared with pyrometallurgical processing, the hydrometallurgical method is more exact, more predictable, and more easily controlled. The main steps in hydrometallurgical processing consist of a series of acid or caustic leaches of solid material. The solutions are then subjected to separation and purification procedures such as precipitation of impurities, solvent extraction, adsorption, and ion-exchange to isolate and concentrate the metals of interest. Consequently, the solutions are treated by electrorefining process, chemical reduction, or crystallization for metal recovery (Safarzadeh *et.al.*, 2007; Ritcey, 2006; Tavlarides *et.al.*, 1987).

A summary of new developments in the recovery of metals from electronic waste by hydrometallurgical techniques is listed in Table 5.6. It can be seen that most of the hydrometallurgical techniques for the recovery of metals are involved in acid leaching and/or halide leaching. This is because acid leaching is the most feasible approach for the removal of base metals resulting in the exposure of precious metals surfaces. However, to develop an environment-friendly technique for the recovery of precious metals from e-waste, more attention should be paid to evaluate the environmental impact of the various techniques.

REGULATIONS DEALING WITH ELECTRONIC WASTE

It is a well-known fact that the environmental quality is dwindling at a very fast pace due to such informal, unplanned, and untrained treatment of E-wastes. But one significant cause for such environmental degradation due to E-wastes is the inability of the law to deter violators. In many countries, there are now legislations and statutes in place specifically to deter such crimes. In India also many environmental legislations and the rules are there, which are dealing with E-waste either directly or indirectly. Such legislations have, inopportunely, not resulted in preventing environmental dilapidation as penal provisions in environmental laws dealing with electronic wastes are weak, lenient, hard to impose, and unlikely to affect 'business as usual.' The situation is aggravated by other problems like slow justice delivery system, poor monitoring and enforcement capacity of regulators, and lack of comprehensive databases to evidence violations, among others.

Table 5.6: Recovery of Metals from Electronic Waste by Hydrometallurgical Techniques (most practiced)

Metals recovered	Main process features	Main product	References
Au	Computer chips were treated in nitric acid to dissolve base metals; the residue was leached with aqua regia; ferrous sulfate precipitation was used for gold recovery	Gold flakes	Sheng & Etsell, 2007
Au and Ag	E-waste with size - 0.5 mm was treated with a combination of KI and I2 or NaCl and bleaching powder; solvent extraction was used for gold and silver recovery	Au and Ag	Shibata & Matsumoto, 1999
Ni	Leaching of nickel from waste multi-layer ceramic capacitors was performed by using 1M HNO3 at 90_C, 90-min reaction time, and 5 g/l pulp density	Ni in solution	Kim *et.al.*, 2007
Au (98%), Pd (96%), Pt (92%), Ag (84%)	H_2SO_4 and MgCl2 for dissolution of base metals; HCl and bromide ions were used to dissolve precious metals; cementation of gold by zinc powder	Au and platinum groupmetals powders	Kogan, 2006
Cu (98%)	Copper was dissolved by sulphuric acid or aqua regia; electrowinning was performed for copper recovery	Cu	Veit *et.al.*, 2006
Cu, Ag (93%), Pd (99%), Au (95%)	Sulphuric acid leaching of copper, chloride leaching of palladium, thiourea or cyanide leaching of gold and silver, activated carbon adsorption of gold, silver, and palladium	AgCl, Cu, Pd, Au	Quinet *et.al.*, 2005
92% for Au, Ag, Pd	HCl or H_2SO_4 for dissolution of base metals, leaching of silver by HNO3, leaching of gold and palladium by HCl and $NaClO_3$; precipitation of Au by FeCl2	Gold sponge	Zhou *et.al.*, 2005
Au	E-scrap was treated with a leaching solution based on NaCl, $CuCO_3$, and HCl	Gold residue	Olper *et.al.*, 2004
Sn, Pb	The solder was dissolved with a solution comprising Ti(IV) and an acid. Tin and lead were recovered by electrowinning	Sn and Pb	Gibson *et.al.*, 2004
Cu, Pb, and Sn	HNO_3 leaching of PCBs, electrodeposition recovery of base metals	Cu, Pb, and Sn	Mecucci & Scott, 2002
Au	Thermal treatment, HNO_3 leaching, and aqua regia leaching for gold dissolution, solvent extraction of gold by diethyl malonate, ferrous sulfate solution was used for gold precipitation	Metallic gold	Chmielewski *et.al.*, 1997
Au and Ni	Leaching of base metals by sulphuric acid and oxidant (ferric sulfate) and aqua regia leaching of precious metals	Ni and Au insolution	Zakrewski *et.al.*, 1992

There are various legislations/rules dealing with E-wastes in environmental laws either directly and indirectly, to name a few are:

1. Electronic waste (management) Amendment rules, 2018.
2. Hazardous and Other Wastes (Management and Transboundary Movement) Rules, 2016.
3. The Environment (Protection) Act, 1986
4. The Air (Prevention and Control of Pollution) Act, 1981
5. The Water (Prevention and Control of Pollution) Act, 1974

Out of these legislations and legal provisions, only a few legislations provide for penal provisions to deal with the menace produced by improper disposal of electronic waste. Improper disposal like burning and segregating electronic waste in open areas and not in a manner in which environmentally sound causes leakage in the environment, which results in pollution to the air, water, and soil.

STRATEGIES TOOK FOR THE MANAGEMENT OF E-WASTE:

Inventory Management – Proper control over the materials used in the manufacturing process is an important way to reduce waste generation. By reducing both the number of hazardous materials used in the process, and the amount of excess raw materials in stock, the quantity of waste generated can be reduced. This can be done in two ways, i.e., establishing material-purchase review and control procedures and inventory tracking system. Developing review procedures for all material purchased is the first step in establishing an inventory management program. Procedures should require that all materials be approved prior to purchase. In the approval process, all production materials are evaluated to examine if they contain hazardous constituents and whether alternative

Non-hazardous materials are available. Another inventory management procedure for waste reduction is to ensure that only the needed quantity of material is ordered. This will require the establishment of a strict inventory tracking system. Purchase procedures must be implemented which ensure that materials are ordered only on an as-needed basis and that only the amount needed for a specific period of time is ordered (Zhang *et.al.*, 2020).

Production-Process Modification – Changes can be made in the production process, which will reduce waste generation. This reduction can be accomplished by changing the materials used to make the product or by the more efficient use of input materials in the production process or both.

Waste reduction can be accomplished by the more efficient use of input 0020wq *(i)* Material change

(ii) Process-equipment modification.

(i) **Material change:** Hazardous material used in the production process may be replaced by the less hazardous material. For example, a circuit board manufacturer can replace the solvent-based product with water-based flux and simultaneously replace the solvent vapor degreaser with the detergent part washer.

(ii) **Process Equipment Modification:** Modifying existing equipment to take advantage of better production techniques can significantly reduce waste generation. For example, in many electronic manufacturing operations, which involve porting a product, such as electroplating or painting, the chemical is used to strip off coating from rejected products so that they can be recoated.

Improvements in the operation and maintenance of process equipment can result in significant waste reduction. This can be accomplished by reviewing current operational procedures and examination of the production process for ways to improve its efficiency. Instituting standard operation procedures can optimize the use of raw materials in the production process and reduce the potential for materials to be lost through leaks and spills. A strict maintenance program, which stresses corrective maintenance, can reduce waste generation caused by equipment failure. An employee-training program is a key element of any waste reduction program. Training should include correct operating and handling procedures, proper equipment uses, recommended maintenance and inspection schedules, correct process control specifications, and proper management of waste materials (Esenduran *et.al.*, 2019).

Hazardous materials used in either a product formulation or a production process may be replaced with less hazardous or non-hazardous material. Implementation of this waste reduction technique may require only some minor process adjustments, or it may require extensive new process equipment (Esenduran *et.al.*, 2019).

For example, a circuit board manufacturer can replace the solvent-based product with water-based flux and simultaneously replace the solvent vapor degreaser with a detergent parts washer. Installing more efficient process equipment or modifying existing equipment to take advantage of better production techniques can significantly reduce waste generation. New or updated equipment can use process materials more efficiently, producing less waste. Modifying existing process equipment can be a very cost-effective method of reducing waste generation. In many cases, the modification can just be relatively simple changes in the way the materials are handled within the process to ensure that they are not wasted. For example, in many electronic manufacturing operations, which involve coating a product, such as electroplating or painting, chemicals are used to strip off coating from rejected products so that they can be recoated. These chemicals, which can include acids, caustics, cyanides, etc., are often hazardous waste and must be properly managed. By reducing the number of parts that have to be reworked, the quantity of waste can be significantly reduced.

- **Volume Reduction** – Volume reduction includes those techniques that remove the hazardous portion of waste from a non-hazardous portion. These techniques are used to reduce the volume, and thus the cost of disposing of waste material. The techniques that can be used to reduce waste-stream volume can be divided into two general categories:
  Source segregation and Waste concentration.
- **Segregation of waste** is, in many cases, a simple and economical technique for waste reduction. Wastes containing different types of metals can be treated separately so that the metal value in the sludge can be recovered.
- **The concentration of a waste** stream may increase the likelihood that the material can be recycled or reused. Methods include gravity and filtration, ultra-filtration, reverse osmosis, freeze vaporization, etc.
- **Recovery and Reuse** – The technique could eliminate waste disposal costs, reduce raw material costs, and provide income from a saleable waste. Waste can be recovered on-site, or at an off-site recovery facility, or through the inter-industry exchange. Several physical and chemical techniques are available to reclaim a waste material such as reverse osmosis, electrolysis, condensation, electrolytic recovery, filtration, centrifugation, etc. for example, a printed circuit board manufacturer can use electrolytic recovery to reclaim metals from copper and tin-lead plating bath (Islam & Huda, 2020; Song *et.al.*, 2019).

However, recycling of hazardous products has little environmental benefit if it simply moves the hazards into secondary products that eventually have to be disposed of. Unless the goal is to redesign the product to use non-hazardous materials, such recycling is a false solution.

CONCLUSION

It is evident from the above discussion, pollution from improper handling of E-waste cannot be ignored owing to the magnitude of health and environmental impacts. To escape from hazardous effects, it is vital to appropriately manage E-waste. Inadequate infrastructure and insufficient budget are two issues that restrict E-waste management. This is high time to follow scientific and safe methods for recycling E-waste. Sustainable E-waste management methods discussed in the article, along with their challenges, might prove to be useful in implementing strategies. Integrating these solutions with existing waste management systems might be a possible way to solve problems related to E-waste management.

REFERENCES

Agrawal, A., Pathak, P., Mishra, D., & Sahu, K. K. (2012). Solvent Mediated Interactions for the Selective Recovery of Cadmium from Ni-Cd Battery Waste. Journal of Molecular Liquids, 173, 77-84.

Aleksandrovich, S., Nicolaevich, E., & Ivanovich, E. (1998). Method of Processing of Products based on Ahalcogenides of base Metals Containing Metals of Platinum Group and Gold. Russian Patent, RU2112064, C22B, 11(02).

Association of Plastics Manufacturers in Europe (APME), 1995. Plastics—a Material of choice for the Electrical and Electronic Industry—Plastics Consumption and Recovery. In: Western Europe, APME, Brussels, 1, 2004.

Awasthi, A.K., Zeng, X., & Li, J. (2016). Environmental Pollution of Electronic Waste Recycling in India: A Critical Review. Environmental Pollution, 211, 259-270.

Balde, C.P., Kuehr, R., Blumenthal, K., Fondeur Gill, S., Kern, M., Micheli, P., ... & Huisman, J. (2015). E-waste Statistics-Guidelines on Classification, Reporting and Indicators", United Nations University, IAS-SCYCLE, Bonn (Germany) 2015, 51 pages (ISBN Print: 978-92-808-4553-2) (with CP Balde, K. Blumenthal, S. Fondeur Gill, M. Kern, P. Micheli, E.

Balde, C.P., Forti, V., Gray, V., Kuehr, R., Stegmann, P., 2017. The Global E-Waste Monitor—2017. United Nations University (UNU), International Telecommunication Union (ITU) & International Solid Waste Association (ISWA), Bonn/Germany/Vienna.

Bhuie, A.K., Ogunseitan, O.A., Saphores, J.D., & Shapiro, A.A. (2004, May). Environmental and Economic Trade-offs in Consumer Electronic Products Recycling: A Case Study of Cell Phones and Computers. In IEEE International Symposium on Electronics and the Environment, 2004. Conference Record. 2004 (pp. 74-79). IEEE.

Bisschop, L. (2016). How e-waste Challenges Environmental Governance. In Hazardous Waste and Pollution (pp. 27-43). Springer, Cham.

Brusselaers, J., Hageluken, C., Mark, F., Mayne, N., & Tange, L. (2005). An Eco-efficient Solution for Plastics-metals-mixtures from Electronic Waste: The Integrated Metals Smelter. 5th Identiplast.

Busselle, L.D., Moore, T.A., Shoemaker, J.M., & Allred, R.E. (1999, May). Separation Processes and Economic Evaluation of Tertiary Recycling of Electronic Scrap. In Proceedings of the 1999 IEEE International Symposium on Electronics and the Environment (Cat. No. 99CH36357) (pp. 192-197). IEEE.

Centre for Science and Environment, 2015. Recommendations to Address the Issues of Informal Sector Involved in E-Waste Handling. Moradabad Uttar Pradesh, http://www.cseindia.org/ userfiles/moradabad-e-waste.pdf. (Accessed 26 March 2018).

Chmielewski, A.G., Urbanski, T.S., & Migdal, W. (1997). Separation Technologies for Metals Recovery from Industrial Wastes. Hydrometallurgy, 45(3), 333-344.

Cooper, T. (2000). WEEE, WEEE, WEEE, WEEE, all the way Home? An Evaluation of Proposed Electrical and Electronic Waste Legislation. European Environment, 10(3), 121-130.

Cui, J., & Forssberg, E. (2003). Mechanical Recycling of Waste Electric and Electronic Equipment: A Review. Journal of Hazardous Materials, 99(3), 243-263.

Cui, J., & Forssberg, E. (2007). Characterization of Shredded Television Scrap and Implications for Materials Recovery. Waste Management, 27(3), 415-424.

Day, J.G. (1984). U.S. Patent No. 4,427,442. Washington, DC: U.S. Patent and Trademark Office.

Dunn Jr, W.E., Carda, D.D., & Storbeck, T.A. (1991). U.S. Patent No. 5,004,500. Washington, DC: U.S. Patent and Trademark Office.

Esenduran, G., Atasu, A., & Van Wassenhove, L.N. (2019). Valuable e-waste: Implications for extended Producer Responsibility. IISE Transactions, 51(4), 382-396.

EU RoHS Directive 2002/95/EC, 2003. http://eur-lex.europa.eu/homepage.html. (Accessed 16 August 2008).

E-Waste Rajyasabha Report, 2011. https://rajyasabha.nic.in/rsnew/publication_electronic/EWaste_in_india.pdf/. (Accessed 26 December 2017).

E-Waste Recycling Facts and Figures, 2018. https://www.thebalance.com/e-waste-recycling-factsand-figures-2878189. (Accessed 25 March 2018).

Gibson, R.W., Goodman, P.D., Holt, L., Dalrymple, I.M., & Fray, D.J. (2003). U.S. Patent No. 6,641,712. Washington, DC: U.S. Patent and Trademark Office.

Gupta, S.M., & McLean, C.R. (1996). Disassembly of Products. Computers & Industrial Engineering, 31(1-2), 225-228.

Ha, N.N., Agusa, T., Ramu, K., Tu, N.P.C., Murata, S., Bulbule, K.A., ... & Tanabe, S. (2009). Contamination by Trace Elements at e-waste Recycling sites in Bangalore, India. Chemosphere, 76(1), 9-15.

Hageluken, C. (2006, May). Improving Metal returns and Eco-efficiency in Electronics Recycling-a Holistic Approach for interface Optimisation between Pre-processing and integrated Metals Smelting and Refining. In Proceedings of the 2006 IEEE International Symposium on Electronics and the Environment, 2006. (pp. 218-223). IEEE.

Hageluken, C., & Art, S. (2007). Recycling of e-scrap in a Global Environment: Opportunities and Challenges. Tackling e-waste towards Efficient Management Techniques, TERI Press, New Delhi, 87-104.

Hoffmann, J.E. (1992). Recovering Precious Metals from Electronic scrap. JOM, 44(7), 43-48.

Ilyas, S., Anwar, M.A., Niazi, S.B., & Ghauri, M.A. (2007). Bioleaching of Metals from Electronic Scrap by Moderately Thermophilic Acidophilic Bacteria. Hydrometallurgy, 88(1-4), 180-188.

Islam, M.T., & Huda, N. (2020). Assessing the Recycling Potential of "unregulated" e-waste in Australia. Resources, Conservation and Recycling, 152, 104526.

Kiddee, P., Naidu, R., & Wong, M.H. (2013). Electronic Waste Management Approaches: An Overview. Waste Management, 33(5), 1237-1250.

Kim, E.Y., Lee, J.C., Kim, B.S., Kim, M.S., & Jeong, J. (2007). Leaching Behavior of Nickel from Waste Multi-layer Ceramic Capacitors. Hydrometallurgy, 86(1-2), 89-95.

Kogan, V. (2006). Process for the Recovery of Precious Metals from Electronic Scrap by Hydrometallurgical Technique. International Patent, WO/2006/013568 (C22B 11/00), WIP Organization.

Kumar, A. (2019). Exploring young Adults'e-waste Recycling Behaviour using an Extended Theory of Planned Behaviour Model: A Cross-cultural Study. Resources, Conservation and Recycling, 141, 378-389.

Lakshmi, S., & Raj, A. (2017). A Review Study of E-Waste Management in India. Asian Journal of Applied Science and Technology (AJAST) Volume, 1, 33-36.

Legarth, J.B., Alting, L., & Baldo, G.L. (1995, May). Sustainability issues in Circuit Board Recycling. In Proceedings of the 1995 IEEE International Symposium on Electronics and the Environment ISEE (Cat. No. 95CH35718) (pp. 126-131). IEEE.

Lehner, T. (2003, May). E&HS Aspects on Metal Recovery from Electronic Scrap. In IEEE International Symposium on Electronics and the Environment, 2003. (pp. 318-322). IEEE.

Li, H., Oraby, E., & Eksteen, J. (2020). Extraction of Copper and the Co-leaching Behaviour of other Metals from Waste printed Circuit Boards using Alkaline Glycine Solutions. Resources, Conservation and Recycling, 154, 104624.

Macaskie, L.E., Creamer, N.J., Essa, A.M.M., & Brown, N.L. (2007). A New Approach for the Recovery of Precious Metals from Solution and from Leachates derived from Electronic Scrap. Biotechnology and Bioengineering, 96(4), 631-639.

Mark, F.E., & Lehner, T. (1999). Plastics Recovery from Waste Electrical and Electronic Equipment in Non-ferrous Processes.

Masud, M.H., Akram, W., Ahmed, A., Ananno, A.A., Mourshed, M., Hasan, M., & Joardder, M.U.H. (2019). Towards the Effective E-waste Management in Bangladesh: A Review. Environmental Science and Pollution Research, 26(2), 1250-1276.

Mecucci, A., & Scott, K. (2002). Leaching and Electrochemical Recovery of Copper, Lead and Tin from Scrap printed Circuit Boards. Journal of Chemical Technology & Biotechnology: International Research in Process, Environmental & Clean Technology, 77(4), 449-457.

Ogata, T., & Nakano, Y. (2005). Mechanisms of Gold Recovery from Aqueous Solutions using a Novel tannin gel adsorbent Synthesized from Natural condensed tannin. Water Research, 39(18), 4281-4286.

Olper, M., Maccagni, M., & Cossali, S. (2004). U.S. Patent Application No. 10/798,143.

Pathak, P., & Srivastava, R.R. (2017). Assessment of Legislation and Practices for the Sustainable Management of Waste Electrical and Electronic Equipment in India. Renewable and Sustainable Energy Reviews, 78, 220-232.

Patil, S.A., & Sharma, N.M. (2015). Electronic Waste-A Literature Review. International Journal of Science and Research (IJSR) ISSN (Online), 2319-7064.

Pradhan, J.K., & Kumar, S. (2014). Informal e-waste Recycling: Environmental Risk Assessment of Heavy Metal Contamination in Mandoli Industrial Area, Delhi, India. Environmental Science and Pollution Research, 21(13), 7913-7928.

Puckett, J., Byster, L., Westervelt, S., 2002. Exporting Harm: The High-Tech Trashing of Asia, The Basel Action Network (BAN) and Silicon Valley Toxics Coalition (SVTC), 2002. https://ban. org/E-waste/technotrashfinalcomp.pdf.

Quinet, P., Proost, J., & Van Lierde, A. (2005). Recovery of Precious Metals from Electronic Scrap by Hydrometallurgical Processing Routes. Mining, Metallurgy & Exploration, 22(1), 17-22.

Ritcey, G.M. (2006). Solvent Extraction in Hydrometallurgy: Present and Future. Tsinghua Science and Technology, 11(2), 137-152.

Robinson, B.H. (2009). E-waste: An Assessment of Global Production and Environmental Impacts. Science of the Total Environment, 408(2), 183-191.

Rodrigues, A.C., Boscov, M.E., & Günther, W.M. (2020). Domestic Flow of e-waste in São Paulo, Brazil: Characterization to Support Public Policies. Waste Management, 102, 474-485.

Safarzadeh, M.S., Bafghi, M.S., Moradkhani, D., & Ilkhchi, M.O. (2007). A Review on Hydrometallurgical extraction and Recovery of Cadmium from various Resources. Minerals Engineering, 20(3), 211-220.

Sepulveda, A., Schluep, M., Renaud, F.G., Streicher, M., Kuehr, R., Christian, H., Gerecke, A.C., 2010. A Review of the Environmental Fate and Effects of Hazardous Substances released from Electrical and Electronic Equipment during recycling: Examples from China and India. Environ. Impact Assess. Rev. 30, 28-41.

Sheng, P.P., & Etsell, T.H. (2007). Recovery of Gold from Computer Circuit Board Scrap using Aqua regia. Waste Management & Research, 25(4), 380-383.

Shibata, J., & Matsumoto, S. (1999). Development of Environmentally Friendly Leaching and Recovery Process of Gold and Silver from Wasted Electronic Parts. Available from: b http://www. environmentalcenter. com/articles/article320/article320. htm N.

Sinha-Khetriwal, D. (2002). The Management of Electronic Waste: A Comparative Study on India and Switzerland. St. Gallen, Switzerland: MS thesis, University of St. Gallen.

Song, S., Duan, Y., Zhang, T., Zhang, B., Zhao, Z., Bai, X., ... & Sun, H. (2019). Serum Concentrations of Bisphenol A and its alternatives in Elderly Population living around e-waste recycling Facilities in China: Associations with Fasting Blood Glucose. Ecotoxicology and Environmental Safety, 169, 822-828.

Sum, E.Y. (1991). The Recovery of Metals from Electronic Scrap. JOM, 43(4), 53-61.

Tavlarides, L.L., Bae, J.H., & Lee, C.K. (1987). Solvent Extraction, Membranes, and ion exchange in Hydrometallurgical dilute Metals Separation. Separation Science and Technology, 22(2-3), 581-617.

Teller, M. (2006). Recycling of Electronic Waste Material. In Sustainable Metals Management (pp. 563-576). Springer, Dordrecht.

Theo, L. (1998, May). Integrated recycling of Non-ferrous Metals at Boliden Ltd. Ronnskar Smelter. In Proceedings of the 1998 IEEE International Symposium on Electronics and the Environment. ISEE-1998 (Cat. No. 98CH36145) (pp. 42-47). Ieee.

Vara, S., Karnena, M.K., Dwarapureddi, B.K., & Chintalapudi, B. (2019). Will Single Use Products Lead to Sustainability?. International Journal of Social Ecology and Sustainable Development (IJSESD), 10(2), 37-52.

Varghese, J., Saritha, V., Bhavya Kavitha, D., Yasaswitha, O., & Karnena, M.K. (2016). Journal of Global Biosciences. Journal of Global Biosciences, 5(3), 3776-3784.

Veit, H.M., Bernardes, A.M., Ferreira, J. Z., Tenório, J.A.S., & de Fraga Malfatti, C. (2006). Recovery of Copper from Printed Circuit boards scraps by Mechanical Processing and Electrometallurgy. Journal of Hazardous Materials, 137(3), 1704-1709.

Veldhuizen, H., & Sippel, B. (1994). Mining discarded Electronics. Ind. Environ.(Switzerland), 17(3), 7-11.

Wang, D., Cai, Z., Jiang, G., Leung, A., Wong, M.H., & Wong, W.K. (2005). Determination of Polybrominated diphenyl ethers in Soil and Sediment from an Electronic Waste Recycling Facility. Chemosphere, 60(6), 810-816.

Wills, B.A., & Finch, J. (2015). Wills' Mineral Processing Technology: An Introduction to the Practical Aspects of ore Treatment and Mineral Recovery. Butterworth-Heinemann.

Zakrewski, J., Chamer, R., & Koscielniak, A. (1992). Method for Recovering Gold and Nickel from Electronic Scrap and Waste. Polish Patent, PL158889B (C22B7/00).

Zeng, X., Duan, H., Wang, F., & Li, J. (2017). Examining Environmental Management of e-waste: China's Experience and Lessons. Renewable and Sustainable Energy Reviews, 72, 1076-1082.

Zhang, B., He, Y., Zhu, H., Huang, X., Bai, X., Kannan, K., & Zhang, T. (2020). Concentrations of Bisphenol A and its Alternatives in Paired Maternal–fetal Urine, Serum and Amniotic Fluid from an e-waste Dismantling Area in China. Environment International, 136, 105407.

Zhang, S., & Forssberg, E. (1997). Electronic Scrap Characterization for Materials Recycling. Journal of Waste Management and Resource Recovery, 3, 157-168.

Zhou, P., Zheng, Z., & Tie, J. (2005). Technological Process for Extracting Gold, Silver and Palladium from Electronic Industry Waste. Chinese Patent, CN1603432A (C22B 11/00).

6

Environment Friendly Technologies

Concept and Need for Sustainability

INTRODUCTION

Environment is basically, the support system that upholds life on earth. It provides the basic requirements to support life such as fresh air that living organisms respire or breathe, food to eat, fresh water for plants & animals and also land where living beings live. There is a rhythm or pattern or natural order in the environment, which keeps the environment in a self-sustaining mode. However, man is in constant interaction with the environment. As a result of developments of civilization over the years; the industrial development; and new breakthroughs in various fields, he has had interventions with Nature. Many of the self-sustaining in-built order in nature are being threatened by way of various human and industrial activities.

ENERGY REQUIREMENTS AND DEVELOPMENT

Energy is a pre-requisite or in fact essential for meeting our developmental needs or accomplishing the development goals for any economy. While moving from a solely agrarian economy and further on the coming of the industrial revolution and later on, with the further developments in Information and Communication Technologies, mankind has come to increasingly depend on various sources for power to run the machinery and equipments, gadgets etc. in our homes and in industrial units.

RENEWABLE ENERGY AND NON-RENEWABLE ENERGY

We can broadly categories our energy sources into two - namely, Renewable Energy and Non-renewable Energy. Renewable Energy refers to the energy that can be generated from renewable sources. Renewable sources are basically those which are in nature and which gets renewed or replenished by the natural processes in the environment. For instance, Water. Water is a natural resource that gets replenished in nature. There is lot of fresh water resources on earth such as the rivers, streams, pounds, springs etc. Apart from this, there are oceans and sea as well. By the process of evaporation, water gets evaporated. This water vapor gets condensed to form clouds. Further, by way of rain or snow etc., it comes down to the earth's surface. Thus, water changes to water vapor form and again to water during this cycle. Water in fact, is getting continuously circulated by this natural process. That is why, we say, water is a renewable resource provided by nature. Another renewable resource we have is from the sun, the solar energy. Sun's light and heat fall on the earth's surface daily and can be considered by us for meeting the energy needs. Yet another one, is the Wind energy, which can be harnessed in areas where there is potential for wind energy.

Now talking about Non-renewable Energy, Non-renewable Energy, on the other hand, it refers to the energy from sources, which cannot be easily replenished, as is the case of renewable energy. Non-renewable energy comes from depleting sources. This means that we need to be concerned about such sources as it cannot be made available for all ages. Therefore, non-renewable sources are not sustainable energy sources and when we use it in the present generation, it is by limiting the future generations to such energy sources. As a big measure towards environment sustainability and environment management, it is imperative that we turn to Renewable sources of energy to meet our energy needs. Every region should explore the scope for use of renewable energy there. This means the scope of using renewable sources of energy needs to be explored. Areas which are abundant with water sources, solar energy, wind etc. are to be assessed for harnessing renewable energy.

Further, it is matter of concern that even now, electricity is not available in many parts of a country, as in case of India. It is required that it is made available to all parts of a nation so that development takes place everywhere. In case of more populous countries, the challenge is higher. It has to be well taken care of, so that infrastructural bottlenecks do not hamper the developmental goals. Depending only a single source of power will have limitations, if the supply-demand gap in power sector is high. Also, the institutional arrangements that are put in place for power needs may not suffice to meet requirements. Environment is the hub of rich natural resources. The rich flora and fauna, streams, rivers, oceans, mountain ranges are not only sources of natural beauty but also are sources of abundant energy. These natural resources found on our planet Earth is the source of rich energy sources which are of great use for mankind. The use of any technology is for a stated purpose. The technological product or the equipment would have been designed to perform certain stated predefined or predetermined tasks that would serve to enhance the efficiency of operations or scale up operations or even be an innovation that can help radically re-engineer the current processes and systems of practice followed in undertaking any activity.

Technological products, by way of its day-to-day use, entail an interaction. By interaction, the technological product operates in an environment - that is a sum total of the surroundings; inclusive of the user of the technology, the inputs or such resources that go into the use or running of the technological product, the output generated out of the technological product. The use of a technological product will have an effect on the environment – this effect can be in three lines - (1) positive effect (2) neutral effect or (3) negative effect. When the product used, adds to the richness of the environment, by any means, then it has a positive effect. When the product used, does not harm or add any richness, then it will of neutral nature. And of more concern, is when the product used has an ill-effect, then it can be said to be of negative effect. This negative effect can be - of a nature of direct effect or of an indirect effect. The negative effect on the environment, can be - of being of a main effect or of the nature of a side effect. Technologies that are designed and developed, taking into cognizance, that the environment in which it operates, is also as important as the use of any such technology and in fact much more - are those designed as Environment friendly Technologies.

THE CONCEPT OF EFT

There are some features or aspects which help us to discern whether the technologies that are in use in our societies and even in our day-to-day lives, are environment friendly or on the other hand, environment harmful. Some of the aspects that are found to be characteristic in environment friendly units are:

- Use environment friendly mechanisms
- Use natural resources
- Preserve or protect our environment
- Maintaining the Ecosystem
- Sustainable development

Any technology that is developed and used, will have certain components or constituting mechanisms such as Materials used, procedure or technological process involved, the effect on life around. That is, basically, there will be some inputs or a set of inputs. The set of specified inputs in the required combination or configuration which will be subject to a specified process – that is, some technological process and further, outputs are generated. So, if we look at the components for managing our environment in an environment friendly approach, we need to focus on Environment friendly technologies. So we need to look even beyond inputs, process and outputs. Retake So the components will encompass for Environment friendly technologies the following:

- Inputs (materials, equipment)
- Process
- Outputs
- Uses
- Beneficiaries - people, industry, flora and fauna, environment
- Environmentally Sustainable.

Inputs - When we talk about inputs for an Environment friendly technology, it will include the materials required, the equipment which will be used, the spare parts/other items etc. The inputs that are used in a EFT should be environment friendly, that is it should by itself, be an input that is Environment friendly. That is why when we are using renewable energy sources, those are environmentally sustainable and hence, Environment friendly. The Materials that we use, would be positive and harmless for our environment, if that used are products which are EF or such products used are such which can be recycled and reused, or the used products are biodegradable waste creation or by-products, as a result of the use of a technological product and is not harmful to society, that is, waste management/by-product should be an environment friendly mechanism

Process - The process entailed in the use of EFT should not be harming the environment. It should be environment friendly. By way of use of any process, there can be changes or implications in the immediate environment in the short run or in the long run. This needs to be taken into cognizance when are looking at technologies or designing solutions, that we aim to make environment friendly.

Noise pollution, air pollution, harmful radiation/other health hazards etc. are some concerns that need to considered in this context. The effect of such processes on living beings - humans, flora, fauna, aquatic life etc. should be examined.

Outputs - The main output in use of EFT, of course, is the desired or intended output for which the EFT has been developed for. For instance, in case of wind turbines, the electrical energy that we are able to harness is the desired output from use of the wind power. While designing EFTs, it is also imperative to consider the possible uses of such EFTs, the beneficiaries of such EFTs, which can be people, industry, flora and fauna, and even the environment itself.

We should analyze any technology that we use in terms of its Cost Benefit study. That is what all costs go into the making and use of the technology. The cost will include not only cost of raw materials, consumables etc. but also cost to the environment where it will be made operational. Another term that is referred in the context of setting up of a new project or plant, is the Environment Impact Analysis. That is, in what way and to what extent the new project, if set up, will impact our environment.

NEED FOR ENVIRONMENT FRIENDLY TECHNOLOGIES (EFT)

We have made great progress in use of industrial equipment, machinery, electronic gadgets, ICT equipment, latest technologies etc. We have also built a greater number of factories, plants, industrial units etc. We have explored and made considerable interventions into the hitherto pristine environment at many places. This has resulted in man-environment interactions that has in some aspects, already affected our environment. For instance, air pollution levels have increased. Non-biodegradable waste has gone into such enhanced levels of which we need to be concerned about, water bodies affected with pollution is noticed at many places. The biodiversity that we have on earth is another important aspect. No doubt, we need to preserve the rich biodiversity we have on planet earth. The different varieties and variants, we have of the different flora especially in the forests, valleys, mountains are to be protected. Activities and developments undertaken by us should be such it does not affect or harm the plant life. Similarly, deforestation, soil erosion, landslides etc. as a result of man's interventions into nature can result in loss of natural vegetation on earth. Plants and trees are very important to maintain the ecosystem and also is life giving for the animal life on earth. Similarly, the fauna on earth is also to be preserved. Deforestation and the resulting reduced forest cover, will affect the wildlife. Many species found only in specific forests and in mountainous regions are being reported to have falling numbers. The quality of life on planet with respect to environment such as fresh air to breathe, clean water for drinking and other purposes etc. are essential for all forms of life on earth. Therefore, whatever developments are undertaken should not degrade our environment. It is essential to bear in mind that whatever development, be it constructions, new power plants, transportation modes etc. should be carefully weighed in terms of its contribution to the environment, especially if there are any negative aspects that emerge from use of machinery, equipment, technologies etc.

Footprints that we leave on the earth will have bearing on the future generations as well. The extent to which we should use the resources on earth, should be taking into consideration the need of the future generations also who will inhabit the same planet. Sustainable development precisely refers to this concept wherein we do not compromise on the needs of the future generations by focusing on the needs of only the current generation. As part of increasing consciousness on the use of various resources, we have started to measure how much of a resource we utilize.

EFT AND SENSITIVITY

Solar Energy is being used in many institutions such as hospitals, educational institutions, business firms etc. to generate electricity. The energy from the sun is being sourced to meet their power requirements. It is interesting to note that they have got clear advantages in implementing energy obtained from renewable sources.

SOLAR FOR TRANSPORTATION

When we talk about solar powered devices, we also need to know that today solar powered transportation is also possible. Solar energy has been considered for use in the transportation sector such as solar buses, solar boats, airports that use solar energy to power etc. These are initiatives which will help us to move towards sustainable transport. This is significant in the context that transportation systems entail huge energy consumption and emissions. So, in terms of air pollution/water pollution etc. these need to be carefully weighed for environment sustainability. Greenhouse gas emissions have been a matter of concern. As per the UNEP (United Nations Environment Programme), the transportation sector is major source of greenhouse gas emissions and also other forms of pollution; and that 95% of the world's transport energy is from fossil fuels. So, it is a major concern and efforts required in place to mitigate greenhouse gases emission. Therefore, moving towards green transport and clean energy is the need. Engaging in environment friendly practices and technologies are essential. We will discuss about some of the environment friendly technologies installed for the transportation sector and also what can be our role in mitigating environment pollution in subsequent modules.

CASE STUDY OF COCHIN INTERNATIONAL AIRPORT LIMITED

Cochin International Airport Limited (CIAL) is the first airport in the world to be solar powered. The foray into solar power began with the setting up of a pilot plant of a capacity of 100kWp in the year 2013. Further, it went on to installation of higher capacity of 1 MW. Considering the huge power requirements on a daily basis and the electricity tariffs to the State Electricity Board, CIAL decided to install solar power plants of capacity adequate to meet its power needs. In this effort, CIAL after taking into consideration the requirements arrived at the designed capacity of 12 MWp, apart from this, a provision to enhance by 2.4 MWp. The project was done in the year 2015 within a short time period of six months. This plant is the major solar plant and generates around 45000 units on an average daily basis, and by this CIAL adorned the rarest of rare distinctions, of being -

the first fully solar powered airport in the world. It is a magnificent sight to see the solar panels laid on around 45 acres of land, suitably configured to generate power of desired capacity. You will recall from our previous modules where we discussed about the principle of working of photovoltaic technology that solar panels convert the solar energy into electricity which is DC or direct current. Inverters are used here too, to convert the DC to AC. Transformers are used to step up and further, connected to the grid. CIAL has gone in for availing the banking facility provided by the State Electricity Board. As per this, instead of having a mechanism of storage using battery, the excess power generated can be given to the grid and such excess power provided can be sourced from the grid. Further, the excess units provided to grid will be paid the electricity board. So here it has the scope for not only being self-sufficient and thereby grid neutral, but also being a contributor towards meeting power requirements outside. The extent of power generation through a renewable source such as solar, is considerable when it is to meet the needs of an airport. So, it only once again highlights to us about the great scope that lies in harnessing solar energy for our needs. Further, in tune with its efforts to remain grid neutral with further expansion plans and new developments such as international terminal, CIAL had taken up setting of additional solar plants in its premises such as the canal top solar project. The carport solar project which is an interesting case where car parking was suitably designed to house solar panels and generate power. This is especially a commendable contribution in a State such as Kerala where the State purchases a good proportion of its power requirements from the Central Grid.

CASE STUDY OF METRO RAIL SYSTEM IN INDIA

The Metro rail system is being increasingly considered as a good mode of urban transport. The metro rail system has certain advantages such as produces less noise and unlike road transport vehicles, emissions are not a matter of concern here. In India also, in many of the big cities, metro rail system has been implemented. Even the metro rail system can be best utilized to generate power using renewable source such as the solar power. The space available along the metro and the roof tops can be considered for optimum utilization.

CASE STUDY OF SOLAR FERRY SERVICE

ADITYA, India's first solar ferry which was inaugurated on 12th Jan 2017. As per its designer, Sandith Thandashery, whom we just listened to, it scores very well on the five important parameters for a passenger ferry which are (Thandasherry, 2018):

(i) Safety;

(ii) Comfort;

(*iii*) Pleasure;

(*iv*) Cost-effectiveness;

(*v*) Eco-friendliness.

It is stated that by annually using ADITYA, the solar ferry, the saving is, in terms of 94 tons of CO_2 and 35000 liters of diesel. So, it is clearly indicating that the solar ferry is a greener & better option for water transport. Further, in terms of cost, it is saving of 22 lakh rupees. This boat has been operational for a year now on the Vaikom - thavanakadavu route and passengers commute via this ferry service. When we talk about this solar ferry boat, the eco-friendly aspect is a big advantage with respect to water transport, primarily due to following aspects. The conventional ferry boats which are diesel powered cause pollution namely- air pollution and water pollution. Emissions from such diesel engine powered boats include CO_2 & other such matter. The gases emitted will affect health of those who operate the boat and that of the passengers. A solar boat helps to not only have avoid diesel but also associated emission or production of CO_2 & such gases. With regard to diesel powered boats, water pollution also is a problem. The oil which is used, may leak from engine, and machinery system during the course of operation of such boats, and this can eventually get easily discharge into the water. Similarly, fuel that is unburned can also be getting released into the water body. This will pollute the water body and also will be dangerous to the aquatic life (Thandasherry, 2018). This institution also has begun using solar energy for the power needs of its office. Few solar panels have been provided on the roof top of the firm is being used to meet some of their power needs. So, as an organization, the Navalt is employing solar power and is a good example for many more institutions to follow environment friendly measures.

SENSITIVITY TOWARDS ENVIRONMENTAL ISSUES

Degradation of the natural environment, extinction of many varieties of flora and fauna and their impact on human lives etc. are now visible all over the world. Though it is enriched with natural resources the situation in India is even more precarious as it is a densely populated country. The sustainable development of the country is facing big challenges due to the environmental pollution, those especially linked to land, water and air. Hence it is a necessity to sensitize these issues in the realm of Environmental Education. Let us have a look into the contemporary environmental issues experienced by us locally and which will later help us to think and act globally.

- Environmental pollution- Land pollution, Air Pollution, Water pollution and Sound pollution.
- Deforestation
- Spoilage of natural resources
- Climate change

ENVIRONMENTAL POLLUTION

Air pollution is one of the worst conditions India faces. The International Energy Agency (IEA) reports that by 2040, India has to face about 9 lakh premature deaths in the country due to the shooting up of air pollution only. As India is at the 11th position out of 20 in pollution rate the life expectancy of newborn children may go down about 15 months. Also, it is a threatening statistic according to the Environmental Performance Index of 14th rank of India among the 180 most polluted countries in the world. Local observations and experiences in the villages of Kerala thrown light into a very big phenomena happening in the flowing water bodies. The word river brings forth an image of flowing water among all the people without the difference of urban or rural, time and space. The traditional concept of running river has been changed now. Almost all the small rivers in the urban places and a few in the rural places (areas) are stagnant with a lot of solid dumps, pollutants and other wastages. But the astonishing seen we see all around is the stagnant water bodies with a layer of precipitated pollutants and solid wastes in dark colors and seen as the habitat of varieties of mosquitoes and microbial organisms. The health mission of Kerala like Arogya Keralam is placing warning boards every nook and corner to avoid stagnation of water to prevent mosquitoes and other microorganisms which cause various kinds of communicable and chronic diseases. Basically, these warning boards are not meant for rivers and such other water resources. They meant the house hold surroundings, drainages and water holding things like utensils, bottles etc. But in the present situation more than this house hold surroundings it is applicable to the water bodies like rivers and ponds. This is a serious issue which seeks immediate solutions from the part of the public and also from the government.

ENVIRONMENTAL DEGRADATION

The rapid growing population, urbanization, economic development, industrialization etc. cause very serious environmental degradation. The natural demographic phenomena like birth, death and human migration taken place and continues its way as usual. The varying and increasing population density demands a lot of infrastructural developments and which results in the huge amount of utilization of natural resources. The technologies and scientific interventions for life facilitations cannot be avoided by the common people. Because convenience factor is the prime concern of our time and for that we compromise a lot with all environmental issues without looking forward and without leaving anything behind except these challenges. India is growing very fast in population to overcome China, the most populous country of the world. In the same manner the imbalance in ecological factors are also growing. In its true sense, we must agree that the general public is not at all bothered about the environmental concerns. It is high time to think and act properly to stick on a developing and sustainable path. Heavy loss of natural resources, heavy pressure on land (land degradation), deforestation, habitat destruction and loss of bio diversity are some of the crucial issues happen due to urbanization. The changing consumption pattern cause rising demand of energy which results in spoilage of natural resources.The infrastructural developments, increase in number of branded expensive motor vehicles, increase in trade and businesses etc. are the economic development indicators of the present days. Even in educational field the status of institutions is indicated by the luxurious facilities provided by the management. Also, it is a trend to rate the quality of the schools on the basis of the amount paid by the parents as donation and other yearly expenses to meet the education of their children. This trend is seen everywhere and in all sectors of life.

Several studies have been conducted on environmental costs and developmental costs and it is found that the majority of the public are of the opinion of increasing developmental costs than environmental costs. It is a clearly evident social truth and common tendency among the public that they always follow superficial and immediate developmental strategies than the philosophical and futuristic dimensions of sustainable development. Environmental quality and sustainability are considered only after the fulfillment of basic needs and sometimes after the fulfillment of all the livelihood requirements even by the government. At the part of government there might have been a number of social development commitments like poverty eradication, employment opportunities, and utilization of development funds from agencies. Also, it is matter of political and democratic governance and policy of the ruling party for getting approval and appreciation from the general public and their voters. We have to agree with the policies taken for eradicating of poverty and to provide a shelter with basic requirements to all. In a civilized society nobody can object these fundamental rights of the citizens in the cost of environmental protection. But sustainability cannot be compromised. Some developed countries advocate this policy as a better thing to attain a developed state of economy in the countries first and then implement developmental activities for environmental sustainability. Earth with pure air, fertile land, clear and pure water, diversity of flora and fauna, cool atmosphere is needed to everyone. Our development should not harm our young one's existence. That is the concern of being educated and educate others environmentally. Education is the best route and destination of the journey of sustainable development and teacher education is the junction for enrooting the technical support and guidelines through interdisciplinary approaches. Thus, the integrity of work education in the process of sustainable development can be assured through environmental education.

Unfortunately, the environmental concerns are being awakened only at the time of crisis management. When a crisis arises, the circumstances will immediately be altered. Behind every movement against environmental threats there will be a learned group committed to educate the public at any cost. We call them activists. But the policy makers and bureaucrats ignore environmental costs to meet their objectives of economic development. Sustainability is not a prime concern for them. Then who can assure environmental sustainability? Solutions have to be found and implemented at personal level and local level. Several studies have been conducted all over the world to determine the reasons of environmental degradation and climate change those having high correlation in different magnitudes. That is just like the relation of deforestation with global warming, carbon emission, water scarcity etc.

Among them global warming becomes very crucial and prime reason for almost all the other challenges. There are many studies which reveal the results of threatening truth of the climate variation due to global warming in India. The highest temperature noticed in India during the summer of 2016 was in Rajasthan, 51 degree Celsius- a real indicator of the increasing rate of global warming over the past five years. The interior areas near the forest boarders are also facing such a challenge. We can again observe the example of the fragile ecological area of Western Ghats of Idukki, one of the most beautiful tourist places of South India. In my own experience when my life started there in the midst of a cold summer- yes it was a cold summer 21 years back in the high range areas- it was not possible to take bath without warm water. There was no fan in any of the houses and it felt as a symbol of luxury only. Now the story has been changed. In summer it is not even to think to sleep at nights without a fan. Then no need to tell about days! This is the change story of a period of almost 21-22 year's duration. The changes of the recent years are not slow as such. The drastic change occurs in the atmospheric temperature is being unpredictable. Another issue India face is the melting of Himalayan glaciers in an alarming rate and its increase in frequency which results in floods and the deadly natural calamities happens in the fertile river banks where the rich yields help us to sustain in food production. The frequent forest fire in summers doubles the risk of global warming. The imbalanced state of layers of earth again threatens us by earthquakes. Totally life becomes a big challenge and a chance. Everything happens only because of our negligence not because of ignorance. This is the context where our role is essential by imparting a fruitful practical education to make us and others to practice on environmental sustainability. In olden days people were planning their livelihood according to the seasons and climate. Now we are not able to predict even the monsoon. We all experience the unpredictable variations and extreme end of weather and thus weather forecasting is being a satire in social media. It is not the fault of the scientific inventions and technology but the repulsion of the extreme level of environmental degradation. Our height of intellect is being defeated by the intensity of natural calamities even though we have several technologies to predict and measure it but no technology to resist it. Hence the only way to be aware is the process of education and the only way to resist is the product of education.

KERALA FLOODS OF 2018- A PARADIGM SHIFT

The Kerala floods of 2018 were a great leveler. All and sundry were put under the same roof- the roof of the rehabilitation camps. Man, machines and government policies all contributed to the disaster. There was allegation of policy paralysis at all levels. One of the fundamental issues that the floods brought into focus was the fact that hard environmental decisions could no longer be postponed. The Gadgil committee had brought into sharp attention the devastation that environmental profligacy would bring on the Western Ghats. Therefore, the report had categorically stated that mining, quarrying and other debilitating activities should be foreclosed in the ghat areas. But profit motive combined with an utter lack of concern for our fellow beings had prevented any concrete action as mentioned in the report. The policy makers also found it convenient to follow the diluted recommendations of the Kasturirangan report. The results are there for all to see. Another constant source of concern is the big dams built on the Ghat areas. The ecology of the Ghat area is least suited for big dams such as the Idukki dam. The result of any mishap associated with the dam is unimaginable. The recipe for the disaster was prepared by an alleged miscalculation about the intensity of the forthcoming rains which prevented authorities from opening the dam's flood gates till the last moment. When they were forced to open the dams at last, a massive deluge resulted that engulfed areas from Idukki to Trivandrum. The fact that massive deforestation had taken place in the ghats made sure that there was little holding capacity for the slopes, hastening the downward flow of water. Illegal mining of sand had left little holding capacity of lands of the plains as well.

As usual, hot political discussions had been aroused. Reasons were highlighted in various dimensions. Our concern in this particular platform for environmental education is focusing on the power of nature and its eternal truth. For the knowledge driven society, it is in the form of scientific evidences. Even though the belief on the power of Nature cannot be denied as it is based on Natural Sciences. It is a fact that no scientific and technologic developments are capable enough to over throw nature's power. India had a fair share of Calamities, natural and manmade over these several decades. Disasters resulting in loss of lives and other assets are still increasing. This is sharply pointing towards the emerging need of sustainable thoughts and practices inculcated through the commitments and love on nature.

Floods, hurricanes, tornadoes, volcanic eruptions, earthquakes, tsunamis, and other geologic processes are natural disasters. Some examples for manmade calamities happened in India:

(a) Bhopal Gas Tragedy
(b) Flyover Collapse happened in Kolkotta Girish Park
(c) Building collapse happened in Lalitha park,
(d) Maha Kumbh Mela Tragey happened in Allahabad.

REASONS FOR THE MANMADE DISASTERS

- Innocence of the people
- Lack of awareness
- Carelessness on environmental matters
- Negligence of the common people
- Lack of scientific knowledge at the end of the people who have not sufficiently educated
- some others who are of orthodox mentality may not have scientific attitude
- Lack of foresight
- Avoidance due to laziness
- Lack of concern with social and environmental matters
- Irresponsibility
- Some may not have any kind of concern to anything and least or little bothered of their accountability

In its broad sense, behind almost all the natural disasters happened in this century, there is a hidden hand of human involvement. That is the main reason behind many of the political and environmental discussions going on in media along with or immediately after the disasters. Whoever is blamed, government or the public is not at all a concern on the environmental point of view. But the facts regarding the intensity of the destruction and its root cause and the limitations of the already existing technological and logistic measures are to be considered with prime concern. It is a general tendency of human being to overcome the difficulties and worries of any kind of disasters immediately after its relief, if the difficulties are of common nature and are affected by many. The theoretical studies done on Anthropological perspectives with regard to environmental sustainability become relevant in this scenario. The theories are Environmental determinism and environmental possibilism. Determinism works on the already determined societal norms. That means it works according to the nature and norms of the society. The nature and norms according to environmental determinism is formed by the determination of type of settlements, their trade, culture and dressing, agriculture etc.

Hence, we can say that the life style of such societies is decided according to the physical environment. But in possibilism it is the perception of the individuals and has to be changed according to the availability of resources and other facilities. Environmental possibilism is the theoretical approach advocates the possibilities adaptive technologies and alternative measures according to the nature of environment. It satisfies the environmental demands in connection with the changing situations. It is against the earlier mentioned environmental determinism. In the context of disasters natural or manmade whatever it is environmental possibilism find its way as a measure to overcome the consequences.

ENVIRONMENTAL POSSIBILISM

- Integrate environmental education as an interdisciplinary approach in all levels of education.
- Attitude towards environment has to be developed in a positive way.
- Try to inculcate the self-responsibility of the individuals in each and every deed in our practical life.
- Develop scientific attitude of the people by adopting apt environmental education techniques.
- The marginal public have to be educated and initiated for the imparting of awareness on sustainable development.
- The effect of sustainable development technologies has to be spread among the public at its maximum.
- The funding allotments done for the grass root level agencies have to be utilized in a transparent manner. Absence of transparency in the processes associated with planning, sanctioning and implementation very often results in debilitation of the overall scheme and ultimately defeating the very purpose for which it was initiated.
- The enthusiasm shown at the first phase of implementation of benign environmental schemes is hardly reflected at subsequent stages. The grandiose elaborations made at the drawing boards is found missing when the implementation takes place. The erosion of substance in such schemes ultimately becomes self-defeating and often works at cross purposes.
- Though laws of the country are often strongly worded, in practice and implementation they are found extremely wanting. This was actively highlighted in landmark cases such as the Ratlam Municipality case where the apex court has attested to this fact in no uncertain terms. When implementation is carried out in letter and spirit, there is no doubt that we shall be beneficiaries of a vibrant environment.

- Development has to go hand in hand with environmental protection. An area of concern is the building norms that exist in our country. Even the existing norms are observed in their violation as is seen in the Mudappa Case. There is an urgent need to combine building norms with protection norms for the environment. Waste management, energy conservation and water resources management have to be integrated into building norms to effectively protect the environment.
- Water recharging through rain water harvesting, though a part of present-day town planning has to be bolstered. The scale and magnitude of its implementation needs extension. The ground loss of water currently experiences and the periodic droughts faced by the country can become a thing of the past if effectively implemented.
- Solar energy is an undying source of clean fuel. The policy makers have taken baby steps towards making solar energy the cornerstone of energy policy, but much needs to be done. The adoption of solar power as the source of energy by Kochi Metro and Cochin International Airport needs commendation. The same needs to be implemented in every house of the country.
- The use of eco-friendly products for everyday use needs promotion. For instance, during the recent floods one of the major pollutants found in Kerala is sodium acrylate used majorly in the production of sanitary napkins and diapers. Needless to state contaminants of this nature change the hue and texture of our ecosystem irretrievably.

CONCLUSION

Calamities unify mankind, perhaps due to the realization that once the material gains have been eroded by an unforgiving nature, everyone is under and even roof. We have witnessed various major calamities. If even an iota of the efforts put out at the time of calamity had been made from time to time, a catastrophe of this scale could have been avoided altogether. Therein lies the message for the future.

REFERENCES

Thandasherry, Sandit (2018). High Fives for Solar Powered Ferry Ops. "Ship & Boat International. January/February 2018. p 18-24.

7

Penalty and Incentive Mechanisms for Coal-based Power Plants

INTRODUCTION

Coal-based power is one of the most resource-intensive and polluting industries. In a long-overdue action, on 07 December 2015, the Ministry of Environment, Forestry and Climate Change (MoEFCC) introduced stricter environmental standards for coal-based thermal power plants (TPPs) under the Environment Protection Act, 1986. The three-fourths of the installed capacity could meet the deadline for particulate matter (PM) and also oxides of Nitrogen (NOx), a massive 70% of the installed capacity could miss the deadline for the sulphur dioxide (SO_2) standard. Installing a control device is critical to comply with SO_2 standards because:

(a) During the retrofit shutdown of SO_2 control technology, power plants had planned an overhaul of PM and NOx control equipment.

(b) The SO_2 control technology also reduces mercury emissions, enabling the mercury requirements to be met.

(c) SO_2 control systems work efficiently only when the PM and NOx standards are met, which is another cross-check of compliance with standards. Since, at this stage, accurate emissions data on SO_2 is unavailable for many plants, a working flue-gas desulphurization (FGD) system in a power station can remain a cross-check.

For these multiple benefits that SO_2 control systems provide, government agencies are closely monitoring the progress of SO_2 standards implementation. However, the delay in progress is evident, and remains unchecked. Any delay in implementation would mean a mockery of the government and the Supreme Court's (SC) efforts to reduce pollution from the sector. The Supreme Court has been closely monitoring the progress of implementation of the new emission norms. Only a few power stations, along with National Thermal Power Corporation (NTPC), are taking significant efforts to comply with the revised norms. This could serve as a spur and bring in urgency in the coal-based power sector to abide by the 2015 emission standard deadlines. The paper also discusses the efficacy of the current deterrence system and the need to strengthen it.

The Indian power sector value chain can be broadly segmented into generation, transmission, and distribution sectors. The distribution companies or DISCOMS supply electricity to consumers like us depending on demand. Demand is the number of electricity units a household or industry or a commercial entity consumes. Depending on this demand, the DISCOMS sign contracts with power generation companies to buy electricity. The power generation companies generate electricity. At an all-India level, the total installed generation capacity was 367,281 megawatts (MW) as on 31 December 2019. This includes coal, gas, thermal, renewable, and other sources of power generation capacity. A DISCOM could buy electricity from a power generation company in its own state or in another state. If the DISCOM signs a power purchase agreement with some other state, then electricity generated by this generation company in the other state is transported with the help of a transmission company. The DISCOM pays the transmission company for its electricity transportation services. India has one large transmission company called the Power Grid Corporation of India Limited (PGCIL) which transports over 50% of the electricity. Apart from PGCIL there are few other state players. India's regional grids (Northern, Eastern, Western, North-Eastern, and Southern) for power transmission are currently integrated into one national grid and can transfer nearly 75,050 MW of power.

POWER MARKET AND ELECTRICITY COSTS

More than 90% of the electricity supplied to customers by DISCOMS is purchased in India through long-term contracts (typically signed for 25 years) with the power stations within their states or in other states. Particularly coal based thermal power stations of over 200,000 MW have signed long term contracts with DISCOMS. Only in the case of an imbalance in the grid, if there is a need for more power than the amount signed in the contracts, do DISCOMS approach the short-term power markets. There are two short-term power markets in operation in India—India Energy exchange and Power exchange India Ltd. Various captive generating power stations of industries sell a portion of the electricity generated in this market. The contract system is the predominant method opted for buying electricity in the Indian power market. The contract system guarantees assured electricity supply to the DISCOM and the power station is guaranteed to get its investment back with 11-16% return on investment. The contracts signed between these thermal power plants and distribution companies guarantee two-part payment of costs as fixed and variable.

Power market and electricity costs Fixed cost is the cost of installing and operating an electricity generation plant. Say, when constructing a 500 MW power station, a company invests Rs 2,500 crore towards purchasing boilers and other equipment and, in addition, it spends Rs 10-20 crore for maintenance by recruiting staff and repairing minor components when needed. This total cost of Rs 2500 crore + Rs 10-20 crore, along with 11-16 percent interest on the investment, is reimbursed to the company as fixed cost in a span of 25 years irrespective of whether it operates or it doesn't as per contracts by the DISCOMS. Typically, fixed cost for a brand-new coal plant is Rs 1.5-2/unit of electricity in the first few years. It falls each year by a few paisa due to depreciation of assets. Depreciation of assets can be understood with the example of a car or a mobile—the resale value of which falls every year compared to its purchase value. If after signing a contract with a generation company the DISCOM does not buy electricity for a few days, months, or years, this fixed cost will still need to be paid on an annual basis by the DISCOM for all 25 years of the contract. The 25 years' time frame is considered as the useful life of the plant; hence contracts are signed for this time period. After 25 years, if the plant is healthy and continues to operate, then the DISCOMS can choose to extend the long-term agreements with these plants and will not pay fixed costs to the plant. Hence some DISCOM companies find it cheap to buy power from old plants which charge no fixed cost.

POWER MARKET AND ELECTRICITY COSTS

The cost of operating the power plant by purchase of coal and oil is variable expense/cost of production. The purchase cost of coal and oil is reimbursed by DISCOMS within a month and a half (45-day cycle) to the power station depending on the actual expenditure. One of the important roles of the distribution companies is to estimate the electricity demand from customers/consumers both in the short-term and the long-term and, accordingly, plan purchase of electricity from generation companies. For this, they measure electricity demand in their locality every 15 minutes and then purchase power based on the needs. The need for electricity is much higher in some hours of the day, which are considered as the hours of peak demand. The peak demand stood at 175,528 MW during FY 2018-19 and 182,533 MW in FY 2019-2020. The demand at the other hours of the day can be very low. The distribution firms therefore sign several contracts with various thermal power stations to ascertain the supply of electricity during peak demands. By signing such agreements each distribution company will create a pool of thermal power plants from which to buy electricity. During non-peak or low electricity demand, the distribution companies buy power from those stations whose cost of generating electricity/variable cost is the lowest among this pool of thermal power stations; however, they will be paying the fixed cost to all the power stations with which they have contracts. The rest of the stations are placed on standby and scheduled only when demand is high. This principle of scheduling cheapest power generating stations by variable cost is called merit order despatch. The concept of MoD exists because of two reasons: (i) variation in fuel prices; and (ii) most of the contracts signed by the DISCOMS are not originally signed by them but rather allotted by the Central Government, and DISCOMS are liable to run the cheapest of the lot. Given that bulk of the power is procured through long-term agreements, the role of MoDs is limited only to variable costs.

SIGNIFICANCE OF CLEAN POWER

To encourage clean power generation, the Indian government, under the Electricity Act, 2003, has asked for the scheduling of renewable energy generating plants on a compulsory basis irrespective of their cost. The Electricity Act, 2003 under section 86 (e) asks the state electricity regulatory commission to ensure distribution companies purchase the quantity of electricity that they (renewable energy companies) produce to satisfy the demands. Accordingly, the state and central electricity grid code regulations have incorporated such clean plants as 'must-run'. Further, they are scheduled for generation even before applying MoD principles discussed above. This means even if the price of electricity generated by renewable sources is over Rs 10 per unit, a state will still have to procure all the electricity generated by renewable sources like solar, wind, small hydro, and biomass. This measure has been introduced to promote running of cleaner, pollution-free power stations. Till date, the installed capacity of renewable power stations in the country is 86,400 MW. Their electricity generation depends on weather conditions like sunlight and wind speed, which makes their production intermittent. Also, payment delays to renewable energy generators and curtailment remains a major hurdle to implementation of the must-run concept. In-fact, the Andhra Pradesh government is renegotiating contracts with renewable energy generators, which were installed few years back, over expensive renewable power. Nearly half the capacity installed in the state is affected with outstanding dues, with an average estimated delay of over 12 months until last year. Curtailment numbers are not available in public domain. According to Wind

Association members in Tamil Nadu, curtailment up to 10-20% is common. Tamil Nadu also has been delaying payments to renewable generators; however, the average estimated delay is less than six months. Overall renewable energy (RE) contribution to Indian power grid remains less than 5%.

The first challenge of the Indian government after transfer of power in 1947 had been ensuring 100% electrification of India. Two years back, India achieved this milestone according to the government. The next challenge is ensuring clean power gets supplied at affordable cost for sustainable development.

COAL-BASED POWER AND LONG-STANDING AGENDA OF ITS CLEAN-UP

Coal continues to be the bulk energy provider, making up 205,312 MW or 89% of the thermal power capacity. About 77% (895 TWh, or terawatt-hour) of the country's total electricity generation is by firing coal in thermal power stations, which are distributed almost equally in the centre, state, and private sector. Coal-based power is one of the most resource-intensive and polluting industries. It contributes to a disproportionate share of industrial-sector air pollution. Coal-based power stations emit 60% of the total particulate matter, 45% of the total sulphur dioxide, 30% of the total nitrogen oxides, and more than 80 percent of the total mercury emitted by all industries in India. To contain the pollution caused by coal-based power plants, MoEFCC introduced stricter environmental standards for coal-based TPPs on 07 December 2015. This was done under the Environment Protection Act, 1986. All TPPs were required to comply with the revised standards within a period of two years—by December 2017. The industry has been giving excuses and the deadline has been pushed to 2022. It is to be noted that 30% of the capacity is still striving to meet the norms. NTPC is gearing up on all fronts to meet the norms. In fact, it has been the only company in the country which has installed a SO_2 pollution control system at NTPC Dadri ever since the announcement of the environmental norms in 2015. All the plants run by the NTPC are meeting the PM norms, they have awarded tenders to a significant capacity to upgrade their systems to meet the NOx norms, and similar tenders have been awarded for over 59,110 MW of their capacity to meet the SO_2 norms. Apart from NTPC, the following plants have already been running with an FGD—CLP India Pvt. Ltd at Jhajjhar, IL&FS Cuddalore, JSW Ratnagiri, Adani Dahanu, few units at Adani Mundra, Tata Trombay; smaller thermal power stations operating with CFBC boilers are meeting the SO_2 norms already. This quarter, four private-run power stations—Reliance Sassan, Reliance Rosa, TAQA Neyveli, and Sterlite Talwandi Sabo TPP with about 7,390 MW (9.5% capacity)—claim to have awarded tenders for installing FGD. Similarly, three state-run power stations—Karnataka Power Corporation

Limited Raichur, Uttar Pradesh Rajya Vidyut Utpadan Limited Parichha and Anpara with a total capacity of about 4,220 MW (6.2%)—claim to have awarded tenders for installation of FGD. These stations stand out in not adopting any delay tactics unlike others and in striving to meet the law.

Power stations which are generating clean energy are incentivized by the country. Today, 86,400 MW (solar, wind, biomass, and small hydro) of renewable capacity or five percent of the total electricity generation in India, from these stations is scheduled as MUST-RUN as per Indian Electricity Grid Code (IEGC) irrespective of their cost. The rest of the power stations in the country are listed after these must-run plants as per their costs and scheduled under MoD.

Similarly, to encourage stations complying with the norms, the plants complying with the norms will be called the 'FIRST-RUN' plants. These plants will also require a certificate from the pollution control board to certify they are complying or are suitably advanced in the direction to comply with the December 2015 environmental norms, mainly in emissions of PM, SO_2 and NOx. A ranking of first-run power stations will have to be made and power procured from them on priority after must-run plants. This can serve as an incentive to motivate power stations which are materializing efforts to meet the new emission norms at the earliest. Fear of no operation or minimal operation can also drive the rest of the non-complying power stations to meet the norms at the earliest.

Fixed costs are paid on plant availability, it does not matter whether electricity is actually bought from the plant or not. So not buying electricity from noncompliant plants does not make much of a difference to them. On the other hand, imposing a penalty on the non-complying power stations by restricting a portion of their operation will reduce the plant availability which in turn will affect the reimbursement of its fixed cost and could motivate the stations to install pollution control equipment at the earliest. It is necessary to incentivize units that are complying and penalize units that are non-complying. The current mechanism of penalty is inadequate to force the plants to comply with the limits. Strong deterrence mechanism should be coupled with the incentive scheme to drive higher compliance.

STATE-WISE CONTRACTS AND SUPPLY: CURRENT SCENARIO

State-wise contract details were found for 166,688 MW of the total 206,014 MW of coal and lignite based thermal power stations in the country. A total of 33 states (including union territories) have signed contracts with coal-based thermal power stations to procure electricity. Majority of the contracts with coal-based thermal power stations are with the state of Maharashtra (about 25,000 MW) followed by ten states which have contracts over 10,000 MW with coal-based thermal power stations—Gujarat,

Uttar Pradesh, Tamil Nadu, Madhya Pradesh, Andhra Pradesh, West Bengal, Haryana, Punjab, Telangana, and Karnataka. Power stations which have already complied with the norms, and stations whose deadline is between 2020 and 2022 to meet the new norms and have awarded tenders to construct FGD systems to control sulphur dioxide, have been considered as capacity which qualify to be first-run/Yellow category in this analysis.

Data was available in the Merit India portal only for 43,365 MW of the 57,624 MW which has been identified as first-run capacity. Accordingly, it was assumed that the rest of the power plants may not have power buying/purchasing agreements/contracts and might be selling power in the short-term markets. On analysing this data, it was found that Maharashtra has the maximum contracts with first-run or cleaner coal-based power capacity—the largest amongst other states in the country with about 6,000 MW of clean power capacity. After Maharashtra come U.P, M.P, Haryana, Punjab, and Gujarat with about 4,000 MW clean power capacity. However, in terms of percentage of total contracts with cleaner coal-based power stations—Himachal Pradesh has the highest at 65% and West Bengal has the lowest at one per cent.

Few states—West Bengal, Dadar, Chhattisgarh, Jharkhand, and Telangana— have less than 20% contracts with cleaner generation. Most of the power stations which supply electricity to these states have to meet the deadline by 2021 and it is very unlikely they will meet the deadlines given their current stages of progress. Imposing a blanket ban on their operations will be difficult. Similarly, implementing first-run concept in these states might not bring in any momentum in pushing other capacity to comply. Also, there might be technical limitations to scheduling first-run plants according to experts. Certain power stations must crucially operate to balance the grid and these are called load centre stations. The regional dispatch centre will be able to comment on the technical feasibility of scheduling all power stations identified on priority list as first-run. Transmission constraint could emerge as a major roadblock in materializing this concept to the fullest. Therefore, the concept of first-run will be successful only by coupling it with a penalty measure. Reducing availability or allowing only part-load operation of power stations could be one option. Notice issued by CPCB to a power station to operate at half its plant load factor can have magnitude effects. Pollution also increases with low-load; therefore, the board should allow operation of the plant for a restricted number of days on full load. Restriction on number of days of operation would imply the plant availability in turn is restricted. The fixed costs to power stations are heavily based on declared plant availability. Only at a 55–60% plant availability (varies widely) will a plant break-even, meaning the cost spent to generate power will be fully recovered with no profits and no loss. Any decrease in availability will pose significant hit to fixed cost recovery—which in a way is a penalty on the power station. Executing this penalty will not require any change/modification in the current legal system; CPCB is empowered to enforce such a measure according to experts.

RECOMMENDATIONS

Need for concerted effort

Need for concerted effort Concerted efforts by stakeholders like the Electricity Regulatory Commission and State Power Departments of these 21 states and 4 union territories, in addition with the co-operation of 15 state pollution control boards where these thermal power stations are located, will be required to implement this concept. The SPCBs advise the Electricity Regulatory Commission on the progress of implementation in TPPs. They will need to designate the plants which qualify for first-run. Electricity regulatory commissions in 21 states and 4 union territories can take cognizance suo-moto under tariff orders, according to a senior official working at the State Electricity Regulatory Commission. Electricity regulatory commissions can also designate first-run plants through notes of recommendation from the state power departments. However, a few of the electricity regulatory commissions say that any such preference will be challenged at the courts by distribution firms/consumers. State electricity regulatory commissions regulate the contracts signed between the distribution companies and power stations, govern the commercial aspects like electricity prices charged to customers, check the authenticity of power generation cost quoted by thermal power stations, make sure merit order despatch principles are adhered with, etc.

Penalty

According to the current regulations, irrespective of whether the power station runs or not, the distribution companies are bound to pay the fixed charges as per the long-term contracts. The current penalty of Rs 30,000-50,000 per MW is not high enough to serve any purpose. To tackle this, CPCB will need to step-in and modify penalty provisions and also give a layout of how the penalty collected will be managed. At least a fine of Rs 20 lakh per MW will need to be imposed by the board.

Restrict Days of Operation

Restrict the number of days a station can operate and thereby reduce availability of plants which are not meeting the targets. This could be an effective measure to push compliance without modifying the current legal system. Reducing availability will impose restrictions in the recovery of fixed costs of the plant which can serve as deterrent to non-compliance.

CONCLUSION

The time has come to look for power from cleaner sources. Power generation, pollution from burning coal, and related impacts on human health cannot be dealt with in isolation. Today, the possibility of affordable clean power would mean power from sources which do not create pollution in the local region/area. In this bracket, renewable power generation capacity of 86,400 MW, hydropower generation capacity of 45,399 MW, natural gas power stations of 24,937 MW, and the coal-based power stations of 57,624 MW can be included. These stations run with minimum level of pollution to the immediate surroundings. Assuming a plant load factor of 20% for hydro, 10% for natural gas, 98% for clean coal, and 20% for renewable energy, up to 553 billion units of electricity can be generated. The peak load demand stood at 175,528 MW during FY 2018-19, and 182,533 MW in FY 2019-2020. The average per unit cost of electricity generated today is Rs 3.5 a unit. One-half of the clean coal-based thermal power stations generate electricity at less than Rs 3.5 per unit. The other half could be more expensive by Rs 0.5-1.5 per unit—which is still significantly lesser than the health cost due to pollution suffered by people. However, the question of fixed cost remains. By scheduling power from cleaner sources necessarily, the burden of fixed cost cannot be removed as long-term agreements have been signed with most coal-based thermal power stations. However, cost of power from cleaner coal generation sources is lower than from renewable energy sources, taking into account the plant load factor of renewable and cleaner coal.

Coal-based power is one of the most resource intensive and polluting industries. On 07 December 2015, the Ministry of Environment, Forestry and Climate Change introduced stricter environmental standards for coal-based thermal power plants under the Environment Protection Act, 1986. Five years after these norms were announced, most plants have neither taken adequate action nor made significant progress towards meeting them.

8

Plastic Waste Disposal and Role of Microorganisms in Bioremediation of Plastics

INTRODUCTION

One of the major environmental threats is the least rate of degradation or non-biodegradability of synthetic organic polymers like plastics under natural condition. The various forms of plastics such as nylon, polycarbonate, polyethylene-terephthalate, polyethylene, polypropylene, polystyrene, polytetraflouro ethylene, polyurethane and polyvinyl chloride are being continuously used in our day-to-day life (Smith, 1964). The word plastic is derived from the Greek word plastikos, which literally translates to 'able to be moulded in to varied shapes. Plastics are polymers that consist of monomers linked together by chemical bonds (Vignesh *et.al.,* 2016). Plastics are defined as the polymers (solid materials) which on heating become mobile and can be casted into specific shapes. They are also called as non-metallic mouldable compounds and the materials that are made from them can be moulded into any desired shape and size (Seymour, 1989). These have greater advantage as they are strong, lightweight, and durable. However, they do have grave disadvantages as they are resistant to biodegradation, leading to pollution, and pose to be harmful to the natural environment (Amal *et.al.,* 2015). Low density polyethylene (LDPE) is viewed to be one of the major causes of environmental pollution. Polyethylene is a polymer made up of several repeating units of monomers called ethylene. The use of this synthetic polymer is growing at a rate of 12% per year and about 140 million tons of synthetic polymers are produced worldwide each year (Sharma *et.al.,* 2015). It causes serious threats to the environment during its production and after its disposal. Microorganisms that can degrade plastics are over 90 genera from bacteria, fungi, among them *Bacillus megaterium, Pseudomonas spp, Azotobacterial spp, Ralstonia eutropha, Halomonas spp* etc (Chee *et.al.,* 2008).

Utilization of plastic materials or articles has found wide application in virtually all aspects of human life in both domestic and commercial environments. There is hardly anything that one will do without encountering plastics or its products (Raziyafathima *et.al.,* 2016). The high consumer demand drove global production to approximately 140 million tons of synthetic polymers, which has increased by 1.74-fold over the past 15 years to about 243 million tons (Sharma *et.al.,* 2015). The rise in production and use of synthetic polymers has on the other hand increase in the amount of global plastic wastes with numerous adverse effects on the environment. This is a concern put forward by a large sector of public including environmental advocates, cultivators, welfare organisations and researchers (Boris Worm *et.al.,* 2017).

TYPES OF PLASTICS

Plastics can be broadly classified into two types. These are the two types of plastics widely in use: thermoplastics and thermosetting polymers. Thermoplastics are plastics that do not undergo chemical change in their composition upon heating and can be moulded to any shape repeatedly. While the thermosetting polymers melt upon heating and can be moulded into various shapes. After they are solidified, they retain the same shape and remain solid forever. In the thermosetting process, a chemical reaction occurs which is irreversible. Thermosets are assumed to have infinite molecular weight. These are made of long polymeric chains with repeating molecular units, known as or derivatives of monomers; each polymer chain will have several thousand repeating units. Vulcanization of rubber is one such thermosetting process. The poly-isoprene is a tacky, slightly runny material, before heating with sulphur, but after vulcanization the product is rigid, non-tacky and retains its shape.

There are several other classifications of plastics based on the properties and chemical nature of the monomer units or the parameters that are relevant for manufacturing or production design. Plastics can also be classified depending on various physical properties, such as density, high tensile strength, and resistance to various chemical products.

PLASTIC DEGRADING MICROORGANISMS

Numerous microorganisms exist and have been confirmed by many researchers globally which have the ability to use polyethylene (one kind of plastic) as a carbon and energy source. This physiochemical ability has been studied only recently. In general, the attachment of microorganisms to the surface of the plastics, followed by the colonization of the exposed surface, is the first stage of growth leading to degradation (Tokiwa *et.al.*, 2009). Degradation of plastics by microorganisms is primarily accomplished by hydrolytic activities of enzymes which specifically cleave the bonds in the polymer releasing monomers and oligomers (Lucas *et.al.*, 2008). Bacteria and fungi are involved in the degradation of plastics (Gu *et.al.*, 2000). For example, Streptomyces spp. and other wood degrading fungi (e.g., *Piptoporus botulinus, Irpex lacteus* etc.) can attach to the surface of the polyethylene and produce extracellular enzymes. These extracellular hydrolytic enzymes degrade polyethylene into respective ethene monomers (Pometto *et.al.*, 1992) (Kim *et.al.*, 2005). Other studies showed that bacteria, such as *Pseudomonas, Streptococcus, Staphylococcus, Micrococcus, Moraxella, Brevibaccillus, and Rhodococcus* (Gilan *et.al.*, 2004; Hadad *et.al.*, 2005), and fungi, including *Aspergillus niger, A. glaucus, Saccharomonospora spp.* and *Actinomycetes spp.* were associated with plastic and plastic like polymer degradation (Swift, 1997; Raaman *et.al.*, 2012).

Studies on biodegradation of plastics such as High Density Polyethene (HDPE), Low Density Polyethene (LDPE), Polypropylene (PP) and Polystyrene (PS) in soils revealed that some fungi and bacteria species are capable of degrading plastics into simple compounds carbon and energy molecules for cellular metabolism. For instance, Yamada-Onodera (2001) reported that the fungus, *Penicillium simplicissimum*, degraded HDPE up to molecular weight of 2800 g/mol (S Yamada-Onodera *et.al.*, 2001). Thermophilic bacteria *Brevibaccillus borstelensis and Rhodococcus ruber* were also reported to assimilate LDPE as a carbon source (Gilan *et.al.*, 2004; Hadad *et.al.*, 2005). Soil inhabiting fungi (e.g., *A. niger, A. japonicas, A. terreus, A. flavus and Mucor sp.*) were also found to have the potential to decompose synthetic plastics although the results were inconclusive (Raaman N *et.al.*, 2012). Also, *Bacillus stearothermophilus and B. pumilus* were reported to degrade Poly Butylene Succinic Acid (PBSA) and Poly lactic acid in soils. This potential is used to compost and activate sludge (Tomita *et.al.*, 2000).

PLASTIC DISPOSAL METHODS

There are four methods of plastic disposal currently being practices all over the world (Webb *et.al.*, 2013):

(a) **Incineration:** technically incineration refers to the burning in order to dispose the plastic waste. Incineration has an advantage that it does not require space to be carried out and there is even the capability for energy recovery in the form of heat (Sinha *et.al.*, 2010). However burning plastic on a large scale releases Polycyclic Aromatic Hydrocarbons, Poly Chlorinated Biphenyls, heavy metals, toxic carbon- and oxygen-based free radicals, significant quantities of greenhouse gases, especially carbon dioxide which lead to major environmental crisis.

(b) **Landfill:** landfill refers to burying the plastic waste in excavated pits. This has been a traditional practice which over several years has shown an impact on the soil quality. Limited oxygen supply and the persistence of anaerobic conditions upon landfill of plastics leads to the release of benzene, toluene, xylenes, ethyl benzenes and trimethyl benzenes, released both as gases and dissolved state (Urase *et.al.,* 2008).

(c) **Recycling:** recycling of plastics can be classified into mechanical processing and chemical processing. Mechanical processing also called mechanolytic recycling involves subjecting the plastic waste to pressure and heat to melt and remould them desired shape. Chemical processing is performed by carrying out chemolysis with a number of compounds, resulting in depolymerisation of the plastic (Awaja *et.al.,* 2005). Depolymerisation can be carried out by hydrolysis (using water), methanolysis (methanol), glycolysis (EG) or aminolysis (e.g., methylamine,) (Awaja *et.al.,* 2005; Sinha *et.al.,* 2010). Each results in different monomer units that can be recovered, but all of the monomers can be used as polymerisation materials to produce new plastic.

(d) **Biodegradation:** It is the process of degrading the plastic waste by employing suitable microbes. The metabolic diversity of microorganisms makes them a useful biodegradation (Iranzo *et.al.,* 2001). Biodegradation is an inviting alternative to all the above practices for waste disposal. A few of the several advantages include that it is an economical process, potentially much more efficient and does not produce secondary pollutants. On the contrary, it may even be possible to obtain useful end products with economic benefit from bacterial metabolism of pollutants, for example, ethanol for use in biofuels (Iranzo *et.al.,* 2001).

DEGRADATION OF PLASTICS

Any physical or chemical change in polymer as a result of several environmental factors, such as light, temperature, moisture, chemical conditions or biological activity can be termed degradation. Processes that induce changes in polymer properties due to physical, chemical or biological reactions resulting in subsequent chemical transformations (formation of structural homogeneities) are categorized as polymer degradation. Degradation with respect to plastics is referred to as the changes in mechanical, optical or electrical characteristics or properties of any plastic material resulting in cracking, erosion, discoloration, phase separation and delamination.

PLASTIC DEGRADATION CAN BE CLASSIFIED INTO THE FOLLOWING BASED ON THE CAUSATIVE AGENTS

(a) **Biodegradation** - This is a natural process by which microorganism (bio-decomposers) breakdown plastics into small units in order to use the carbon and energy sources for subsequent growth and energy utilization (Sharma *et.al.*, 2015; Sen *et.al.*, 2015). This process can occur through hydrolytic biodegradation and oxidative biodegradation (Bonhomme, *et.al.*, 2003).

(b) **Photo degradation** - This is brought about by the action of sunlight. Photo degradation can result in an alteration in the physical and chemical structure of the plastic, usually as a result of sunlight in outdoor exposure (Yousif *et.al.*, 2013).

(c) **Thermo-oxidative degradation** - This is caused by slow oxidative breakdown at moderate temperatures.

(d) **Thermo-degradation** - This is caused by the degrading action of plastics at high temperatures.

(e) **Hydrolysis** - This involves breakdown of polymers or oligomers of plastic on reaction with water molecules. This releases monomers to the environment (Hakkarainen *et.al.*, 2004; Andrady, 2011).

BIODEGRADATION OF PLASTICS

Plastics are used as potential substrates by heterotrophic microorganisms (Glass and Swift G., 1989). Microorganisms such as bacteria and fungi are prominently involved in the degradation of both natural and synthetic plastics (Gu *et.al.*, 2000).

The biodegradation of plastics proceeds actively and differ indefinitely depending on parameters like different soil conditions, properties and physical characteristics of the plastic disposed and the microbial composition of the soil (because the microorganisms that are responsible for the process of degradation differ from each other and they have their own optimal growth conditions in the soil). Biodegradation is specifically governed by different factors that include characteristics of polymer, type of organism, and nature of pre-treatment.

The characteristics of polymer such as mobility, crystallinity, molecular weight, functional groups and substituents present in its structure, and plasticizers or additives when added to the polymer all play a significant role in the time and extent of degradation (Gu *et.al.*, 2000).

Several organizations are involved in setting standards for biodegradable and compostable plastics: the U.S. Composting Council (USCC), the American Certification System of Biodegradable Products Institute (BPI), the Environment & Plastics Industry Council, the American

Society for Testing and Materials (ASTM), the European Committee for Standardization (CEN), Japan's Greenplum program, and the British Plastics Federation. The restrictions and regulations from these organizations help create biodegradable and compostable products that meet the increasing worldwide demand for more environmentally friendly plastics. Biodegradable polymers decompose into carbon dioxide, methane, water, inorganic compounds or biomass by the actions of microorganisms (Greene, 2007). Biodegradable polymers used for producing biodegradable agricultural films include inter alia, copolyesters, poly(vinyl)alcohol, poly(vinyl)chloride, acylated starch-plastic, modified starch and vegetable oil (Kyrikou, 2007).

BIODEGRADATION OF SYNTHETIC PLASTICS

The degradation of most synthetic plastics in nature is a very slow process that involves environmental factors, which follows the action of wild microorganisms (Albertsson 1980; Cruz-Pinto *et.al.,* 1994; Albertsson *et.al.,* 1994). The oxidation or hydrolytic cleavage by enzyme generates functional groups that improve the hydrophilicity of polymer. This is the primary mechanism for the biodegradation of high molecular weight polymer. Subsequently, the main chain of polymer is degraded resulting in polymer of low molecular weight with feeble mechanical properties. This makes them more accessible for further microbial assimilation (Albertsson *et.al.,*1990; Albertsson *et.al.,* 1987; Huang *et.al.,* 1990). Poly (vinyl alcohol), poly (lactic acid), polycaprolactone, and polyamides are some examples of synthetic polymers with oligomeric structures that can succumb to biodegradation. The rate of degradation is affected by several physical properties such as crystallinity and orientation of the monomers and morphological properties such as surface area of the polymers (Huang *et.al.,*1992).

STEPS OF PLASTIC BIODEGRADATION BY MICROORGANISMS

There are four steps involved in the biodegradation of plastic:

1. **Bio-deterioration:** This refers to the superficial degradation of plastics by physical and chemical deterioration that is a result of the activities of microbial communities and other bio-decomposers.
2. **Bio-fragmentation**: This refers to the catalytic activity of extracellular hydrolytic enzymes secreted by microorganisms that breaks down polymeric plastics into smaller oligomers, dimers or monomers. Some of the enzymes secreted include Alkane hydroxylase, Lipases, Esterase, Protease and Lactase.
3. **Assimilation:** This refers to the integration, transport or assimilation of molecules or monomers from the surroundings into the cytoplasm of microbes during metabolism.

4. **Mineralization:** This is the last phase where microorganisms utilize the assimilated monomers in the energy pathways to break them down completely to simple oxidised metabolites or micro-molecules like CO_2, N_2, CH_4 and H_2O (Lucas *et.al.*, 2008). These are ultimately released to the natural environment.

BIODEGRADABLE POLYMERS

In Poland, 3 to 10% of the mass of waste materials is constituted by synthetic materials and every year it rises by 3%. This results in the increase in the volume of waste dumps. The most efficient solution to the problem is the replacement of conventional synthetic fibres with biodegradable polymers. Biodegradable materials may be divided into three groups: the mixtures of synthetic polymers and substances which are easy digestible by microorganisms (inter alia, modified natural polymers, natural polymers such as starch and cellulose), synthetic materials with groups that are susceptible to hydrolytic microbial attack (for example, polycaprolactone) and the bio polyesters from bacterial sources. The most popular and important biodegradable polymers are aliphatic polyesters [e.g., polylactide, poly(ε-caprolactone), polyethylene oxide, poly(3-hydroxybutyrate), polyglycolic acid] and thermoplastic proteins (Liao *et.al.*, 2009). The major advantages of biodegradable plastics are that they can be composted with organic wastes and returned to enrich the soil, their use will not only reduce ecological stress and loss of habitat to wild animals caused by dumping of conventional plastics, but will also lessen the labour cost for the removal of plastic wastes in the environment because they are degraded naturally, their decomposition will help increase the longevity and stability of landfills by reducing the volume of garbage, they could be recycled to useful monomers and oligomers by microbial and enzymatic treatment (Tokiwa *et.al.*, 2007).

FUTURE PROSPECTIVE

Recent trend in research has observed, the development of the methods for manufacture of such polymers. Using biodegradable polymers in many fields of industry, instead of synthetic materials, may significantly help protect the natural environment. On the other hand, it is important to isolate several microorganisms like bacteria, fungi, zooplanktons, phytoplankton from the natural environment which possesses the enzymatic machinery that suitable degrade the disposed plastics. Such microorganisms can be found in several sources like soil, dumps, ocean bed and even the gut of few arthropods which feed on plastic. Such a modern approach developed for remediation combined and applied with such microorganisms will help solve plastic waste problem through bioremediation. This will ensure an eco-friendly and sustainable development of mankind where in all the other life forms can coexist.

Use of plastic in general has gained a subtle predominance over the past three decades. With increase in the use of plastic enrooted the need to effectively dispose the waste generated by it. Plastic waste disposal is gaining importance with higher awareness about the ill-effects of plastics among several sectors of the society. Industries largely depend upon plastics for various purposes and hence turn out to be major pollutants. Considering the hazards of its disposal, there is an immediate need to replace the conventional plastics with the bio-degradable ones. Our planet needs to be protected by this menace as effectively and expeditiously so as to ensure a sustainable wellbeing of all the species on it. Biodegradable materials or isolation of microorganisms which can degrade these synthetic polymers can be viewed as an eco-friendly alternative to the traditional disposal practices. This review emphasises on the relevance and requirement of many such research activities in the near future aimed at effectual and powerful annihilation of plastics and their wastes from the world.

CONCLUSION

In recent years, public has shown interest and concern over environmental issues. The problem of plastic pollution is now really a mess for the mankind. There is no part of the world untouched from its impacts. In the present era of globalization some thought must be given to plan safe disposal of products before making it commercial. This review has covered the major concerns about the plastics and their types, uses and degradability. Technical and economic problems connected with materials recycling have induced scientists to search for new materials that may be organically recycled. Synthetic polymers' negative influence on the natural environment creates many problems with waste deposition and utilization.

Nowadays, there are few biodegradable water-soluble polymers available commercially, in spite of the obvious and pressing need for environmental protection. Biodegradable polymers have been researched, but polymers based on renewable and abundantly available sources (especially like starch) are most desirable. The major advantages of biodegradable polymers are that they can be composted with organic wastes and returned to enrich the soil, their use will not only reduce injuries to wild animals caused by dumping of conventional plastics but will also lessen the labor cost for the removal of plastic wastes in the environment because they are degraded naturally, their decomposition will help increase the longevity and stability of landfills by reducing the volume of garbage, they could be recycled to useful monomers and oligomers by microbial and enzymatic treatment. To solve plastic waste problem there is an immediate need to fund research for the production of biodegradable plastics.

REFERENCES

Albertsson, A.C. (1980) The Shape of the Biodegradation Curve for Low- and High-density Polyethylene's in Prolonged series of Experiments. Eur Polym J, 16: 623-630.

Albertsson, A.C. and Karlsson, S. (1990) The Influence of Biotic and Abiotic Environments on the Degradation of Polyethylene. Prog Polym Sci, 15: 177-192.

Albertsson, A.C., Andersson, S.O. and Karlsson, S. (1987) The Mechanism of Biodegradation of Polyethylene. Polym Degrad Stab, 18: 73-87.

Albertsson, A.C., Barenstedt, C. and Karlsson, S. (1994) Abiotic Degradation Products from Enhanced Environmentally Degradable Polyethylene. Acta Polym, 45: 97-103.

Alshehrei, F. (2017). Biodegradation of Synthetic and Natural Plastic by Microorganisms. Journal of Applied & Environmental Microbiology, 5(1), 8-19.

Amal A. Hussein., Al-Mayaly, I.K., & Khudeir, S.H. (2015). Isolation, Screening and Identification of Low-Density Polyethylene (LDPE) degrading Bacteria from Contaminated Soil with Plastic Wastes. Journal, Vol, 1(4), 1-14.

Andrady, A.L. (2011). Microplastics in the Marine Environment. Marine Pollution Bulletin, 62(8), 1596-1605.

Awaja, F., & Pavel, D. (2005). Recycling of PET. *European Polymer Journal, 41*(7), 1453-1477.

Bonhomme, S., Cuer, A., Delort, A.M., Lemaire, J., Sancelme, M., & Scott, G. (2003). Environmental Biodegradation of Polyethylene. Polymer Degradation and Stability, 81(3), 441-452.

Chee, J.W., Amirul, A.A., Muhammad, T.T., Majid, M.I.A., & Mansor, S.M. (2008). The influence of Copolymer Ratio and Drug Loading Level on the Biocompatibility of P (3HB-co-4HB) synthesized by Cupriavidus sp. (USMAA2-4). Biochemical Engineering Journal, 38(3), 314-318.

Cruz Pinto, J.J.C., Carvalho, M.E.S., & Ferreira, J.F.A. (1994). The Kinetics and Mechanism of Polyethylene Photo Oxidation. Die Angewandte Makromolekulare Chemie: Applied Macromolecular Chemistry and Physics, 216(1), 113-133.

Glass, J.E., & Swift, G. (1989). Agricultural and Synthetic Polymers, Biodegradation and utilization. In ACS Symposium series (Vol. 433, pp. 9-64).

Greene, J. (2007). Biodegradation of Compostable Plastics in Green yard-waste Compost Environment. Journal of Polymers and the Environment, 15(4), 269-273.

Gu, J.D., Ford, T.E., Mitton, D.B. and Mitchell R. 2000. Microbial Degradation and Deterioration of Polymeric materials. In: Review, editor. The Uhlig Corrosion Handbook. 2nd Edition. New York: Wiley; 439-60.

Hadad, D., Geresh, S., & Sivan, A. (2005). Biodegradation of Polyethylene by the Thermophilic bacterium Brevibacillus borstelensis. Journal of Applied Microbiology, 98(5), 1093-1100.

Huang, J.C., Shetty, A.S., & Wang, M.S. (1990). Biodegradable Plastics: A Review. Advances in Polymer Technology, 10(1), 23-30.

Huang, S.J., Roby, M.S., Macri, C.A., & Cameron, J.A. (1992). The Effects of Structure and Morphology on the Degradation of Polymers with Multiple Groups. Special Publication-Royal Society of Chemistry, 109(1), 149-149.

Iranzo, M., Sainz-Pardo, I., Boluda, R., Sanchez, J., & Mormeneo, S. (2001). The use of Microorganisms in Environmental remediation. Annals of Microbiology, 51(2), 135-144.

Kim, Y., Yeo, S., Kum, J., Song, H.G., & Choi, H.T. (2005). Cloning of a Manganese Peroxidase cDNA Gene repressed by Manganese in Trametes versicolor. The Journal of Microbiology, 43(6), 569-571.

Kyrikou, I., & Briassoulis, D. (2007). Biodegradation of Agricultural Plastic Films: A Critical Review. Journal of Polymers and the Environment, 15(2), 125-150.

Liao, H.T., & Wu, C.S. (2009). Preparation and Characterization of Ternary Blends composed of Polylactide, Poly ([-caprolactone) and Starch. Materials Science and Engineering: A, 515(1-2), 207-214.

Lucas, N., Bienaime, C., Belloy, C., Queneudec, M., Silvestre, F., & Nava-Saucedo, J.E. (2008). Polymer Biodegradation: Mechanisms and Estimation Techniques–A Review. Chemosphere, 73(4), 429-442.

Luckachan, G.E., & Pillai, C.K.S. (2011). Biodegradable Polymers-a review on recent trends and emerging Perspectives. Journal of Polymers and the Environment, 19(3), 637-676.

Mierzwa-Hersztek, M., Gondek, K., & Kopeæ, M. (2019). Degradation of Polyethylene and Biocomponent-Derived Polymer Materials: An Overview. Journal of Polymers and the Environment, 27(3), 600-611.

Orr, I.G., Hadar, Y., & Sivan, A. (2004). Colonization, Biofilm formation and Biodegradation of Polyethylene by a Strain of Rhodococcus Ruber. Applied Microbiology and Biotechnology, 65(1), 97-104.

Pometto, A.L., Lee, B.T., & Johnson, K.E. (1992). Production of an extracellular Polyethylene-degrading Enzyme (s) by Streptomyces species. Appl. Environ. Microbiol., 58(2), 731-733.

Raaman, N., Rajitha, N., Jayshree, A., & Jegadeesh, R. (2012). Biodegradation of Plastic by Aspergillus spp. isolated from Polythene Polluted sites around Chennai. J Acad Indus Res, 1(6), 313-316.

Raziyafathima, M., Praseetha, P.K., & Rimal, I.R.S. (2016). Microbial Degradation of Plastic Waste: A Review. Chemical and Biological Sciences, 4, 231-42.

Sen, S.K., & Raut, S. (2015). Microbial Degradation of Low Density Polyethylene (LDPE): A Review. Journal of Environmental Chemical Engineering, 3(1), 462-473.

Seymour, R.B. (1989). Polymer Science before and after 1899: Notable Developments during the Lifetime of Maurits Dekker. Journal of Macromolecular Science—Chemistry, 26(8), 1023-1032.

Sharma, J., Gurung, T., Upadhyay, A., Nandy, K., Agnihotri, P., & Mitra, A.K. (2015). Isolation and Characterization of Plastic degrading Bacteria from Soil collected from the dumping Grounds of an Industrial Area. Int J Adv Innov Res, 3, 2278-7844.

Sharma, M., Sharma, P., Sharma, A., & Chandra, S. (2015). Microbial Degradation of Plastic—A Brief Review. CIBTech Journal of Microbiology, 4(1), 85-89.

Sinha, V., Patel, M.R., & Patel, J.V. (2010). PET Waste Management by Chemical Recycling: A Review. *Journal of Polymers and the Environment*, *18*(1), 8-25.

Smith, W.M. (Ed.). (1964). Manufacture of Plastic (Vol. 1). Reinhold Pub. Corp..

Swift, G. (1997). Non-medical Biodegradable Polymers: Environmentally Degradable Polymers. Handbook of Biodegradable Polymers. Hardwood Academic, Amsterdam, 473-511.

Tokiwa, Y., & Calabia, B. P. (2007). Biodegradability and Biodegradation of Polyesters. Journal of Polymers and the Environment, 15(4), 259-267.

Tokiwa, Y., Calabia, B.P., Ugwu, C.U., & Aiba, S. (2009). Biodegradability of Plastics. International Journal of Molecular Sciences, 10(9), 3722-3742.

Tomita, K., Kuroki, Y., Hayashi, N., & Komukai, Y. (2000). Isolation of a Thermophile Degrading poly (butylene succinate-co-butylene adipate). Journal of Bioscience and Bioengineering, 90(3), 350-352.

Urase, T., Okumura, H., Panyosaranya, S., & Inamura, A. (2008). Emission of Volatile Organic Compounds from Solid Waste Disposal Sites and importance of Heat Management. *Waste Management & Research*, 26(6), 534-538.

Vignesh, R., Deepika, R.C., Manigandan, P., & Janani, R. (2016). Screening of Plastic degrading Microbes from various Dumped Soil samples. *Int Res J Eng Tech*, 3(4), 2493-2498.

Webb, H.K., Arnott, J., Crawford, R.J., & Ivanova, E.P. (2013). Plastic Degradation and its Environmental Implications with special reference to Poly (ethylene terephthalate). *Polymers*, 5(1), 1-18.

Worm, B., Lotze, H.K., Jubinville, I., Wilcox, C., & Jambeck, J. (2017). Plastic as a Persistent Marine Pollutant. Annual Review of Environment and Resources, 42, 1-26.

Yamada-Onodera, K., Mukumoto, H., Katsuyaya, Y., Saiganji, A., & Tani, Y. (2001). Degradation of Polyethylene by a Fungus, Penicillium simplicissimum YK. Polymer Degradation and Stability, 72(2), 323-327.

Yousif, E., & Haddad, R. (2013). Photodegradation and Photostabilization of Polymers, especially Polystyrene. Springer Plus, 2(1), 398.

9

Safe use of Wastewater in Agriculture through Bioremediation Process

INTRODUCTION

A major concern now days internationally and nationally is of quantity and quality of irrigation water. There is a conflicting problem as on one hand there is an increasing scarcity of freshwater availability and on the other side wastewater generation has enormously increased. Wastewater generation is linked with increasing urbanisation, population pressure, industrialisation and all these have created a huge pressure on managing this wastewater which otherwise will create socio-economic and environmental problem (Chaidez *et.al.*, 2014). Before going into the details of wastewater, let us be clear about wastewater term.

Wastewater is any water which is not intended to be used directly for human consumption. In general wastewater is 99.9% water and rest are pollutants which we intend to remove or which makes it a wastewater. This 0.1% contains organic matter, inorganic compounds, nutrients, pathogens and toxic metals. Generally, municipal wastewater is a mix of domestic wastewater, storm water and industrial wastewater. Domestic wastewater is the water which is discharged from households, schools and other institutions of a place. While industrial wastewater refers to wastewater generated from the industries. The composition of industrial wastewater differs with the industry type (Hussain *et.al.*, 2002). As demand for water is increasing, the per capita availability of water has declined and day by day it is widening which is posing threat for human existence. Around 36% of global population lives in water scarce regions and as per the estimate by World Bank (2019), this will reach to more than 50% by

2050. Therefore researchers globally are focussing on measures for conserving water and at the same time it is appropriate time now to find ways to use wastewater as a resource and reuse it in agriculture (Hussain *et.al.*, 2002) as it will promote water security and resilience to climate variability in long term. In many regions of the world especially in water scarce areas falling under arid and semi-arid regions as well as peri urban and peri-industrial area where competition for water is very high among different sectors like industries, agriculture, domestic use, landscape etc. agriculture is the largest sufferer. Since agriculture uses more than 80% of freshwater use of wastewater for irrigation purpose is common. It depicts use of wastewater for irrigation by different countries. As there is no official figure of wastewater use for irrigation in India therefore it did not have mention of India. As per one estimate by Raychaudhuri *et.al.* (2017), 62000 million litres per day of wastewater is produced in India of which only 27% is treated and rest is untreated. This untreated wastewater is being used by farmers in peri urban and peri industrial areas for their crop irrigation under water scarce situation. More than 73000 ha area is being irrigated with wastewater (Raychaudhuri *et.al.* 2017). International Water Management Institute estimated irrigation potential with wastewater in class I and II cities of India. Volume of treated wastewater and untreated wastewater generated from these cities are 11787 MLD and 326467 MLD respectively which has the potential to irrigate approximately 70722 and 1032213 ha of area respectively.

CURRENT STATUS OF WASTEWATER USE IN AGRICULTURE

Although proper documentation related to use of wastewater is lacking but we cannot deny its use of irrigation especially in peri-urban and peri-industrial area. There are many benefits for which farmers prefer to use wastewater like round the year availability, nutrient present in it which reduces fertilizer cost and overall production cost (Banerjee, 2016; Rachana and Subhasis, 2019). In spite of all these benefits still wastewater use has many limitations. In most of the developing and under developed nation's use of untreated sewage is prevalent which is associated with many health hazards like bacterial, viral and protozoan diseases. Many types of parasitic worms like hookworm, roundworm etc. are prevalent. Additionally, depending on wastewater source heavy metals, persistent pollutants, and emerging pollutants are present which not only poses threat to soil but through the food chain and cycle reaches to human being and animals (Mateo-Sagasta *et.al.*, 2013). Many instances in the past has been found where persistent pollutants have created more havoc to the animals/plants/ human beings of higher hierarchy in the food chain via bio-magnification. Therefore globally the focus is on safe use of wastewater in agriculture. Treatment of wastewater is the most appropriate option where wastewater is converted into bilge water which can be discharged back into the environment. But operation and maintenance cost of treatment plants is very high because of which most of the treatment plants are not functional even after establishment. For example, India only treats 37% of its total sewage water generated and rest goes directly on land or nearby water bodies creating risk for its users (CPCB, 2016). Keeping this in view in 2017, United Nations emphasized on wastewater with the theme 'Why Waste Water'- which was about reducing the use of water and reusing wastewater for sustainable development. Thus out of many ways of reusing wastewater most economical and sustainable option is bioremediation which has been discussed in detail in below section.

BIOREMEDIATION PROCESS

Bioremediation refers to use of bio or living entities to degrade, alter or remove toxic/undesirable compounds or pollutants from the wastewater. Here organisms play a key role and rate of bioremediation depends on the catabolic activities of the microorganism which use wastewater as a source of food for their energy requirement. These microorganisms can either be native to contaminated site or it can be brought and adjusted to the new site Bioremediation provides ample scope to use wastewater irrigation safely in agriculture.

Bioremediation process has benefit as it can be done directly on contaminated site reducing its cost and space. Although bioremediation seems simple in application, the process is not that easy as it involves organism which needs to adapt to a site, moreover they should use the contaminant as their energy source in the process of degradation. In other words, efficiency of bioremediation process depends on contaminant properties as well as microorganism ability (Mora-Ravelo *et.al.*, 2017). Bioremediation process is mainly classified in two broad categories i.e. *ex-situ and in-situ. In-situ* bioremediation refers to the process where contaminants are biologically degrades to simple products like carbon dioxide and water or other transformed product at the site only. This is a preferred process since it involves low cost and maintenance, additionally it is environmentally sustainable (Megharaj *et.al.*, 2011). Ex-situ refers to remediating contaminated site after taking the pollutants from one place to the site of treatment (Azubuike *et.al.*, 2016). All the bioremediation process can be categorised into three types depending on the process involved. The first one is Bio-attenuation: also known as natural attenuation where naturally the remediation process goes on at the contaminated site. Second one is bio-stimulation: here the natural process of bioremediation is stimulated externally by supplying either water, energy, electron donors or acceptors which enhances the remediation process by increasing the metabolic process of microorganism. Third process is bio-augmentation:

here according to the dominant contaminant to be removed from a site, well known microbes are added externally which have the capability to degrade these contaminants (Ying, 2018). The type of bioremediation process to be used will depend on environmental plus microbial condition like site property, climate, quality and quantity of pollutants present etc. (Ying, 2018).

USE OF BIOREMEDIATION FOR WASTEWATER TREATMENT

Although there are numerous bioremediation techniques but most common ones being practised in wastewater remediation is phytoremediation, chelation, methylation and precipitation (Martínez-Prado *et.al.*, 2011).

PHYTOREMEDIATION

Phytoremediation is made of two words i.e. phyto- means plants and remediation- to rectify. As per United Nations, phytoremediation is defined as the use of living green plants for in-situ removal/degradation/reduction of contaminants in the affected area of soil, water or groundwater. Phytoremediation can be done to remediate metals like lead, zinc, cadmium, copper, nickel, mercury, nickel etc., metalloids like arsenic, inorganic compounds like nitrate, phosphate, ammonium; radioactive compounds, petroleum compounds, pesticides, herbicides, chlorinated compounds (Favas *et.al.*, 2014). Phytoremediation process is broadly divided into six types namely phytoextraction, phytodegradation, phytovolatilisation, rhizofiltration, phytostabilisation and rhizodegradation. Detail are being given below:

(i) *Phytoextraction*: Phyto-extraction refers to extraction of metals or organic compounds by plants from contaminated sites. In this process, pollutants are absorbed by plants and are translocated to above ground biomass. Plants are harvested from the contaminated site. This process is suitable where contamination is of low to moderate levels.mn. Plants selected for phytoextraction should be tolerant type which are able to tolerate high concentration of toxic metals or compounds in their body. The plants must be fast grower with high biomass production (Farraji, 2014). Phytoextraction can be continuous or induced process. Continuous phytoextraction refers to the process where plants accumulate high level of toxic metals/compounds in their parts during the entire life cycle of plants. Induced phytoextraction means the extraction process is enhanced via use of chelators at any particular plant stage at which the plants extraction capacity is highest (Farraji, 2014). For example chelators like EDTA or low molecular weight acids have the ability to enhance the efficiency of phytoextraction. In a study done by Mirza *et.al.* (2010) where species *Arundo donax* was tested for arsenic from wastewater under greenhouse condition. Arsenic concentration of upto 600 µg L^{-1} was extracted from *A. donax* spp. and above that concentration (1000 µg L^{-1}), plant started oxidative stress. Therefore *A. donax* was found suitable for phyto-extracting arsenic from wastewater. Similarly, Monferran *et.al.* (2012) showed *Potamogeteon pusillus* leaves and roots tolerant towards Cr and Cu which can be used for phytoextraction of these metals from contaminated water.

(ii) *Phytodegradation:* Phytodegradation or phytotransformtion is breaking of organic compounds by plants. Breakdown of organic compounds or contaminants is done either by metabolic activities within the plants or via metabolites released by plants. These plants via metabolites such as nitro-reductases, dehalogenase, oxygenase etc. degrade organic compounds present in plants (Farraji, 2014). Plans photodegrades contaminants either by uptake, metabolism or translocation to different plat parts (Ferraji, 2014). Nutrient load reduction in wastewater through microalgae is one of the emerging option (Akpor *et.al.*, 2014) as these microalgae can assimilate nutrients in their cells. These microalgae are variedly used to degrade chlorinated solvents, insecticides and pesticides and many other inorganic and organic nutrients (Akpor *et.al.*, 2014). Plants ability to metabolise these nutrients determines the efficacy of the process. When a toxic compound is taken by plants the first stage is activation of compounds by the action of different metabolites like flavin, monooxygenase etc. then its conjugation in plant parts and lastly the plant compartmentalises it in different parts preferably vacuoles or apoplast which ensures safe disposal of these toxic compounds (Akpor *et.al.*, 2014).

(iii) *Phytovolatilsation:* As the name suggest, phytovolatilsation refers to volatilisation of contaminants via plant parts. Here plant takes up contaminants from the affected site transforms them into volatile form which then vaporises in the air via plant parts (Farraji, 2014). This process is used for remediation of volatile organic compounds either through stem and leaves (known as direct volatilisation) or from soil due to root activity of plant (indirect volatilisation) (Limmer & Burken, 2016). A classic example of volatilisation is removal of Selenium. Selenium as a toxic element is found in most of the arid and semi-arid regions of the world with seleniferous soils originating from marine sediments. Selenite can leach from soil to groundwater or nearby surface water which through bioaccumulation can reach to human and

plants. Plants are effective in removing selenium from contaminated site (Adel *et.al.*, 1999). When selenium is absorbed by plant roots and translocated to shoots it is volatilised into dimethyl selenide which gets volatilised from the stem or leaves. Hyperaccumulators of Se are mostly from *Fabaceae* group including *Brassica juncea, Brassica napus,* Stanleya, Astragalus spp. etc. (Adel *et.al.*, 1999).

Another example of phytovolatilsation is constructed wetlands used for remediation of wastewater. It can be used to remediate industrial, domestic, municipal or agricultural wastewater. In this process helipohytes takes contaminants from the wastewater which are then taken up by plants with the assistance of microbial activities and are transformed to different secondary products and released from the plants (Stottmeister *et.al.*, 2003).

(iv) *Rhizofiltration:* Rhizofiltration in simple terms refers to filtration by roots. It is the adsorption or absorption into plant roots of contaminants present in soil solution. It is a preferred technique to remediate groundwater. Plants are grown hydroponically in contaminated water where they take up contaminants alongwith water. When the roots gets saturated with the contaminants they are taken off from the site and fresh plants are again grown in these contaminated water (Abdullahi, 2015; Dushenkov *et.al.*, 1995). Very popular example of it is use of Sunflower plants for remdiation of groundwater from radioactive contaminants in Ukraine (Abdullahi, 2015). In another study by Elias *et.al.* (2014) where water hyacinth was used to treat ceramic industry wastewater containing organic pollutants and heavy metals like Cd, Cr, Cu, Mn, Zn, Fe and B. Studies showed that most of the metal and organic pollutant absorption was through roots of the plants with an efficiency of 99%. Rhizofiltration ability of *Carex pendula* (wetland plant) was tested against lead in wastewater. C.pendula showed tolerance level of 1600mg/kg when water concentration in wastewater was 10 ppm. Results showed that C. pendula is an effective plant for rhizofiltration of lead from wastewater (Yadav *et.al.*, 2011)

Rhizofiltration is mostly used for wastewater remediation especially for heavy metals as it is cost-effective and environmental friendly. Moreover the best part is that accumulated metals can be recovered from root system which after extraction can be used as bio-ore. As this technique is in-situ so it does not disturbs the ecological balance of the site as well as it is aesthetically pleasing which makes it more sustainable option for metal recovery of heavy metals (Yadav *et.al.*, 2011)

(v) *Phytostabilisation:* Phytostabilisation refers to immobilisation of contaminants in the soil/water via accumulation and adsorption by the plants roots or rhizospheric zone. In this process movement of contaminant is restricted by plant roots so that they are spread by erosion or water movement (OB and Muchie, 2010).

In a study done at urban stream sediments of the Nakivubo in Kampala, Uganda found that *Commelina benghalensis* (L.) and *Cynodon dactylon* (L.) bioaccumulation factor was more than 1 compared to translocation factor with respect to Pb, Cd and Zn which showed that these plant spp. can be utilised for phytostabilisation of heavy metals in these area (Sekabira *et.al.*, 2011)

(vi) *Rhizodegradation:* Rhizodegradation means degradation of compounds (mostly organic contaminants) by rhizospheric microorganism for nutrient use in plants. This process is also known as phytostimulation. Under this process microbial activity is enhanced in rhizospheric zone via plant exudates such as carboxylic acid, carbohydrates or proteins are released from plant which enhances microbial activity and hence degrades organic contaminats present in soil or water (Ferraji, 2014). Some examples of rhizodegradation by plants are- *Hibiscus cannabinus* for used lubricating oil, *Plantago major* for Imidachlorpid insecticide, *Sorghum bicolor* for crude oil, willow spp. for perchloeate removal from soil and water (Ferraji, 2014). Table 9.1. describes the phytoremediation techniques in brief citing some examples.

MERITS AND LIMITATIONS OF PHYTOREMEDIATION PROCESS

There are many advantages associated with phytoremediation techniques (Koptsik, 2014) some of them are:

1. It can be used to remediate a wide range of contaminants including organic, inorganic and radionuclides.
2. As *in-situ* remediation occurs, it reduces the quantum of waste which enters into landfills or dump sites
3. Again as it is *in-situ*, it reduces the soil disturbance and spread of pollutants.
4. As compared to other chemical or traditional methods, it is less costly or cheaper technique.
5. The technique of phytoremediation is simple which is easy to use and maintain. At the same time it is renewable one which can be easily adopted in field with least technical skill requirement.
6. It is environmentally safe, aesthetically pleasant and socially acceptable method.
7. It is less noisy method.

Table 9.1: Different phytoremediation techniques with some examples

Phytoremediation type	Process description	Medium	Type of contaminants	Plants involved
Rhizodegradation/ Phytodegradation	Degradation of contaminants in rhizosphere assisted by microorganism	Soil, Sludge	Aromatic, aliphatic and petroleum hydrocarbons, pesticides, chlorinated solvents	Grasses Alfalfa Hybrid poplar Cassia Brassica spp.
Phytostabilisation	Stabilisation of contaminants by plants through complexation or absorption	Sediments, soil, sludge	Mostly metals like Pb, Fe, Cu, Cr, As, Ni radionuclides etc.	Sunflower Chenopodium
Phytoextraction	Extraction of contaminants by roots and accumulation in upper parts like shoots or vacuoles	Sediments, soil, sludge	Mostly metals like Pb, Fe, Cu, Cr, As, Ni radionuclides etc.	Sunflower Brassica Alyssum
Rhizofiltration	Removal of contaminants by roots	Wastewater Groundwater Surface water	Metals, Radionuclides	Lemna Eichhornia
Phytovolatilisation	Contaminants are volatilised from leaves or other exposed surfaces of plants	Soil Sediments	Organic and inorganic contaminants including metals	Poplar Scirpus

Source: Dhir, 2013.

Limitations (Koptsik, 2014)

The benefits of phytoremediation are many but still this technique has some limitations which has not made it very popular amongst industrialist to adopt at wider scale:

(i) This technique is restricted within the rhizospheric zone and contaminants removal depends on solubility and availability of pollutants so that plants can take them up.

(ii) It is time consuming process, can take several years (2-15 years) to remediate a contaminated site.

(iii) Remediation via phytoremediation can be successful only if the contaminats level is low-medium.

(iv) After phytoextraction of contaminants mostly heavy metals, proper disposal is a concern and challenge to tackle. Although bio-ores have come into role as one of the option for removal of these contaminants but still its technology is not very sound to be used at commercial scale.

(v) Plants can grow under certain agro-climatic condition and any change in it may affect their remediating capacity.

(vi) Sometimes introduction of a plant species in a certain area for remediation purpose can cause menace as it may be a threat to biodiversity of that place.

(vii) Variation in agronomic practices may render ineffectiveness in phytoremediation capacity.

In one publication by Carolyn Beans in PNAS (2017) titled 'Phytoremediation advances in the lab but lags in the field'. The author stated that despite phytoremediation being a successful technology still it is mostly limited to lab studies or pilot study. Major lacuna is time intensive where plants years to remediate which discouraged industrialist to invest in this technique. Secondly, there are more than 1000 publications on phytoremediation but they all are limited to lab studies and very limited number of publication showed long term field studies in this regard which may precisely determine the total time and cost involved in remediating a contaminated site considering all the factors in a given area. Therefore long term studies on phytoremediation is utmost important to make it a successful technology at commercial level.

Depending on contaminant type the whole phytoremediation process can be categorised into three broad categories:

(i) Remediation of inorganic contaminants site.

(ii) Remediation of organic contaminants site.

(iii) Remediation of both inorganic and organic contaminants site.

With increasing pressure on freshwater resources with burgeoning population and in turn increased demand for food, energy and other resources have put tremendous pressure on our water resources. With agriculture being the largest user of freshwater resources, the brunt of impact of pollution and climate change is bear by agriculture focusing on irrigation water around the world. Pollution by saltwater intrusion, algal blooms, soil erosion, improper sanitation, detergents, pesticides, chemicals etc. have posed serious concern (Falconer & Humpage, 2005)

Although understanding of remediation after categorising it into organic or inorganic pollutants is easy to understand but in in real we find places or wastewater contaminated with organic as well as inorganic pollutants called as co-contaminated sites. In these areas, first of all analysis of the wastewater is required and then depending on the major type of pollutant whose concentration is high action is taken upon. In these areas, phytoremediation activity is affected by interaction of different substances which affects their form and availability. In these areas, different pollutant affects plant-microbe interaction and therefore the micro-environment changes within the wastewater or a particular site. Therefore, engineered microorganism or plants are best suited for remediation of this type of affected wastewater.

In an attempt to remove 4-chlorophenol from wastewater both photocatalysis and biological treatment was done. Pre-treatment of Titanium dioxide as photocatlayst. Integrating biological treatment with photochemical showed greater remediating efficiency to 4-chlorophenol. A concentration of 400 ppm of 4-chlorophenol in wastewater took 264 hr when only biodegradation was done while the same was done in 96 hr when both photolysis and biological treatment was applied (Goel *et.al.*, 2010). An attempt was made by Gupta and Ali (2004) where lead and chromium present in wastewater was removed through bagasse fly ash obtained abundantly from local sugar industry in India. The mechanism involved was particle diffusion and reaction was exothermic in nature. With column flow rate of 0.5 ml min^{-1} removal efficiency through adsorption was 95-98%. In another study phenol was removed from wastewater using palm seed coated carbon through film diffusion method. For phenol concentration of 25 ppm palm seed coated carbon showed removal efficiency twice as effective compared to commercially available activated carbon in the pH range of 4-9 (Rengaraj *et.al.*, 2002). Trovaslet *et.al.* (2007) tested the efficacy of white rot fungi for treating the dye in wastewater. From fungal strain *Pycnoporus sanguineus* MUCL 41582 laccases was extracted and isoenzyme LAC-1 was tested for textile industry effluents. As textile industry effluents mostly contains either sodium sulphate or sodium hydroxide and LAC-1 showed promising result as the affinity was very high. Algae consortia are also great agents for bioremediation. In an attempt by Mahapatra *et.al.* (2014), algae was grown in reactors and was tested for filtered wastewater. Results showed that 86% total organic carbon, 90% total nitrogen, 89% ammoniacal nitrogen, 70% total phosphorous and 76% ortho phosphate were removed from the wastewater. It showed that algae consortia if replicated in sewage receiving ponds or lakes can help in remediation of wastewater that too in decentralised manner. Not only this, algae are good source of energy so at one place we will be able to meet some energy demand with reduction in GHG emission.

Algae mainly removes nutrients or contaminants by assimilation in their body as in general different algal species have different nutrient removal capability under certain optimum environmental condition. From livestock wastewater algae species *Chroococcus* removed 80% of ammoniacal and nitrate nitrogen and total phosphorous (Prajapati *et.al.*, 2014). In another study of effluent of anaerobic digestion *Arthrospira maxima and Tetradesmus obliquus* removed 98-99% of nitrogen while *Phaeodactylum tricornutum and Botryococcus braunii* removed 80-89% of phosphorous. One of the nutrient removal system is High rate algae pond (HRAP). Many studies have been done which removes nutrients and other contaminants. HRAP removed 51-57 % of P, 80-85% of ammoniacal N and 50-60% of total nitrogen from anaerobic digested wastewater (Nhat *et.al.*, 2014). Dominant algal species in *HRAP* were *Cyanobacteria, Planctomycetes Alpha, beta, gamma epsilon, delta-proteobacteria, Firmicutes, and Bacteroidetes* (Nhat *et.al.*, 2018). Although algae offers many benefits but its production at commercial level handles many challenges which makes its economic production unfeasible. Most important one is harvesting and dewatering of microbial cells, stabilising nutrient level in water. Therefore existing techniques does not seems practically feasible and economically profitable (Sharma and Malaviya, 2016). Fungus aided algal association is one technique which is getting attention as harvesting efficiency gets enhanced. Therefore algal assisted fungal biomass is a renewable and sustainable association for remediation of wastewater (Muradov *et.al.*, 2015). Because of the filamentous nature, fungi offers many benefits over algae or bacteria as it can tolerate high flow pressure, can be handled and cultured easily. Fungi have high tolerance and uptake ability towards metals (Salvadori *et.al.*, 2014).

As we know that waste from industries are more toxic compared to domestic or municipal wastewater. Not only we need to reduced chemical oxygen demand, colour or nutrients from it but more concern is dyes used in the industries. As dyes are colourful, therefore they impact light diffusion in water impacting the organism activities (Salvadori *et.al.*, 2014). Sharma and Malaviya, (2016) tested for chromium resistant ascomycetes fungi *(Cladosporeum perangustum and Penicillium commune*) isolated from tannery wastewater. These fungi were used for remediation of tannery wastewater. *Paecilomyces lilacinus* and *Fusarium equiseti* were used for the remediation purpose. Nylon mesh was used to immobilise fungal consortia in a bioreactor where results were promising. These fungi consortia were able to remove 82% of chemical oxygen demand, 86% colour, and 100% chromium (VI) and 92% total lead in 5 days. These treated wastewaters were then tried in wheat crop which showed around 50% germination as compared to untreated wastewater.

Industries particularly electroplating, leather, tannery effluents contains large amount of heavy metal. Fungi can remove these from wastewater through bioaccumulation and biosorption. Joshi *et.al.* (2011) isolated some fungi namely *Phanerochaete chrysosporium, Aspegillus awamori, Aspergillus flavus, Trichoderma virid* from sewage and industrial effluents. Most of these fungi were able to tolerate 400 ppm of heavy metals namely lead, chromium, cadmium and nickel. Results showed that lead, cadmium, chromium and nickel showed bioaccumulation of 60 ppm, 16ppm,0.6 ppm and 0.6 ppm respectively by Pb3 (*Aspergillus terreus*), *Trichoderma viride, Cr8 (Trichoderma longibrachiatum*), and *isolate Ni27 (A. niger)* respectively, which proves the bioremediation capacity of these fungal strains in removal of heavy metals from industrial effluents.

Macrophytes are another group of aquatic system which have the potential for remediation of wastewater. Now a days with increasing load of nutrients growth of macrophytes is massive in the water system. These plants helps in stabilising surface of water, provides physical filtration for water. It also provides allows oxygen transfer which enhances degradation of organics in wastewater (Lone *et.al.*, 2014). In this regard to test the efficacy of three macrophytes viz. water lettuce, water hyacinth and duckweed were used which were grown locally in the Taxila area of Pakistan (Shah *et.al.*, 2014). These were evaluated in terms of biological oxygen demand, chemical oxygen demand, nitrogen and phosphorous. After 10 days of retention of wastewater with these macrophytes it was tested for their removal efficiency. Water hyacinth showed 50%, 47%, 41% and 19% removal of BOD, COD, N and P respectively. Duckweed removed 33% BOD, 27% COD, 18% N and 15% P. Similarly, water lettuce was able to reduce BOD, COD, N and P by 33%, 26%, 18% and 15% respectively (Shah *et.al.*, 2014). This shows that macrophytes are not only weeds for aquatic ecosystem but at the same time they can do appreciable remediation from wastewater as well. Thus we can say that not only plants but different other microorganism also play a crucial in bioremediation of wastewater which needs to be exploited at commercial scale.

WASTEWATER REUSE IN AGRICULTURE

When we talk of wastewater reuse it can be (i) direct or indirect use- Direct use refers to the use of wastewater from source (municipal/sewer/ industrial effluents) directly. Indirect use refers to the use of water in which wastewater is being discharged like river or lake water. In the latter case wastewater, which is being used in diluted form where farmers may do not know about the use of wastewater in its irrigation (ii) Treatment level of wastewater: It determines the condition/quality of wastewater. Now this treatment level can be either untreated, treated or reclaimed wastewater (requires additional treatment to meet the desired standard of wastewater for use) and (iii) its intended or unintended use: whether farmers use the wastewater knowingly or unknowingly in agriculture. (Jeong *et.al.*, 2016). The above methods for irrigation is being followed in developed countries where the regulatory measures are followed strictly. In India scenario is different, as infrastructure for collection and treatment is inadequate, most of the wastewater flows into water system directly. As discussed, earlier use of this water is round the year with some nutritional benefits farmers use this in irrigation (Saldias *et.al.*, 2015). Although this is beneficial in terms of water availability but it poses health risk to the farmers, users, soil and overall ecosystem of that place. Therefore, one thing is institutional focus on this issue and essential regulatory framework to deal with wastewater and use this wastewater in agriculture in safer ways. As we all accept that wastewater irrigation can no longer be ignored or stopped with increasing water scarcity. Therefore, going for bioremediation measures can help to lessen the burden of wastewater treatment system and can decentralise it (Saldias *et.al.*, 2015).

CONCLUSION

The agricultural sector is the major user of freshwater resources and in future with increasing water scarcity major chunk of pressure will fall upon this sector only. Therefore, we need to take precautions and a step forward to use the wastewater as irrigation source. It is desirable to utilise the wastewater safely to minimise any ill health effect on soil as well as humans. Therefore, bioremediation should be considered as a feasible and futuristic technology for safe use of wastewater in agriculture. Irrigation of non-food crops is a much safer option which is already in practice at many places and its wings are extending in horticultural crops as well. However further research is required to validate the advantages of bioremediation process for cleaning and make water safe for irrigation with international standards. It's high time that we turn this practice in planned and controlled manner for sustainable agriculture with sustainable ecosystem.

REFERENCES

Abdullahi, M.S. (2015). Soil Contamination, Remediation and Plants: Prospects and Challenges. Soil Remediation and Plants; Khalid, RH, Muhammad, S., Munir, O., Ahmet, RM, Eds, 525.

Adel Zayed, Elizabeth Pilon-Smits, Mark deSouza, Zhi-Qing Lin, and Norman Terry. Chapter 4- Remediation of Selenium-Polluted Soils and Waters by Phytovolatilization; Edited Book Phytoremediation of Contaminated Soil and Water by Terry, N., & Banuelos, G.S. (1999). CRC Press.

Akpor, O.B., Otohinoyi, D.A., Olaolu, D.T., & Aderiye, B.I. (2014). Pollutants in Wastewater Effluents: Impacts and Remediation Processes. International Journal of Environmental Research and Earth Science, 3(3), 050-059.

Azubuike, C.C., Chikere, C.B., & Okpokwasili, G.C. (2016). Bioremediation Techniques–classification based on site of Application: Principles, Advantages, Limitations and Prospects. World Journal of Microbiology and Biotechnology, 32(11), 180.

Banerjee, A. (2016). Wastewater use for Agriculture in India: A Background Review. Wastewater Use for Agriculture in India, 1-12.

Beans, C. (2017). Core Concept: Phytoremediation Advances in the Lab but Lags in the Field. Proceedings of the National Academy of Sciences, 114(29), 7475-7477.

Bishnoi, N.R. and Garima (2005). Fungus-an Alternative for Bioremediation of Heavy Metal Containing Wastewater: A Review. Journal of Scientific and Industrial Research, 64, 93-100.

Chaidez, C., Soto, M., & Jiménez, M. (2014). Water: Waste, Recycling and Irrigation in Fresh Produce Processing. In Global Safety of Fresh Produce (pp. 119-132). Woodhead Publishing.

CPCB BULLETIN VOL. I, JULY 2016, Updated on December 6th, 2016.

Dhir B (2013). Phytoremediation: Role of Aquatic Plants in Environmental Clean-Up. Springer.

Dushenkov, V., Kumar, P.N., Motto, H., & Raskin, I. (1995). Rhizofiltration: The use of Plants to remove Heavy Metals from Aqueous Streams. Environmental Science & Technology, 29(5), 1239-1245.

Elias, S.H., Mohamed, M., Nor-Anuar, A., Muda, K., Hassan, M.A.H.M., Othman, M.N., & Chelliapan, S. (2014). Ceramic Industry Wastewater Treatment by Rhizofiltration System-application of Water Hyacinth Bioremediation. The IIOAB Journal, 5(1), 6.

Falconer, I.R., & Humpage, A.R. (2005). Health Risk Assessment of Cyanobacterial (blue-green algal) Toxins in Drinking Water. International Journal of Environmental Research and Public Health, 2(1), 43-50.

Farraji, H. (2014). Wastewater Treatment by Phytoremediation methods. Wastewater Engineering: Advanced Wastewater Treatment Systems, 194.

Favas, P.J., Pratas, J., Varun, M., D'Souza, R., & Paul, M. S. (2014). Phytoremediation of Soils Contaminated with Metals and Metalloids at Mining Areas: Potential of Native Flora. Environmental Risk Assessment of Soil Contamination, 3, 485-516.

Goel, M., Chovelon, J.M., Ferronato, C., Bayard, R., & Sreekrishnan, T.R. (2010). The Remediation of Wastewater Containing 4-chlorophenol using Integrated Photocatalytic and Biological Treatment. Journal of Photochemistry and Photobiology B: Biology, 98(1), 1-6.

Gupta, V.K., & Ali, I. (2004). Removal of Lead and Chromium from Wastewater using Bagasse Fly Ash—a Sugar Industry Waste. Journal of Colloid and Interface Science, 271(2), 321-328.

Hussain, I., Raschid, L., Hanjra, M.A., Marikar, F., & Van Der Hoek, W. (2002). Wastewater use in Agriculture: Review of Impacts and Methodological issues in Valuing Impacts (Vol. 37). IWMI

Jeong, H., Seong, C., Jang, T., & Park, S. (2016). Classification of Wastewater reuse for Agriculture: A Case Study in South Korea. Irrigation and Drainage, 65, 76-85.

Joshi, P.K., Swarup, A., Maheshwari, S., Kumar, R., & Singh, N. (2011). Bioremediation of Heavy Metals in Liquid Media through Fungi Isolated from contaminated Sources. Indian Journal of Microbiology, 51(4), 482-487.

Koptsik, G.N. (2014). Problems and Prospects Concerning the Phytoremediation of Heavy Metal Polluted Soils: A Review. Eurasian Soil Science, 47(9), 923-939.

Limmer, M., & Burken, J. (2016). Phytovolatilization of Organic Contaminants. Environmental Science & Technology, 50(13), 6632-6643.

Lone, P.A., Bhardwaj, A.K., & Shah, K.W. (2014). Macrophytes as Powerful Natural Tools for Water Quality Improvement. Research Journal of Botany, 9(2), 24-30.

Mahapatra, D.M., Chanakya, H.N., & Ramachandra, T.V. (2014). Bioremediation and Lipid Synthesis through Mixotrophic Algal Consortia in Municipal Wastewater. Bioresource Technology, 168, 142-150.

Martínez-Prado, A., Pérez-López, M., Pinto-Espinoza, J., Gurrola-Nevarez, B., Osorio-Rodríguez, A. (2011): Biorremediación de suelo contaminado con hidrocarburos empleando lodos residuales como fuente alterna de nutrientes. – Revista Internacional de Contaminación Ambiental 27(3): 241-252.

Mateo-Sagasta, J., Medlicott, K., Qadir, M., Raschid-Sally, L., & Drechsel, P. (2013). Proceedings of the UN-water project on the Safe use of Wastewater in Agriculture.

Megharaj, M., Ramakrishnan, B., Venkateswarlu, K., Sethunathan, N., & Naidu, R. (2011). Bioremediation Approaches for Organic Pollutants: A Critical Perspective. Environment O International, 37(8), 1362-1375.

Mirza, N., Mahmood, Q., Pervez, A., Ahmad, R., Farooq, R., Shah, M.M., & Azim, M.R. (2010). Phytoremediation Potential of Arundo donax in Arsenic-contaminated Synthetic Wastewater. Bioresource Technology, 101(15), 5815-5819.

Monferrán, M.V., M.L. Pignata, D.A. Wunderlin. 2012. Enhanced Phytoextraction of Chromium by the Aquatic Macrophyte Potamogeton pusillus in Presence of Copper. Environmental Pollution 161: 15-22.

Mora-Ravelo, S.G., Alarcon, A., Rocandio-Rodriguez, M., & Vanoye-Eligio, V. (2017). Bioremediation of Wastewater for Reutilization in Agricultural Systems: A Review. Applied Ecology and Environmental Research, 15(1), 33-50.

Muradov, N., Taha, M., Miranda, A.F., Wrede, D., Kadali, K., Gujar, A., ... & Mouradov, A. (2015). Fungal-assisted Algal Flocculation: Application in Wastewater Treatment and Biofuel Production. Biotechnology for Biofuels, 8(1), 24.

Nhat, P.V.H., Ngo, H.H., Guo, W.S., Chang, S.W., Nguyen, D.D., Nguyen, P.D., Bui, X.D., Zhang, X.B & Guo, J.B. (2018). Can algae-based Technologies be an Affordable Green Process for Biofuel Production and Wastewater Remediation? Bioresource Technology, 256, 491-501.

OB, A., & Muchie, M. (2010). Remediation of Heavy Metals in Drinking Water and Wastewater Treatment Systems: Processes and Applications.

Rachana Dubey and Subhasis Swain. Wastewater use in Agriculture: Issues and Prospects. Agriculture & Food: e- Newsletter Volume 1, Issue 10, 2019.

Raychaudhuri, S., Raychaudhuri, M., Rautaray, S.K., Parida, S., & Kumar, A. (2017). Urban Wastewater–A Potential Irrigation source for Summer Paddy (Oryza sativa L.) in India.

Rengaraj, S., Moon, S.H., Sivabalan, R., Arabindoo, B., & Murugesan, V. (2002). Agricultural Solid Waste for the Removal of Organics: Adsorption of Phenol from Water and Wastewater by Palm Seed Coat Activated Carbon. Waste Management, 22(5), 543-548.

Saldías, C., Speelman, S., Amerasinghe, P., & Van Huylenbroeck, G. (2015). Institutional and Policy Analysis of Wastewater (re) use for Agriculture: Case Study Hyderabad, India. Water Science and Technology, 72(2), 322-331.

Salvadori, M.R., Ando, R.A., Oller Do Nascimento, C.A., & Correa, B. (2014). Bioremediation from Wastewater and Extracellular Synthesis of Copper Nanoparticles by the Fungus Trichoderma koningiopsis. Journal of Environmental Science and Health, Part A, 49(11), 1286-1295.

Sekabira, K., Oryem–Origa, H., Mutumba, G., Kakudidi, E., & Basamba, T.A. (2011). Heavy Metal Phytoremediation by Commelina benghalensis (L) and Cynodon dactylon (L) Growing in Urban Stream Sediments.

Shah, M., Hashmi, H.N., Ali, A., & Ghumman, A.R. (2014). Performance Assessment of Aquatic Macrophytes for Treatment of Municipal Wastewater. Journal of Environmental Health Science and Engineering, 12(1), 106.

Sharma, S., & Malaviya, P. (2016). Bioremediation of Tannery Wastewater by Chromium Resistant Novel Fungal Consortium. Ecological Engineering, 91, 419-425.

Stottmeister, U., Wießner, A., Kuschk, P., Kappelmeyer, U., Kästner, M., Bederski, O., ... & Moormann, H. (2003). Effects of Plants and Microorganisms in constructed Wetlands for Wastewater Treatment. Biotechnology Advances, 22(1-2), 93-117.

Trovaslet, M., Enaud, E., Guiavarc'h, Y., Corbisier, A.M., & Vanhulle, S. (2007). Potential of a Pycnoporus Sanguineus laccase in Bioremediation of Wastewater and Kinetic Activation in the Presence of an Anthraquinonic Acid Dye. Enzyme and microbial technology, 41(3), 368-376.

World Bank. 2019. From Waste to Resource: Shifting Paradigms for Smarter Wastewater Interventions in Latin America and the Caribbean (English). Washington, D.C.: World Bank Group.

Yadav, B.K., Siebel, M.A., & van Bruggen, J.J. (2011). Rhizofiltration of a Heavy Metal (Lead) Containing Wastewater using the Wetland Plant Carex pendula. CLEAN–Soil, Air, Water, 39(5), 467-474.

Ying, G.G. (2018). Ecological Risk Assessment of Pesticides used in Agriculture. In Integrated Analytical Approaches for Pesticide Management (pp. 67-79). Academic Press.

10

Solid Wastes and their Sustainable Management Practices

INTRODUCTION

Solid waste is every type of solid substance which arises from human and other organisms and considered as unwanted. Solid wastes can be organic or inorganic fractions and generally do not carry any value to any organism. Wastes can be kitchen refuse, packaging, clippings, cloth, bottles, paper, cans, and dry batteries. There are different types of solid wastes on the basis of biodegradability, inertness, e-wastes, composites and domestic. All these wastes are generated from industrial processes and domestic activities (Kumar *et.al.*, 2018).

Expanding population, growing economies and fast urbanization has incredibly accelerated the metropolitan waste generation rate in developing nations (Guerrero *et.al.*, 2013). Cities typically are responsible for waste generation (Burnley, 2007; Sujauddin *et.al.*, 2008). Solid waste is one of the important byproducts of urban lifestyle, which is growing faster due to rapid urbanization. In the last 1 year, the world population increased from 2.9 to 3 billion, but waste generation increased from 0.68 to 1.3 billion tons, and per capita generation increased from 0.64 to 1.2 kg/day, which become almost double within 10 years. A prediction was made on the basis of increasing solid waste generation; about 4.3 of urban population will generate 1.42 kg/capita/day of municipal solid waste by 2025. However, per capita solid waste generation varied in different countries and different cities within a country (Mian *et.al.*, 2017). There are different associated risks of solid wastes and their treatment technologies. Like leachates in landfill sites cause soil and groundwater pollution, gaseous emissions from combustion, incineration, pyrolysis and waste to energy processes cause air pollution and climate change, solid waste smell and its presence in any area creates nuisance (De and Debnath, 2016).

SOLID WASTES, TYPES, AND SOURCES

There are different types of solid waste that are released from different sources and they are described briefly in the following:

(a) Biodegradable waste

This waste type include any waste organic material which can be degraded into carbon dioxide, water, methane or simple organic molecules by micro-organisms and other living things. These wastes are decomposed by composting, aerobic and in-aerobic digestion. These wastes are decomposed by the above processes domestically as well as commercially with the purposes of reduction of waste volumes with the aim to reduce harm to human health and impact on the environment and production of useful products and use them wherever possible. It is important to choose correctly the composition of various biodegradable wastes and ensure proper temperature regime (Kliopova *et.al.*, 2019).

Biodegradable waste is commonly damped, combusted or buried into the soil. As the biodegradation rate of organic wastes is low, and also leads to the emission of gas which cannot be captures and contribute to the greenhouse effect. The amount of gasses emitted through this process is estimated about 30% of the global methane emissions (Nowicki *et.al.*, 2016). To control the gaseous emissions from degradation of biodegradable wastes, production of activated carbon adsorbents from this type of waste has become a very interesting alternative to its combustion, recycling or composting (Biedenbach *et.al.*, 2015). Activated carbon act as efficient adsorbents used for purification of gases and liquids because they have large surface area and micro-porous structure, ensuring very good sorption capacity towards a wide range of gasses and other substances. It also advantage that activated carbon also produced from any waste substance containing carbon in it. Therefore, taking into regard the high cost of activated carbon production from fossil coals along with the economic and ecological aspects, recently much attention has been paid to the use of organic waste for this purpose. The post-agricultural production waste is easily available, renewable and inexpensive, that is why the activated carbons obtained from this type of waste have been subjected to adsorption tests from gas and liquid phases.

(b) Recyclable

Any waste material which can be used again for beneficial purpose is often called as Recyclable waste. It is the method of renovating waste materials into new and useful materials and objects or reusing them as a whole. It is best alternative to conventional waste disposal method as it saves natural resource materials and help in lowering greenhouse gasses. It can prevent the wastage of potentially useful resources and materials, and reduce the consumption of fresh raw materials, thereby reducing energy usage, air pollution (from incineration), and water pollution (from landfilling). Recycling is a major constituent of modern waste reduction strategy of 3Rs (Reduce, Reuse, and Recycle). Thus, it aims at environmental sustainability by substituting raw material inputs. International Standardization Organization also set some standards related to recycling such as ISO 15270:2008 for plastics waste and ISO 14001:2015 for environmental management control of recycling practice (Hohenthal *et.al.*, 2019; Roychoudhuri and Debnath, 2020).

Materials which can be recycled include glass, paper, cardboard, metal, plastic, tires, batteries, and electronic equipments. These materials are either delivered to recycling center and sorted, cleaned, and reprocessed into new materials destined for manufacturing new products. Due to rapid economic growth and population increase, problems of environmental pollution, climate change, and resource depletion have become increasingly serious in the world. Recyclable waste recycling is becoming one of the key approaches to simultaneously respond to the above issues, and governments have begun to regulate and promote source separation and urban waste recycling in recent years. There are three main types of recycling: primary, secondary, and tertiary. In primary recycling, wastes are recycled into same things i.e. like paper into more paper. In secondary recycling process, wastes are modified to use for any-other way i.e. cutting plastic bottle to use it in garden, and tertiary recycling include complete transformation of the waste into a new product by chemical processes, burning or any-other process (Zhang *et.al.*, 2016; Zhao *et.al.*, 2018; Zink *et.al.*, 2018; Shi *et.al.*, 2019).

(c) Inert

Any type of waste which cannot be decomposed biologically or chemically reactive and does not decomposed. It is the major part of the waste and covers up to 50% of the total generated wastes which poses a challenge of its management. It also has major contribution in affecting human health and the environment as it contains many types of secondary pollutants trapped in it. Inert wastes include demolition waste, plastic, rubber, ceramic and debris etc. Its management only include its recycling as filling and base material for floors, concrete aggregate, building material and tiles, etc. (Mendoza *et.al.*, 2017; Tatsuno *et.al.*, 2019).

Many Governments has set up storage facilities for inert waste management i.e. French Ministry of Environment workgroup defined three types of storage facilities according to the nature of the inert waste viz:

1. Type F facility stores plaster, asbestos-cement and certain inert industrial wastes.
2. Type G facility stores demolition waste mixed with certain industrial wastes.
3. Type H facility stores non-polluted soil from works and sorted demolition wastes and technically separable plaster certain industrial wastes (Emmanuel *et.al.*, 2002).

(d) E-waste

It is electronic waste of discarded electrical devices. Used electronics are refurbished, reuse, resale, or metals used in their mother and circuit boards are recovered for reuse in new equipments. Casual management of e-waste in developing countries can lead to environmental pollution and adverse human health effects as electronic scrap components such as CPUs contain potentially harmful materials such as lead, cadmium, beryllium, or brominated flame retardants. Recycling and disposal of e-waste may involve significant risk to the health of workers and their communities. Electronic Equipment Directive has classified e-waste into ten categories: Large household appliances (including cooling and freezing equipments), small household appliances (computers), consumer electronics (television), lamps, toys, tools and medical devices, monitoring and control instruments, and Automatic dispensers. On the other hand, some categorize e-wastes into six categories, namely: (1) Temperature exchange equipment (air conditioners, freezers), (2) Screen and monitors, (3) Lamps, (4) Large equipment (washing machines, electric stoves), (5) Small equipment (microwave, electric shaver), and (6) Small IT and telecommunication equipment (mobile phones, printers). Products in each category vary in longevity profile, impact, and collection methods, among other differences (Ilankoon *et.al.*, 2018; Narbón-Perpiñá and Prior, 2020). In 2016, Asia imported significant amount of the most extensive volume of e-waste (18.2 Mt), accompanied by Europe (12.3 Mt), America (11.3 Mt), Africa (2.2 Mt), and Oceania (0.7 Mt). The smallest in terms of total e-waste made, Oceania was the largest generator of e-waste per citizen (17.3 kg), with hardly 6% of e-waste gathered and recycled. Europe is the second largest e-waste generator per citizen with an average of 16.6 kg. America generates 11.6 kg and solicits only 17% of the e-waste caused in the provinces, which is commensurate to the assortment count in Asia (15%) (Kumar *et.al.*, 2017; Dutta and Goel, 2017).

(e) Composite

Composite is aggregate of two or more materials. This type of waste creates tons of problems as it is hard to deal with multiple type of wastes at a time. To date, there has been no successful attempt to recycle the composite materials and hence the waste is increasing day by day. Composite waste include liquid waste, organic waste, solid and recyclable rubbish, and hazardous waste.

Composite recycling has been an issue in research over the last decade and some methods were proposed: pyrolysis, oxidation in a fluidized bed, and chemical recycling. Among them, pyrolysis is currently the only process with commercial scale implementations (Hu *et.al.*, 2017; Li *et.al.*, 2017).

(f) Domestic

Domestic waste means any no putrescible waste, consisting of organic and in-organic materials, such as paper, cardboard, yard clippings, wood, or similar materials, generated in a dwelling, including the real property upon which it is situated, containing four living units or less. Household waste, also known as domestic waste or residential waste, is disposable materials generated by households. This waste can be comprised of hazardous and non-hazardous waste. Non-hazardous waste can include food scraps, paper, bottles, etc. which can be recycled or composted (Mian *et.al.*, 2017). Domestic waste is waste that is generated as a result of the ordinary day-to-day use of a domestic premise and is either: collected by or on behalf of a local government as part of a waste collection and disposal system. During the last decade, a growing interest in recycling of domestic waste has emerged, and action plans to increase the recycling of domestic waste have been agreed by many governments. The implementation of new systems and equipment for the collection of domestic waste has been separated at the source. However, only limited information exists on possible occupational health problems related to such new systems. Occupational accidents are very frequent among waste collectors. Based on current knowledge, it appears that the risk factors should be considered as an integrated entity, i.e. technical factors (poor accessibility to the waste, design of equipment) may act in concert with high working rate, visual fatigue due to poor illumination and perhaps muscle fatigue due to high workload (Ihedioha *et.al.*, 2017).

SOLID WASTE GENERATION AND ASSOCIATED ENVIRONMENTAL RISKS

Around the world, waste generation rates are rising. In 2016, 2.01 billion tons of solid waste was generated with the rate of 0.74 kg/person/ day. It is estimated that annual waste generation will be increased up to 70% with rapid increase in population in 2050. In Pakistan, 5.5 million USD are invested in a composting project in Lahore. Due to this facility, 150,000 tons of carbon dioxide equivalents are reduced, and compost production increased from 300 to 1000 tons/day (World Bank, 2019). Solid waste is generated from 0.283 to 0.612 kg/capita/day in Pakistan and its growth rate is 2.4%/year (Nintendo *et.al.*, 2019). The following are the main problems regarding solid waste management in Pakistan:

- No existence of waste collection system.
- Waste is dumped or thrown into the streets.
- Wastes are not categorized properly.
- No existence of enough sanitary landfill sites.
- No awareness among citizens about waste management and associated environmental risks.

These all factors contributes in spreading human health diseases and environmental pollution.

(g) Health Hazards

There are numerous environmental and human health impacts associated with solid wastes as described:

- Gasses originated from wastes cause skin and eye infections.
- Dust generated during wastes handling cause breathing problems.
- Bees and flies breed on rotting garbage and spread diseases like diarrhea, dysentery, typhoid, hepatitis and cholera.
- Mosquitoes also breed on waste piles and transmit malaria and yellow fever.
- Dogs, cats and rats dwelling on waste spread diseases including plague and flea born fever.
- Waste collectors face different diseases like intestinal, parasitic and skin diseases (Lal *et.al.*, 2016; Ihedioha *et.al.*, 2017; Mustafa *et.al.*, 2017).

SOLID WASTES MANAGEMENT TECHNOLOGIES AND THEIR TYPES

Solid waste management is regarded as a centralized process and this is mostly based on the economic status of countries (Srivastava *et.al.*, 2014). The first step in solid waste management is making strategy and its monitoring. The modern waste management strategies are expensive and mostly used by developed countries (Hassan *et.al.*, 2016). The following solid wastes management technologies are used generally and divided into two types i.e., ancient and modern solid waste management technologies.

(h) Ancient

The old solid waste management technologies include recycling, open burning, dumping into seas and rivers, and plowing crop residues directly into the fields.

(i) Recycling

One of the most sustainable means of solid waste management is recycling, as stated in the literature. This process does not adversely affect human health, social conditions, and the environment. This sustained technique does not diminish the quality of life due to poor economic conditions (Troschinetz & Mihelcic, 2009). There is a clear difference between the research conducted on recycling in developed countries as compared to the developing countries. The recycling facilities in the developed countries are heavily industrialized that are produced as a result of the daily life activities of a citizen. The technical applications are focused on the developed countries, including tools and models (Daskalopoulos *et.al.*, 1998). In developing countries, the focus is on the research on recycling for direct factors, practical, and elements related to waste management. The competency is the best indicator actual behavior of society towards the different strategies of solid waste management. If the concept and the proper way to recycle the waste is understood by any community, it is easier to persuade them to adopt it (Corral-Verdugo, 1997).

The plastic has contributed a lot in water and land pollution. The problem with it is its non-degradability and not degraded well. The primary recycling is employed to recycle plastic. First cycling is the reintroduction of scrap, single-use plastic edges, and its parts to the extrusion cycle to make products like the plastic. A material from scrap plastic has a similar feature to the original ones. This type of recycling must be only done with semi-clean scrap, that's why it is not mostly selected by the recyclers. A significant number of our daily life products are produced by recycling like pipes, door profiles, windows, grocery shoppers, and blinds (Al-Salem *et.al.*, 2009). There is another type of recycling known as chemical recycling. This is feasible for those heterogeneous and contaminated waste materials for those which cannot be separated, or their separation is economically not suitable. This is one of the best ways to protect the environment from the plastics. It may be done in closed-loop recycling or open-loop recycling based on the products made from different types of plastics. In closed-loop recycling, the same products are manufactured from which they were made. It may be made entirely from recycled products or a mixture of them. The PET packaging products are its example. In open-loop, recycled plastics are utilized for different products than the one they were made from (Ragaert *et.al.*, 2017).

(ii) Open Burning

Open burning is one of the most common strategies to manage solid waste in the developing countries of the world. This is mostly done in open places. The masses are not aware of its ill effects on humans. The people find it the easiest way to get rid of solid waste. The problem of waste has been aggravated by an increase in solid waste in Thailand. This problem was mainly due to change in client behavior, growth in population, inadequate facilities to tackle waste, and economic expansion. These are the main reasons causing every house to adopt their own techniques in the elimination of this waste. Open burning is one of the main strategies adopted by many people (Pansuk *et.al.*, 2018).

One of the main concerns with open burning is its effects on the environment and human health. There are a lot of emissions from open burning, which are very toxic to human health. The open burning has a direct role in air pollution and climate change due to greenhouse gases from solid waste due to open burning. For example, in Thailand, 4.09 kilo tones/year solid waste is burnt by open burning and emit 0.61 kilo tones of nitrous oxide, 499 kilo tones carbon dioxide, and 26 kilo tones/year of methane in 2016. Sulfur dioxide, carbon monoxide, and many other air pollutants are added in the environment by open burning in Thailand (Pansuk *et.al.*, 2018).

(iii) Dumping into Seas and Rivers

It is a common practice to dump solid waste into the rivers and seas. This has played havoc for the marine and freshwater ecosystems. There is a significant concern about the pollutants being added in these systems by the solid waste. This is mostly seen in developing countries where the authorities do not have any mechanism to check the composition of solid waste. The only source for this kind of dumping is the anthropogenic activities. The huge population growth along the seas and rivers have resulted in increased spill in them. In a short-term period, the degradation of these activities has reached the health of the population across the coastal areas. The pollutants included in them are heavy metals, hydrocarbons from oil, nitrate and phosphates, fertilizers, pesticides, and insecticides. Eutrophication is caused by the nutrients in the waters and estuaries near the shore. In the river, the ecosystem is maintained by the steady discharge of the water from the river with that of salty water of the sea in the estuary. The sediment load from the river is balanced by ocean erosion in the delta and its adjacent coastal areas. Due to the industrial zones, many persistent organic pollutants are added in the solid waste. This solid waste, when dumped in the seas or rivers, directly affects the life in the water systems. The other significant source of pollutants in the seas and rivers is sewage waste. The solid waste, along with the sewage sludge, is also very damaging to the sea and river life. The sandstorms are one of the unique ways to pollute water systems. The pollutants are carried by the strong winds into the river or the sea (Daoji & Daler, 2004).

The solid waste being dumped in the rivers also composed of papers, files, bottles, cans, bags, cigarette packaging, and many other products. Most of the waste from the construction is thrown in nearby water reservoirs. The primary mode of transmission of solid waste in rivers, canals, streams, and seas is the drainage system of different cities. It is also observed that they may get stuck in the plantings along the beaches. Most of it is dumped in rivers and seas. The drainage system is also blocked by the solid waste leading to the more production of sediments due to absence of protection of surfaces, and the natural discharge is maximized, the degradation of water quality and the entrance of pollutants in the food chain (Salles *et.al.*, 2012).

(iv) Ploughing in the Fields

Ploughing in the fields is related to waste management in rural areas. The ploughing is the physical manipulation of soil in the field. Firstly, it is essential to note the type of solid waste being added in the fields. It may be crop residues or any chemical wastes. Crop residues or any organic substance buried in the fields by ploughing these in soils. The wastes added in soils should be degradable necessarily. Ploughing and tillage is done in the fields after crop harvesting. It is also done by collecting wastes from other areas and ploughing in fields. Many farmers in the developing countries also burn the crop stubbles in fields that is the primary cause of smog in these areas. The major drawback of using ploughing is that they mostly take out heavy objects from the field (Abdoli *et.al.*, 2008).

(v) Modern

Many modern strategies are being applied to deal with solid waste. These technologies are mostly used in the developed countries of the world. The advanced waste management strategies are presented in fig. 1 and are discussed below;

(vi) 3Rs

The 3Rs (Reduce, Reuse, and Recycle) strategy of waste management is widely used in developing countries. It is the strategy that is sustainable and acceptable in society. The developed countries are focusing on the development of sustainable solid waste management. This is one of the best ways to conserve the environment. But this is not adopted by the developing countries due to their expensive instrumentation and installation. There are many concerns in the developing world on which they focus. 3Rs are way more sophisticated systems as compared to ancient strategies. First, the awareness of a reduction in solid waste is being created in developed countries. People are encouraged to use of disposable things. Many policies are made to address the problem of reduction in solid waste. There are many analyses being done by the researchers of this field. The reduction policy is made by keeping in view the waste generated from a single household to the factory. The economic advantage of reducing waste may be an essential point to raise the importance of this issue in the world. Reusing has been used for many years in the developed world. The reusing must be done such that there is minimal use of the physical and chemical modifications. There are a number of economic, environmental, and social advantages of reuse. The reusing of certain materials must be done under the proper conditions because they may require special requirements for it. Recycling of the materials is the last approach in 3Rs. This is the most utilized technique for solid waste treatment being applied in many developing countries (Mena *et.al.*, 2011). Following are the benefits of using 3Rs:

- The developing countries can attract foreign investment by emission reduction credits.
- The organic gas can be produced by adopting these methods, which can be used for energy production purposes.
- The power generation can be efficiently done.
- It is eco-friendly approach and replenishes the nutrients in the soil.
- Reduced greenhouse gas emissions.
- These approaches may increase the GDP of the country by creating new jobs (Chowdhury *et.al.*, 2014).

(vii) Composting

As the sizes of the cities and urban areas are increasing the solid waste production is also growing. This has led to the development of modern strategies. Composting is one of the most critical strategy to tackle waste. The organic waste produced by the landfills can be made into such a product that may be used to enhance agricultural productivity. The volume of the waste is considerably reduced by composting. It is a biological process that involves the conversion of much heterogeneous organic waste into organic matter rich substances under the controlled conditions of oxygen, moisture, and temperature along with the microbial population. The organic substances such as vegetables, leaves, fruits, manure, sludge, and other waste are converted by microorganisms into humus like materials. These materials can be used as an organic fertilizer in the fields. Fungi, bacteria, and actinomycetes are the decomposers employed in the process of composting. The basic concept of composting is the microbial decomposition of organic substances. The decomposers release enzymes which convert complex materials into simpler ones. The composting, done in the presence of oxygen is called aerobic and the composting done in the absence of oxygen is called anaerobic composting. Vermicomposting, in-vessel composting, biomineralization, open windrows, controlled microbial composting and aerated static pile composting are other composting systems which are employed to convert wastes into useful soil fertility enhancing products (Atalia *et.al.*, 2015).

(viii) Landfilling

Landfilling is one of the most economical strategies for managing solid waste. This technique is often confused with open dumping. To avoid this confusion, scientists classified some conditions. The following conditions must be fulfilled by a site to be called as landfill site:

- There should be anaerobic environment.
- There should be one daily cover at least.
- There should be connected pipe system for collection of leachates.
- There should be natural ventilation facility (Hassan *et.al.*, 2000).

The second system of classification is based on operational purposes. Level (I) include controlled tipping. Level (II) has a landfill having embankment and daily covering of soil. Level (III) has a leachate recirculation system. Level (IV) contains a treatment system for leachate (Idris *et.al.*, 2004).

(ix) Incineration

It is energy producing process which is carried-out in engineered facility and employs thermal decomposition at high temperatures to destroy and reduce waste volumes. Generally, combustible wastes or wastes with significant organic contents are considered suitable for incineration. However, any solid waste which pose hazards to environment can be incinerated. Different incineration technologies have been developed for handling various types and physical forms of hazardous wastes. The significant sub-systems which may be incorporated into a solid waste incineration system are waste preparation and feeding, combustion chamber, air pollution control, and residual/ash handling facility. The selection of an appropriate system combination of these components is primarily a function of the physical and chemical properties of the waste stream or streams to be incinerated (Oppelt, 1987).

(x) Fermentation

The organic fractions of the municipal solid wastes and other biodegradable solid substrates like agricultural wastes have to be conveniently treated to reduce their environmental impact and to recover energy and material while massive disposal treatments e.g., landfill or incineration should be avoided. An obvious choice to achieve this goal is given by the anaerobic digestion and co-digestion processes for methane production. However, anaerobic fermentation processes can be used for the production of valuable products. In fact, aerobic fermentation is an effective bioprocess for the production of volatile fatty acids and other low weight organic compounds such as lactic acid and alcohols. These can used for the production of methyl and ethyl-esters to be added to gasoline because of their high octane number (between 103 and 118), as a low cost external carbon source for the production of biopolymers, like poly-hydroxy-alkanoates, for sustainment of the biological processes for nutrient removal in waste water treatment plants, still, for anaerobic fermentation with a high hydrolysis rate being the first step of the anaerobic digestion process for biogas production when treating organic wastes with a high biodegradability (Bolzonella *et.al.*, 2005).

(xi) Pyrolysis

It is one of the most efficient and environmental-friendly strategies. It also has many operational advantages over other approaches. If it is adopted at a large industrial scale, it has proven to be very economical in terms of fuel pricing. The pyrolysis is defined as a procedure in which the degradation is thermally achieved in an inert environment of long-chain organic substances either in the presence of a catalyst knows as catalytic pyrolysis or in the absence of catalysis called Thermal Pyrolysis. The long-chain complex organic compounds are converted into simpler molecules by control the flow of heat and pressure. The by-products of this procedure are known as tars. The long residence time is required to operate this process. The most common solid waste materials used in the pyrolysis are plastics. Due to the utilization of plastic, it has gained much fame in the market. About 80% of daily life plastic is composed of thermosets and thermoplastics. These are converted products like those of fossil fuels. The setup of the pyrolysis may range from a micro-industry level to a large scale. It is dependent on the type of reactors installed, and the kind of plastic added. The factors affecting the rate of pyrolysis are the pressure, temperature, type of catalyst, heat transfer limit, and residence time (Al-Salem *et.al.*, 2017).

(xii) Biomethanation

It is the process of extraction of methane gas from waste burning (Yan *et.al.*, 2019). Different types of feed-stock like rice straw and other crop residues, livestock dung and fruit and vegetable leaves remains that contain high amounts of organic material in them, are used for methane generation and biogas production (Negi *et.al.*, 2018). Anaerobic digestion is commonly used to extract methane gas from different types of wastes (Donoso-Bravo *et.al.*, 2016).

(xiii) Waste to energy/Refused derived fuel

Due to energy shortage and increased demands and rapid depletion of fossil fuels resources, researchers are doing work on cheap, reliable and sustainable sources of energy. Different solid wastes are used for energy production through burning and digestion (Kothari *et.al.*, 2010). As food is necessity of every human, the wastes produced during food production, processing and consumption. About one third of food produced globally is left as waste which allows the sustainable production of energy from the food wastes through combustion, digestion and fermentation processes (Uçkun Kiran *et.al.*, 2014). In USA, energy production from municipal solid waste management consists of recycling, composting and combustion with energy production from them (Psomopoulos *et.al.*, 2009).

(xiv) Plasma Gasification

Plasma gasification is comparatively a newer advancement in existing technologies in which solid wastes are changed to energy-filled products (Sanlisoy and Carpinlioglu, 2017). This technology is capable of providing sustainable disposal for various wastes as well as providing the energy requirements of the world (Favas *et.al.*, 2017). Different types of wastes like industrial and municipal wastes are used in this process for energy generation. This process also have the advantages of reducing the chances of soil and groundwater pollution because wastes are burned and used for energy generation. By using this technology, up to 71.8% energy recovery can be obtained from feed-stock (Messerle *et.al.*, 2016; Wang *et.al.*, 2019).

SUSTAINABLE WASTE MANAGEMENT

There is an increased concern about the wastes management whose production is increasing day by day. Increasing environmental concerns like soil and groundwater pollution, it is necessary to remove the solid wastes or use them for any purposeful use. For this, different solid waste conversion to energy technologies are being used for sustainable waste management and energy production.

(i) Agricultural Wastes

Due to increased agricultural crop residues production, their management is necessary because these are produced in huge amounts all over the world. Agricultural wastes are conventionally burned in the fields, used as fuels in homes, or incorporated in the fields after chopping by rotavators. Agricultural wastes contain different types of useful substances in them which can be used for different purposes like biochar production for use as biosorbent, carbon sequestration enhancement, biofuels production like biodiesel, and recovery of cellulose, fibers and biopolymers etc. which are used in medicine and food industry (Mostafa *et.al.*, 2018). These wastes also used as removal agents of dyes from industrial effluents. As depicted from the various experiments that up to 90% of removal efficiency of dyes from industrial effluents can be achieved (Singh *et.al.*, 2017).

Production of biofuels from agricultural wastes also helps in reduction of greenhouse gasses by reducing fossil fuels combustion and reduced emissions of different gasses when crop residues are set to fire in the fields (Wang *et.al.*, 2018; Yilmaz *et.al.*, 2018). Bio-oil production from different agricultural wastes are also practiced by pyrolysis which shows good potential to produce bio-oils from agricultural crop residues (Hawash *et.al.*, 2017).

(ii) Industrial Wastes

Due to increasing industrialization, industrial wastes generation is also increasing. This increasing waste generation polluting the soil and water pollution. To avoid the pollution, different technologies are being used for effective removal and management of these wastes. Bricks manufacturing from industrial wastes is now being used as alternate of conventional bricks (Andreola *et.al.*, 2016; Wiemes *et.al.*, 2017). By using combustion and digestion, energy is also produced from different types of industrial wastes. Electricity is produced from sugarcane bagasse, different sludges and used in the industrial as well as supplied for domestic use (Contreras-Lisperguer *et.al.*, 2018; Hassan *et.al.*, 2019). Green cements are also produced by converting industrial wastes into geopolymers and using the product as replacement of conventional cement. Geopolymers derived cement product is eco-friendly (reduction of 60% consumption and carbon emissions as compared to conventional cement production) and also has the advantage of industrial waste disposal (Zhang *et.al.*, 2017).

(iii) Domestic Wastes

Rapid urbanization has resulted in large amounts of municipal wastes generation. Increase in municipal solid wastes results in increased pollution levels in environment, which must be managed accordingly. So, there must be any effective way of municipal solid waste disposal (Polyakova *et.al.*, 2018).

Some strategies of their disposal are using them as fuel by mixing with other wastes, use them as soil conditioners and fertilizers (Tikiz and Pehlivan, 2018). These wastes are also used as biosorbents for heavy metals (Quintas *et.al.*, 2019), processing for production of composts (Jiya *et.al.*, 2019), use of different fruit peel extracts for bio-control agents (El-Gendy *et.al.*, 2016) and production of electricity (Ayodele *et.al.*, 2017).

(iv) E-Wastes

Electronic waste or E-waste is one of the growing waste streams all over the world. It posse different hazardous environmental impacts. Heavy metals in e-waste cause soil and water pollution, piles of e-wastes present a bad image of the area. In the world, 41 million tons of e-waste was produced in 2014. It is increasing with the rate of 3-5% each year. This poses a challenge to the researchers to devise a proper method to cope with this problem (Kumar *et.al.*, 2017; Tansel, 2017).

Recycling is the strategy which is being used since the ages. Recycling of e-waste is a necessity to address the pollution problems and shortage of mineral resources for electronics industry as well as to reduce the environmental pollution and human health risks (Zeng *et.al.*, 2017). Recycling and demolishing is also done to recover the precious rare earth elements like metal recovery from printed circuit boards, hard disc drives and displays (Garlapati, 2016; Isildar *et.al.*, 2018).

COST TO BENEFIT RATIOS OF DIFFERENT WASTE MANAGEMENT TECHNOLOGIES

(i) Fuel Production

Energy production from different solid wastes is now widely considered for a sustainable approach for energy production and waste disposal simultaneously. This approach is very cost-effective as feedstock is usually the wastes which are headache otherwise. Cost-benefit analysis for waste to energy was done and it was revealed that it has more benefits than fossil fuels in combination with reducing global warming potential of greenhouse potential (Wang *et.al.*, 2016). Waste cooking oil is used for energy generation for production of biodiesel. By spending 0.946 USD, we can obtain benefits of 1.298 USD (Mohammadshirazi *et.al.*, 2014; Singhabhandhu and Tezuka, 2010; Zhao *et.al.*, 2016). Landfilling and energy recovery from the wastes is a beneficial industry. It can be depicted in the study in which authors showed an estimated benefit of 1.92 million USD to 16.63 million USD earning in a single year by a single landfill site in China (Zhou *et.al.*, 2015).

(ii) Recycling

Recycling is a win-win strategy in which, used or scrap products are reused or sold to the areas where these products are needed. It has more benefits than the costs (Pickin, 2008). By recycling, different types of resources are used again and again. Developed countries send their old equipments to developing countries adopting new technology by giving old technology to developing countries is a mode of recycling e-waste. For example, old models of equipment's are sold at cheaper prices to developing countries. By adopting this method, they get rid of their e-wastes as well as earn some money by selling their e-waste (Tanskanen, 2013).

SOLUTION AND RECOMMENDATIONS

As indicated in the chapter, there are numerous ways by which solid wastes can be disposed-off in a sustainable way. Wastes to energy, pyrolysis, biomethanation, combustion, incineration and fermentation techniques are extensively used for energy and biofuels production. Generally, above mentioned technologies are thought to be useful and eco-friendly. But, there are some issues associated with these, like air pollution levels may increase near pyrolysis, incineration and combustion facilities. Gasses emissions can contribute in climate change and increase health problems in nearby areas. Some techniques require sophisticated and costly equipment and setups like Biomethanation, pyrolysis and fermentation, and some require labor to run the processes. These issues should be scientifically studied and addressed accordingly.

FUTURE RESEARCH DIRECTIONS

Sustainable solid wastes management is an innovative approach by which solid wastes are collected, treated, reused or processes for fuel and energy production. But due to the issues of air pollution in the case of combustion, pyrolysis etc., research should be done to invent or modify the ways of fuels and energy production without harming the air as it is already polluted due to excessive carbon and other greenhouse gas emissions. Landfilling cause soil and groundwater contamination by leaching of heavy metals and other contaminants. All these issues must be addressed to minimize these risks with continuous and wise use of available resources for environmental health and its improvements along with fuel and energy production.

CONCLUSION

Different types of solid wastes pose environmental threats. They cause environmental pollution by contaminating soil, water air and other biotic components. Solid wastes are of different types like agricultural wastes (crop residues, animal dung, fruit peels, thinning and pruning wastes), industrial wastes (sewage sludge, wastewater, ash, and miscellaneous solid wastes) and domestic solid wastes. Their management is of great concern in modern era. There are different approaches which are used for solid waste management like dumping into sea, landfilling, and open burning. But these management strategies are not eco-friendly and poses environmental threats. With the progress in science and technology, scientists invented various sustainable methods to cope with problems associated with solid waste management and energy shortage collectively. They devised the methods of fuel production from crop residues, sewage sludge and animal dung. They produced biogas, biodiesel, and electricity from solid wastes by processes like incineration, digestion, methanation, pyrolysis and plasma gasification etc. These methods are well studied and cost effective. Future studies are being done to assess the more advance method of energy recovery from wastes having less emission so that we can totally eradicate the climate change problems originated by use of fossil fuels.

REFERENCES

Abdoli, M., Samieifard, R., & JALILI, G.M. (2008). Rural Solid Waste Management.

Al-Salem, S., Antelava, A., Constantinou, A., Manos, G., & Dutta, A. (2017). A Review on Thermal and Catalytic Pyrolysis of Plastic Solid Waste (PSW). *Journal of Environmental Management*, 197, 177-198.

Al-Salem, S., Lettieri, P., & Baeyens, J. (2009). Recycling and Recovery Routes of Plastic Solid Waste (PSW): A Review. *Waste Management*, 29(10), 2625-2643.

Andreola, F., Barbieri, L., Lancellotti, I., Leonelli, C., & Manfredini, T. (2016). Recycling of Industrial Wastes in Ceramic Manufacturing: State of Art and Glass case Studies. *Ceramics International*, 42(12), 13333-13338.

Atalia, K., Buha, D., Bhavsar, K., & Shah, N. (2015). A Review on Composting of Municipal Solid Waste. *Journal of Environmental Science, Toxicology and Food Technology*, 9(5), 20-29.

Ayodele, T., Ogunjuyigbe, A., & Alao, M. (2017). Life Cycle Assessment of Waste-to-energy (WtE) Technologies for Electricity Generation using Municipal Solid Waste in Nigeria. *Applied Energy*, 201, 200-218.

Biedenbach, D.J., Kazmierczak, K., Bouchillon, S.K., Sahm, D.F., & Bradford, P.A. (2015). In vitro Activity of Aztreonam-avibactam against a Global Collection of Gram-negative Pathogens from 2012 and 2013. *Antimicrobial Agents and Chemotherapy*, 59(7), 4239-4248.

Bolzonella, D., Fatone, F., Pavan, P., & Cecchi, F. (2005). Anaerobic Fermentation of Organic Municipal Solid Wastes for the Production of Soluble Organic Compounds. *Industrial & Engineering Chemistry Research*, 44(10), 3412-3418.

Burnley, S.J. (2007). A Review of Municipal Solid Waste Composition in the United Kingdom. *Waste Management*, 27(10), 1274-1285.

Chowdhury, A.H., Mohammad, N., Haque, M.R.U., & Hossain, T. (2014). Developing 3Rs (Reduce, Reuse and Recycle) Strategy for Waste Management in the Urban Areas of Bangladesh: Socioeconomic and Climate Adoption Mitigation Option. *IOSR Journal of Environmental Science, Toxicology and Food Technology (IOSR-JESTFT)*, 8(5), 9-18.

Contreras-Lisperguer, R., Batuecas, E., Mayo, C., Díaz, R., Pérez, F., & Springer, C. (2018). Sustainability Assessment of Electricity Cogeneration from Sugarcane Bagasse in Jamaica. *Journal of Cleaner Production, 200*, 390-401.

Corral-Verdugo, V.C. (1997). Dual 'Realities'of Conservation Behavior: Self-Reports vs Observations of Re-use and Recycling Behaviour. *Journal of Environmental Psychology*, 17(2), 135-145.

Daoji, L., & Daler, D. (2004). Ocean Pollution from Land-based Sources: East China Sea, China. *Ambio*, 107-113.

Daskalopoulos, E., Badr, O., & Probert, S. (1998). An Integrated Approach to Municipal Solid Waste Management. *Resources, Conservation and Recycling*, 24(1), 33-50.

De, S., & Debnath, B. (2016). Prevalence of Health Hazards associated with Solid Waste Disposal-A Case Study of Kolkata, India. *Procedia Environmental Sciences*, 35, 201-208.

Donoso-Bravo, A., Ortega-Martinez, E., & Ruiz-Filippi, G. (2016). Impact of Milling, Enzyme Addition, and Steam Explosion on the Solid Waste Biomethanation of an Olive Oil Production Plant. *Bioprocess and Biosystems Engineering*, 39(2), 331-340.

Dutta, D., & Goel, S. (2017). Electronic Waste (E-Waste) Generation and Management. In *Advances in Solid and Hazardous Waste Management* (pp. 249-266). Springer, Cham.

El-Gendy, N.S., Hamdy, A., Fatthallah, N.A., & Omran, B.A. (2016). Recycling of some Domestic Wastes to Produce Green Corrosion Inhibitors and Biocides for Sulfate Reducing Bacteria. *Energy Sources, Part A: Recovery, Utilization, and Environmental Effects*, 38(24), 3722-3732.

Emmanuel, E., Perrodin, Y., Keck, G., Blanchard, J.-M., & Vermande, P. (2002). *Effects of Hospital Wastewater on Aquatic Ecosystem.* Paper Presented at the Proceedings of the XXVIII Congreso Interamericano de Ingenieria Sanitaria y Ambiental. Cancun, México.

Favas, J., Monteiro, E., & Rouboa, A. (2017). Hydrogen Production using Plasma Gasification with Steam Injection. *International Journal of Hydrogen Energy*, 42(16), 10997-11005.

Garlapati, V.K. (2016). E-waste in India and Developed Countries: Management, Recycling, Business and Biotechnological Initiatives. *Renewable and Sustainable Energy Reviews*, 54, 874-881.

Guerrero, M., Re, M., Kazimierski, L.D., Menéndez, Á.N., & Ugarelli, R. (2013). Effect of Climate change on Navigation Channel Dredging of the Parana River. *International Journal of River Basin Management*, 11(4), 439-448.

Hassan, M.N., Rahman, R.A., Chong, T.L., Zakaria, Z., & Awang, M. (2000). Waste Recycling in Malaysia: Problems and Prospects. *Waste Management and Research*, 18(4), 320-328.

Hassan, S.A., Jameel, N.G.M., & Sekeroglu, B. (2016). Smart Solid Waste Monitoring and Collection System. *International Journal*, 6(10).

Hassan, S.H., Abd el Nasser, A.Z., & Kassim, R.M. (2019). Electricity Generation from Sugarcane Molasses using Microbial Fuel Cell Technologies. *Energy*, 178, 538-543.

Hawash, S.I., Farah, J.Y., & El-Diwani, G. (2017). Pyrolysis of Agriculture Wastes for Bio-oil and Char Production. *Journal of Analytical and Applied Pyrolysis*, 124, 369-372.

Hohenthal, C., Leon, J., Dobon, A., Kujanpää, M., Meinl, G., Ringman, J., & Forsström, U. (2019). The ISO 14067 Approach to Open-loop Recycling of Paper Products: Making it Operational. *Journal of Cleaner Production*, 224, 264-274.

Hu, J., Huang, Y., Yao, Y., Pan, G., Sun, J., Zeng, X., Wong, C.-P. (2017). Polymer Composite with Improved Thermal Conductivity by Constructing a Hierarchically Ordered Three-dimensional Interconnected Network of BN. *ACS Applied Materials & Interfaces*, 9(15), 13544-13553.

Idris, A., Inanc, B., & Hassan, M.N. (2004). Overview of Waste Disposal and Landfills/dumps in Asian Countries. *Journal of Material Cycles and Waste Management*, 6(2), 104-110.

Ihedioha, J.N., Ukoha, P.O., & Ekere, N.R. (2017). Ecological and Human Health Risk Assessment of Heavy Metal Contamination in Soil of a Municipal Solid Waste Dump in Uyo, Nigeria. *Environmental Geochemistry and Health*, 39(3), 497-515.

Ilankoon, I.M.S.K., Ghorbani, Y., Chong, M.N., Herath, G., Moyo, T., & Petersen, J. (2018). E-waste in the International Context–A Review of Trade Flows, Regulations, Hazards, Waste Management Strategies and Technologies for Value Recovery. *Waste Management*, 82, 258-275.

Isildar, A., Rene, E.R., van Hullebusch, E.D., & Lens, P.N.L. (2018). Electronic Waste as a Secondary Source of Critical Metals: Management and Recovery Technologies. *Resources, Conservation and Recycling*, 135, 296-312.

Jiya, A., Ijah, U.J., Galadima, M., & Akpan, U. (2019). Isolation of Microorganisms Associated with Biodegradation of Household Domestic Wastes for Biogas Production in Niger State, Nigeria. *Journal of BioMedical Research and Clinical Practice*, 2(1), 70-76.

Kliopova, I., Staniskis, J.K., Stunzenas, E., & Jurovickaja, E. (2019). Bio-nutrient Recycling with a Novel Integrated Biodegradable Waste Management system for Catering Companies. *Journal of Cleaner Production*, 209, 116-125.

Kothari, R., Tyagi, V.V., & Pathak, A. (2010). Waste-to-energy: A way from Renewable Energy Sources to Sustainable Development. *Renewable and Sustainable Energy Reviews*, 14(9), 3164-3170.

Kumar, A., Holuszko, M., & Espinosa, D.C.R. (2017). E-waste: An Overview on Generation, Collection, Legislation and Recycling Practices. *Resources, Conservation and Recycling*, 122, 32-42.

Kumar, A., Holuszko, M., & Espinosa, D.C.R. (2017). E-waste: An Overview on Generation, Collection, Legislation and Recycling Practices. *Resources, Conservation and Recycling,* 122, 32-42.

Kumar, A., Samadder, S.R., Kumar, N., & Singh, C. (2018). Estimation of the Generation Rate of Different Types of Plastic Wastes and Possible Revenue Recovery from Informal Recycling. *Waste Management,* 79, 781-790.

Lal, R.M., Nagpure, A.S., Luo, L., Tripathi, S.N., Ramaswami, A., Bergin, M.H., & Russell, A.G. (2016). Municipal Solid Waste and Dung Cake Burning Discoloring the Taj Mahal and Human Health Impacts in Agra. *Environmental Research Letters,* 11(10), 104009.

Li, K., Yang, F., Zhang, G., Song, S., Li, Y., Ren, D., Song, C.-P. (2017). AIK1, a Mitogen-activated Protein Kinase, Modulates Abscisic Acid Responses through the MKK5-MPK6 Kinase Cascade. *Plant Physiology,* 173(2), 1391-1408.

Mena, C., Adenso-Diaz, B., & Yurt, O. (2011). The causes of Food Waste in the Supplier–retailer Interface: Evidences from the UK and Spain. *Resources, Conservation and Recycling,* 55(6), 648-658.

Mendoza, F.J.C., Altabella, J.E., & Izquierdo, A.G. (2017). Application of inert Wastes in the Construction, Operation and Closure of Landfills: Calculation Tool. *Waste Management,* 59, 276-285.

Messerle, V.E., Ustimenko, A.B., & Lavrichshev, O.A. (2016). Comparative Study of Coal Plasma Gasification: Simulation and Experiment. *Fuel,* 164, 172-179.

Mian, M.M., Zeng, X., Nasry, A.A.N.B., & Al-Hamadani, S.M. (2017). Municipal Solid Waste Management in China: A Comparative Analysis. *Journal of Material Cycles and Waste Management,* 19(3), 1127-1135.

Mian, M.M., Zeng, X., Nasry, A.A.N.B., & Al-Hamadani, S.M. (2017). Municipal Solid Waste Management in China: A Comparative Analysis. *Journal of Material Cycles and Waste Management,* 19(3), 1127-1135.

Mohammadshirazi, A., Akram, A., Rafiee, S., & Bagheri Kalhor, E. (2014). Energy and Cost Analyses of Biodiesel Production from Waste Cooking Oil. *Renewable and Sustainable Energy Reviews,* 33, 44-49.

Mostafa, N.A., Farag, A.A., Abo-dief, H.M., & Tayeb, A.M. (2018). Production of Biodegradable Plastic from Agricultural Wastes. *Arabian Journal of Chemistry,* 11(4), 546-553.

Mustafa, M.F., Liu, Y., Duan, Z., Guo, H., Xu, S., Wang, H., & Lu, W. (2017). Volatile Compounds Emission and Health Risk Assessment during Composting of Organic Fraction of Municipal Solid Waste. *Journal of Hazardous Materials,* 327, 35-43.

Narbón-Perpiñá, I., & Prior, D. (2020). Management of Waste Electrical and Electronic Equipment in European Union Countries: A Comparison. In *E-waste Recycling and Management* (pp. 127-141). Springer, Cham.

Negi, S., Dhar, H., Hussain, A., & Kumar, S. (2018). Biomethanation Potential for Co-digestion of Municipal Solid Waste and Rice Straw: A Batch Study. *Bioresource Technology,* 254, 139-144.

Nintendo, E., Nintendo, E., Miyamoto, S., Tezuka, T., & Kondo, K. (2019). *The Legend of Zelda.* Paper Presented at the Spin.

Nowicki, M.A., Castro, N.J., Plesniak, M.W., & Zhang, L.G. (2016). 3D Printing of Novel Osteochondral Scaffolds with Graded Microstructure. *Nanotechnology,* 27(41), 414001.

Oppelt, E.T. (1987). Incineration of Hazardous Waste. *JAPCA,* 37(5), 558-586.

Pansuk, J., Junpen, A., & Garivait, S. (2018). Assessment of Air Pollution from Household Solid Waste Open Burning in Thailand. *Sustainability*, 10(7), 2553.

Pickin, J. (2008). Representations of Environmental Concerns in Cost–benefit Analyses of Solid Waste Recycling. *Resources, Conservation and Recycling*, 53(1), 79-85.

Polyakova, V., Degaev, E., & El Haddad, P. (2018). *Reduction of Ecological and Economic Risks in Utilization of Solid Domestic Wastes and Construction Waste.* Paper Presented at the MATEC Web of Conferences.

Psomopoulos, C.S., Bourka, A., & Themelis, N.J. (2009). Waste-to-energy: A Review of the Status and Benefits in USA. *Waste Management*, 29(5), 1718-1724.

Quintas, P.Y., Dotto, G.L., Da Silva, S.M., & Escudero, L.B. (2019). Removal of Thallium from Environmental Samples using a Raw and Chemically modified Biosorbent Derived from Domestic Wastes. *Environmental Science and Pollution Research*, 26(31), 32285-32297.

Ragaert, K., Delva, L., & Van Geem, K. (2017). Mechanical and Chemical Recycling of Solid Plastic Waste. *Waste Management*, 69, 24-58.

Roychoudhuri, R., & Debnath, B. (2020). Risk Assessment of E-Waste Recycling with a Focus on ISO 9000 Standard. In *Sustainable Waste Management: Policies and Case Studies* (pp. 431-440). Springer, Singapore.

Salles, A., Wolff, D., & Silveira, G. (2012). Solid Wastes Drained in an Urban River Sub-basin. *Urban Water Journal*, 9(1), 21-28.

Sanlisoy, A., & Carpinlioglu, M.O. (2017). A Review on Plasma Gasification for Solid Waste Disposal. *International Journal of Hydrogen Energy*, 42(2), 1361-1365.

Shi, X., Luo, C., Lu, H., & Yu, K. (2019). Primary Recycling of Anhydride Cured Engineering Epoxy using Alcohol Solvent. *Polymer Engineering & Science*, 59(s2), E111-E119.

Singh, H., Chauhan, G., Jain, A.K., & Sharma, S.K. (2017). Adsorptive Potential of Agricultural Wastes for Removal of Dyes from Aqueous Solutions. *Journal of Environmental Chemical Engineering*, 5(1), 122-135.

Singhabhandhu, A., & Tezuka, T. (2010). The Waste-to-energy Framework for Integrated Multi-waste Utilization: Waste Cooking Oil, Waste Lubricating Oil, and Waste Plastics. *Energy*, 35(6), 2544-2551.

Srivastava, R., Krishna, V., & Sonkar, I. (2014). Characterization and Management of Municipal Solid Waste: A Case Study of Varanasi City, India. *Int. J. Curr. Res. Acad. Rev*, 2(8), 10-16.

Sujauddin, M., Huda, S., & Hoque, A.R. (2008). Household Solid Waste Characteristics and Management in Chittagong, Bangladesh. *Waste Management*, 28(9), 1688-1695.

Tansel, B. (2017). From Electronic Consumer Products to e-wastes: Global Outlook, Waste Quantities, Recycling Challenges. *Environment International*, 98, 35-45.

Tanskanen, P. (2013). Management and Recycling of Electronic Waste. *Acta materialia*, 61(3), 1001-1011.

Tatsuno, H., Nishina, K., Shibayama, Y., Osaka, T., & Hirakawa, M. (2019). Focus Adjustment System for an Image Display Device. In: Google Patents.

Tikiz, I., & Pehlivan, H. (2018). Experimental Investigation for Alternative Use of Agricultural and Domestic Wastes. *Kýrklareli Üniversitesi Mühendislik ve Fen Bilimleri Dergisi*, 4(1), 142-152.

Troschinetz, A.M., & Mihelcic, J.R. (2009). Sustainable Recycling of Municipal Solid Waste in Developing Countries. *Waste Management*, 29(2), 915-923.

Uçkun Kiran, E., Trzcinski, A.P., Ng, W.J., & Liu, Y. (2014). Bioconversion of Food Waste to Energy: A Review. *Fuel,* 134, 389-399.

Wang, M., Mao, M., Zhang, M., Wen, G., Yang, Q., Su, B., & Ren, Q. (2019). Highly Efficient Treatment of Textile Dyeing Sludge by CO_2 Thermal Plasma Gasification. *Waste Management,* 90, 29-36.

Wang, W., Zeng, C., Sardans, J., Zeng, D., Wang, C., Bartrons, M., & Penuelas, J. (2018). Industrial and Agricultural Wastes Decreased Greenhouse-gas Emissions and Increased Rice Grain yield in a Subtropical Paddy Field. *Experimental Agriculture,* 54(4), 623-640.

Wang, Y., Geng, S., Zhao, P., Du, H., He, Y., & Crittenden, J. (2016). Cost-benefit Analysis of GHG Emission Reduction in Waste to Energy Projects of China under Clean Development Mechanism. *Resources, Conservation and Recycling,* 109, 90-95.

Wiemes, L., Pawlowsky, U., & Mymrin, V. (2017). Incorporation of Industrial Wastes as Raw Materials in Brick's Formulation. *Journal of Cleaner Production,* 142, 69-77.

Yan, M., Khoshnevisana, B., Tsapekos, P., Fotidis, I., & Angelidaki, I. (2019). *Continuous Biomethanation of Organic Fraction of Municipal Solid Waste under Extreme Ammonia Levels.* Paper presented at the 16th World Congress on Anaerobic Digestion.

Yilmaz, E., Wzorek, M., & Akçay, S. (2018). Co-pelletization of Sewage Sludge and Agricultural Wastes. *Journal of Environmental Management,* 216, 169-175.

Zeng, X., Yang, C., Chiang, J.F., & Li, J. (2017). Innovating e-waste Management: From Macroscopic to Microscopic Scales. *Science of the Total Environment,* 575, 1-5.

Zhang, W., Yang, J., Wu, X., Hu, Y., Yu, W., Wang, J., ... & Kumar, R.V. (2016). A Critical Review on Secondary Lead Recycling Technology and its Prospect. *Renewable and Sustainable Energy Reviews,* 61, 108-122.

Zhang, Z., Zhu, Y., Yang, T., Li, L., Zhu, H., & Wang, H. (2017). Conversion of Local Industrial Wastes into Greener Cement through Geopolymer Technology: A Case Study of High-magnesium Nickel Slag. *Journal of Cleaner Production,* 141, 463-471.

Zhao, X., Xia, Y., Zhan, L., Xie, B., Gao, B., & Wang, J. (2018). Hydrothermal Treatment of e-waste Plastics for Tertiary Recycling: Product Slate and Decomposition Mechanisms. *ACS Sustainable Chemistry & Engineering,* 7(1), 1464-1473.

Zhao, X.-g., Jiang, G.-w., Li, A., & Wang, L. (2016). Economic Analysis of Waste-to-energy Industry in China. *Waste Management,* 48, 604-618.

Zhou, C., Gong, Z., Hu, J., Cao, A., & Liang, H. (2015). A Cost-benefit Analysis of Landfill Mining and Material Recycling in China. *Waste Management,* 35, 191-198.

Zink, T., Geyer, R., & Startz, R. (2018). Toward Estimating Displaced Primary Production from Recycling: A Case Study of US Aluminum. *Journal of Industrial Ecology,* 22(2), 314-326.

11

Agro-residue Generation, Theoretical Surplus and Availability for Power Sector

INTRODUCTION

During the last decade, Northwest India has been experiencing dreadful pollution due to crop residue burning, especially in Punjab, Haryana and Uttar Pradesh (Leah, 2018). After rice is harvested in October, farmers have only a handful of days to remove crop stubble from their fields before rabi crops are ready to be sown. Earlier, only a small portion of the stubble used to be burnt, but in recent years, shortage of labour, use of common harvester technology, a short lead time between kharif and rabi crops, and insufficient market linkages to utilize crop residue have resulted in a significant shift towards agro-residue burning. NASAs satellite images reveal that the operative area of crop burning in northern India extends from the India–Pakistan border into Uttarakhand, Haryana, Himachal Pradesh, Delhi and Uttar Pradesh. According to two 2014 studies (Anon, 2019a), the country generates 600-700 million tonnes of crop residue, of which around 16% was burnt on farms (Moonmoon *et.al.*, 2014). The government has come out with various policies to curb crop burning, but recent figures of residue burning vary between 85-100 million tonnes (Niveta *et.al.*, 2018). Three states— Uttar Pradesh, Punjab and Haryana—contributed around 60% of the crop burning in 2008-09. In Uttar Pradesh, nearly 22 million tonnes (23% of the total) of agro-residue was burnt; 20 million tonnes (21%) in Punjab; and 9 million tonnes (10%) in Haryana. Crop residue burning adds significant emissions load to our already choked cities. When 1 tonne of crop residue is burnt on the field, it releases approximately 1,400 kg of CO_2, 58 kg of CO, 11 kg of particulate matter (PM), 4.9 kg of NOx and

1.2 kg of SO_2. Due to such high emissions, crop residue burning has become a major environmental problem. PM emissions from crop burning in one year are more than 17 times the total annual particulate pollution in Delhi from all sources—vehicles, industries, garbage burning, etc. Similarly, the total national annual emissions of CO_2 from crop residue burning are more than 64 times the total annual CO_2 emissions in Delhi. For SO_2, the total national annual emissions from crop residue burning are about five times the total annual SO_2 emissions in Delhi. Burning of crop residue releases sooty black carbon which is one of the most prominent contributors to climate change. Another study estimated 42,000 premature deaths in 2010 were attributable to crop residue burning alone (Siddharth, 2018). According to the System of Air Quality and Weather Forecasting and Research (SAFAR), crop residue burning contributed around 10-20% to Delhi–NCRs air pollution during October-November 2019.

This rose to as high as 44% during peak burning days (Pratik, 2019; Anon, 2019b). During this period, air pollution in Delhi is about 12-20 times higher than the threshold for safe air as defined by the World Health Organization (Moonmoon *et.al.*, 2014). Besides increased levels of PM and smog that cause health hazards, crop residue burning also causes loss of biodiversity of agricultural lands, and deterioration of soil fertility. Further, it is a huge nutrient loss to the farmers as frequent residue burning leads to catastrophic loss of microbial population and reduces the levels of nitrogen and carbon in the top soil profile, which is important for crop root development. It is a huge monetary loss in terms of health impacts on people and soil.

CROP-WISE AGRO-RESIDUE GENERATION

Agro-residue or crop residue is the sum total of plant materials left after removal of the main crop. The residue could be of different sizes, shapes, forms, and densities like straw, stalks, leaves, fibrous materials, etc. Crop residue can also be by-products of the post-harvest processes of crops such as cleaning, threshing, linting, sieving and crushing, e.g. rice husk and sugarcane bagasse.

Different crops generate different amounts of gross residue. The proportion of crop yield to residue yield is termed residue production ratio (RPR). For example, a tonne of rice and wheat crop yield generate 1.5 tonne gross crop residue, so their RPR is 1.5. Surplus residue is the residue left after competing uses (such as cattle feed, animal bedding, heating and cooking fuel, organic fertilizer, etc.) are fulfilled. Research suggests that different kinds of crops have different utilizations in terms of fodder, fertilizer, and in households; in turn, their surplus availability varies as well. For example, 60-70% of wheat residue is directly consumed or stored as fodder, whereas for certain rice varieties, use of residue as fodder can be as low as 10-20%. Thus, surplus residue availability may vary from 10-70% depending on other competing uses of a crop. Based on crop utilization in various states, on an average, nearly one-third of gross residue can theoretically be considered surplus residue.18 Bagasse (sugarcane residue) is considered an agro-industrial waste that does not have any competing use, so, in theory, all of it is considered surplus residue. Sugarcane, rice, wheat, maize, and cotton contribute over 90% to India's crop production. Hence, the bulk of India's agro-residue comes from these crops. In the year 2016-17, India generated around 560 million tonnes of gross agro-residue. Rice (33%) contributed the most to the gross residue, followed by wheat (31%) and sugarcane (20%). The theoretical surplus of 260 million tonnes can be further categorized into:

(i) Residue left on the field, 140 million tonnes (rice, wheat, cotton and maize) and,

(ii) Agro-industrial residue of 120 million tonnes (100 million tonnes bagasse, and the rest rice husk and wheat pods).

India is a largely agrarian country with around 50% of its population engaged in farming activities (Sushruth, 2018). Uttar Pradesh produces nearly one-fourth (130 million tonnes) of India's total agro-residue. Punjab, West Bengal, Madhya Pradesh, Maharashtra and Bihar are the other top agro-residue producers.

ESTIMATES OF THEORETICAL AGRO-RESIDUE GENERATION AND SURPLUS AVAILABILITY

As per information available on the Ministry of New and Renewable Energy (MNRE) website, current availability of biomass in India, covering both agricultural and forestry residue, is an estimated 500 million tonnes per year and surplus biomass availability is estimated at about 120-150 million tonnes per year (Anon, 2020a). As per the Central government's biomass portal (biomassportal.gov), surplus biomass availability from agriculture is 145 million tonnes and from forestry it is about 104 million tonnes, which gives us a total of about 250 million tonnes. As per NITI Aayogs Expression of Interest (EOI), 620 million tonnes of agro-residue are generated annually in India, based on an estimate for 2014 (Anon, 2019c). Thus, the government itself is not able to provide clear figures of biomass availability. In 2018, Technology Information, Forecasting and Assessment Council (TIFAC), an autonomous organization under the Department of Science and Technology, surveyed a total of 662 districts of India. The data collected by the survey covered production statistics from 2010-11 to 2015-16 (based on data availability and accessibility) for eleven selected crops–rice, wheat, maize, sugarcane, cotton, gram, tur, groundnut, mustard, soybean and castor. The study estimated that the total dry biomass generated annually from the selected eleven crops in the three seasons averaged at about 682.61 million tonnes. Rice straw and husk (33%), wheat straw (22%), sugarcane tops and bagasse (17%) and cotton (8%) accounted for almost 80% of the residue among the selected crops. The top five states in terms of biomass generation were Uttar Pradesh, Maharashtra, Madhya Pradesh, Punjab and Gujarat. It was estimated that 178 million tonnes of surplus crop residue are available in India annually; 26% of the overall identified crop residue generation (Niveta *et.al.*, 2018). Other research suggests that agro-based residue generation is around 686 million tonnes, out of which 234 million tonnes residue is estimated as surplus for bio-energy generation (Moonmoon *et.al.*, 2014).

Stubble burning is a major source of pollution in Northwest India. To deal with this problem, significant investments are required in the form of direct capital and as subsidy to improve farming practices, set up costly biomass plants, or find other uses for agro-residue. This economic support has to be a continuous intervention. On the other hand, it is also a well-established fact that even with the rapid growth in the renewable sector, India has to continue its reliance on coal to meet its base load demand. Coal-based power plants are resource-intensive and add up to a significant pollution load on the environment. Many of these power stations have become old and will be shut down due to their higher emissions, and replaced with new plants using cleaner coal technology. The dilemma for India is that at a time when countries around the world have stopped investing in new coal power plants, will it be prudent for the country to replace old coal power plants with new ones?

It is clear that standalone solution to these two problems (stubble burning and use of coal to generate power) will burn a hole in the exchequers pocket, and even after that, returns on investment cannot be guaranteed. But what if we were to see the broader picture and make one problem the solution to the other problem? This can be achieved by identifying older units operating at a satisfactory efficiency within safe operating parameters, and promoting co-firing of biomass in them–a cost-effective method to address pollution as well as a clear climate change mitigation strategy.

BIOMASS CO-FIRING

Co-firing is the process of utilization of a certain portion of biomass with the existing base fuel. Currently, three co-firing technologies are widely used in coal plants: direct co-firing, indirect co-firing, and parallel co-firing. Co-firing is direct when biomass and coal are fired in the same boiler; and indirect when combustion or gasification of biomass occurs in a separate unit. As biomass enters the coal boiler, some technical issues may arise, depending on its properties and the boiler type. However, direct co-firing has been undertaken in stoker, cyclone, fluidized bed combustion (FBC) and pulverized coal combustion (PCC) boilers. FBC boilers are designed to utilize a wide variety of fuels, hence they are technically much more suited to co-firing very high percentages of biomass.

MAJOR DRIVERS OF BIOMASS CO-FIRING IN COAL POWER PLANTS

Replacement of coal with agro-residue in power generation can result in a sharp decrease in the pollution load, especially in regions where agro-residue burning is prevalent. Firstly, it will directly reduce crop residue burning. Secondly, it will directly reduce the equivalent emissions from existing coal use. Thirdly, when agro-residue is burnt in power plants in controlled conditions in the presence of pollution control technologies, emissions of PM, SO_2, NOx and CO will significantly decrease. It can save substantial investment in new biomass power plants and coal power plants by renovating old power plants at a minimum cost.

Key drivers of biomass co-firing are as follows:

(i) Initial capital investment Biomass co-firing banks on existing investment and infrastructure at coal-fired power plants and incurs only relatively modest retrofitting cost. Retrofitted boilers can fire biomass when supplies are plentiful but switch back to coal when supplies are low. The major driver of this initiative will be the capital cost requirement per MW. At lower co-firing ratios of 5-10%, there is no or miniscule capital cost and even for higher co-firing ratios, the cost will be just 10-20% of a standalone biomass plant.

(ii) Efficient burning for biomass Co-firing increases efficiency of biomass-energy conversion, by firing in a larger plant that can accommodate superheaters, economizers and reheaters compared with a smaller plant firing biomass alone. Biomass co-firing has little or no-impact on the efficiency of existing power plant operations. Thus, they operate at an efficiency of 34-38% in comparison with 24-30% efficiency of biomass power plants.

(iii) Mechanism for extending life of existing power plants Co-firing has played an important transitional role in the decarbonization of the coal fleet and has extended the lives of power plants in Europe, USA and UK.

(iv) Breaking supply chain constraints for biomass utilization Transportation constitutes a significant portion of the total cost of biomass utilization. Biomass needs to be shredded onsite before transportation to increase its density. Transportation in any form over more than 50 km becomes unviable for a 10-15 MW biomass plant. This is not a constraint for bigger coal power plants where biomass can be used in co-firing. Economies of scale

and the comparative cost of transporting coal and biomass tilt the balance in favour of the latter in such cases. A major constraint in the use of biomass is the non-availability of agro-residue around the year. Since agro-reside is generated at a specific time in the year, i.e., at the time of harvest, it can be procured in bulk only at that time. However, smaller industries or biomass power plants do not have the capacity to buy or pre-order in large quantities. In turn, this affects the biomass procurement capacity of pellet or briquette manufacturers since they have limited working capital available. It is possible to have a perennial biomass supply chain, but that will make it costlier than coal. By paying higher and fixing contracts with pellet manufacturers, availability of sufficient working capital to procure the required biomass and to store it for round-the-year use can be made possible. At lower co-firing ratios (0-10%), the variation in the cost will be too little to matter, but it will keep increasing as the co-firing ratio goes up. A higher co-firing ratio will require government support in terms of subsidy or other incentives as received by renewables, or the additional cost will need to be passed on to consumers through tariffs.

(v) Tackling pollution as well as climate change simultaneously One of the key drivers of the introduction of biomass co-firing to conventional coal-fired power stations was its potential to reduce CO_2 footprints of the sector. It can help meet climate change mitigation targets as well as pollutant compliance regulations.

CO_2

The greatest advantage of biomass co-firing is that it reduces CO_2 emissions. Co-firing is a cheap and quick method to achieve modest scaling-down of CO_2 emissions at a coal-fired power plant. The calorific value of agro-residue pellets is comparable to Indian coal. Thus, technically, it can directly reduce CO_2 emissions equivalent to the coal it replaces. However, since biomass supply has higher transportation footprints with respect to coal because of its scattered availability, for 10% biomass co-firing, CO_2 emissions reduction may be slightly lower (than 10%), depending on the distance over which it needs to be transported.

NOx

NOx emissions from biomass co-firing are difficult to predict because they vary depending on the type of biomass, and the firing technology (boiler or burner) and operating conditions. NOx content in the emissions is due to two factors—inherent nitrogen in the fuel and thermal NOx. Different types of biomass can have higher or lower nitrogen content with respect to coal. While burning biomass, a greater proportion of nitrogen is released as volatile compounds, thus results in lower NOx emissions. Thermal NOx emissions concentration is dependent on the combustion temperature. The moisture content in biomass can lower peak flame temperatures and, thus, thermal NOx. As per research studies, NOx emissions from biomass firing tend to decrease linearly with respect to the blending percentage (Dayton, 2002).

SO_2

SO_2 emissions depend solely on the sulphur content in the fuel. Agro-residue has much lower sulphur content (0-0.2%) with respect to coal (0.3-0.7%). Moreover, biomass ash contains higher levels of alkali and alkaline earth compounds than coal ash and can retain a greater fraction of sulphur. The proportion of sulphur retained typically increases from 10% in coal ash to 50% in pure biomass ash (Rohan, 2012). Biomass co-firing can, therefore, significantly reduce SO_2 emissions.

GLOBAL PROGRESS ON BIOMASS CO-FIRING

Biomass co-firing can be considered a transitional option towards a completely carbon-free power sector. According to the International Energy Agencys (IEA) Roadmap on Biomass Heat and Power, biomass-based power generation will increase by at least a factor of ten from today until 2050, accounting for 7.5% of the global electricity generation. For the foreseeable future, this biomass-based power generation will be almost entirely based on combustion and co-firing technologies (Jaap, 2019). To promote biomass co-firing, European countries and US offer policy incentives or have mandatory regulations to increase share of renewables in the electricity sector. Currently, 230-250 power and combined heat and power plants using co-firing techniques are in operation, a significant portion of them in Europe. Apart from UK, Denmark, Germany and Netherlands, many other European countries such as Finland, Sweden, Russia, Belgium, Austria, Hungary, Italy and Spain are using biomass co-firing technologies in their power plants. All major coal-fired power plants in UK have adopted biomass co-firing. Currently, 86 out of 560 coal-fired power plants in the US use biomass co-firing technologies and this number is expected to increase in the coming years. A number of Asian countries such as Japan, China and South Korea have already adopted co-firing technologies. In 2018, a 50 MW (84% co-firing) circulating fluidized bed (CFB) plant was installed at Mombetsu, Japan. Another, 112 MW thermal power plants were commissioned at Hibikinada in 2019. At this plant, coal and wood pellets are separately pulverized and fed into the boiler. Its biomass blend ratio is approximately 30% (Anon, 2019c). Biomass production and trading have also increased in countries where new investors are becoming more interested in investing in biomass co-firing. China, the world's largest agro-residue generator, has drafted extensive policy to manage it. The countrys predominant focus has been on biogas and co-firing.

Co-firing percentages of 5-10 is well tested and can be adopted without major modifications and additional investment. Many plants across the world have adopted co-firing of up to 20% with minor modifications and little investment. However, very few plants have gone beyond 20% co-firing because of technical issues that arise due to differences in fuel composition and other operational issues. These issues may be of less importance if a power plant is approaching the end of its operating life.

IMPLEMENTATION OF BIOMASS CO-FIRING

There are three major points of interest regarding implementation of biomass co-firing in thermal power plants: modifications required in the existing setup, impact on various performance parameters, and data on actual implementation from plants that have adopted co-firing.

The delivery, storage and handling of biomass pose challenges different from those posed by coal for the following reasons:

- Due to its geographically scattered availability, it is mostly transported on trucks
- Low density and high volume require comparatively larger storage areas that should be covered because of hygroscopic nature of biomass
- High flammability and high abrasion resistance require dedicated fire prevention and suppression systems
- Increased fire risk from pellets may also require large-scale dust extraction systems to minimize the hazard.
- Covered conveyor and storage facilities are required to minimize the spread of dust for prevention of fire and to protect biomass from ingress of water, which reduces the quality of the fuel.

Trials at existing power stations suggest that existing infrastructure is sufficient for low co-firing ratios (< 10%). Modifications to existing infrastructure and operations might be required depending on the nature of the biomass utilized, the co-firing ratio and the delivery method. Several modifications to existing coal plants might be required based on the above parameters.

These include:

- Dedicated covered storage areas
- Modified fuel feeding systems
- Modified or new milling equipment

- Modified or new combustion systems
- Possible boiler modifications
- Modifications in existing emissions control technologies.

IMPACT ON CRITICAL PARAMETERS

The majority of biomass fuels tend to be relatively rich in alkali metals, especially potassium. In some cases, they are rich in phosphates. They have higher moisture content, relatively high chlorine content, and relatively low sulphur and ash contents. The impact of these parameters on various power plant performance parameters can be discussed as follows.

- **Boiler efficiency**

Lower energy density of biomass may pose limitations in existing fuel handling systems; for example, conveyors, mills or primary air pipe work can reduce the primary energy delivered and, hence, the boiler output. In addition, increased propensity for slagging and fouling at co-firing ratios greater than 10% can also decrease heat transfer in the boiler. However, as the co-firing experience in existing power stations demonstrates, this increased risk can be managed without any loss of boiler performance.

- **Particulate matter and fly ash**

Most biomass fuels have lower ash content than typical coals. Still, it is difficult to predict the PM and fly ash generation. The effect is site-specific, and depends on the type of biomass and the performance of the installed particulate collection equipment. The concentrations of some trace elements can be significantly higher in certain biomass materials than in coal. However, there is no evidence that these elevated levels have led to compliance issues in existing plants that have switched to co-firing. Biomass fly ash behaves differently from coal ash. Biomass ash can have electrical properties that reduce effectiveness of electrostatic precipitators (ESPs) in capturing fine particles from the fuel (flue) gas stream. Modifications in ESP operations may be required to mitigate this effect at higher co-firing ratios.

- **Impact on fly ash properties**

Thermal power plants are required by law to ensure 100% utilization of the ash they produce. Potential uses of fly ash and bottom ash depend on their composition. Coal ash is already in demand for various applications. Co-firing coal and biomass should also allow use of the ash in a similar manner. Experts believe that up to 10% co-firing will only have a minor impact on fly ash properties. However, at higher co-firing ratios, fly ash should be tested or analysed on a case-by-case basis depending on chemical characteristics of the co-fired biomass. In fact, in some respects, biomass fly ash outperforms coal fly ash. Biomass enhances the pozzolanic reaction (CaOH with fly ash) significantly, presumably because it contains amorphous rather than crystalline silica, the former reacting more readily with CaOH in the mix. This reaction ultimately improves the strength of the concrete beyond that developed by cementitious reactions. Experimental studies have shown that biomass-containing fly ash is superior to pure coal fly ash. Other studies indicate only a modest impact of biomass-containing fly ash on concrete properties, with an increased aerating agent requirement being one issue needing further attention. Otherwise, biomass-containing fly ash qualitatively behaves similar to coal fly ash. It is essential that Bureau of Indian Standards (BIS) analyse and define fly ash quality standards at various co-firing ratios so that fly ash can be utilized in the construction sector. Biomass ash may have more widespread applications, including as a soil improver and fertilizer, adsorbents and as a source of high value char.

Co-firing in old power stations

In India, older units are retired based on a combination of one or more of the following factors:

- If they are more than 25 years old
- If they are unsafe to operate
- If they have poor efficiency, high coal consumption and high CO_2 emissions (15-25% higher than new plants)
- If they emit high levels of SO_2 and NOx due to absence or non-viability of pollution control technology
- If cooling towers to reduce water consumption are absent or non-viable.

In India, the safe operating life of a power plant is considered to be 25 years. But experts believe that 25 years should not be used as a direct benchmark as a number of coal-fired plants operating across the world are as old as 40-50 years. The operational life of a plant is greatly dependent on the quality of operation and maintenance. Even in India, units do invest in renovation and modernization, and life extension projects to extend the life of power plants beyond the operating life of 25 years. Under such circumstances, retiring plants at the age of 25 can have an impact on cost recovery and financial sheets of distribution companies (discoms). It would be unwise to retire an old unit working safely and efficiently, unless other reasons push it towards retirement. Other reasons for retirement can be higher CO_2 emissions in comparison to new clean coal technology plants and not meeting environmental compliance standards. New supercritical plants have an average efficiency of 38-40% whereas old units can have efficiencies in the range of 32-36%. In terms of CO_2 emissions, new supercritical and ultra-supercritical units will have CO_2 emissions in the range of 750-850 g/kWh in comparison to 950-1,100 g/kWh in older units using subcritical technology. Clearly, an older unit will emit 15-25% higher

CO_2 per unit of electricity generated if it is not replaced with new efficient units. With the introduction of new environmental norms in 2015, plants need to make huge investment in reducing their PM, SO_2 and NOx emissions. Additional investment in older units for pollution control means that these units need to be operated for more years to recover the cost. This investment will ensure compliance with standards for critical pollutants from older units but questions about high CO_2 emissions will still remain.

ECONOMICS OF BIOMASS CO-FIRING

The cost of conversion of coal power plants is dependent on biomass co-firing ratios and the technological choices made in each individual case. Recent estimates of the CAPEX for co-firing have reduced by 40% and for full conversion by 48% since 2011 (Anon, 2020b). CAPEX costs include pre-development and construction costs including boiler modifications, construction of biomass storage facilities and modifications in the material handling system. The OPEX costs comprise mainly of fixed and variable operation and maintenance costs, insurance, labour and use of service (UoS), which is the use of the transmission network. The majority of the OPEX cost is associated with labour requirements for operation of the plants. To assess the cost impact and benefits achieved, we have analysed two scenarios. The first scenario is illustrated through a new 800 MW supercritical unit and the second scenario is illustrated through four old units of 200 MW each. The units are shifted to biomass co-firing at different co-firing ratios. A new supercritical or ultra-supercritical plant has a capital cost of around Rs 4-6 crore per MW, and is equipped with flue gas desulphurization (FGD) and selective catalytic reduction or selective non-catalytic reduction (SCR/SNCR) to meet stringent pollution norms. All this cost amounts to around Rs 4,500-5,500 crore for an 800 MW supercritical or ultra-supercritical plant. If installed today, such a plant will need to be run till 2050 or more to recover the cost. Recovery is getting progressively difficult due to continuously falling plant load factor of coal power plants with rapid growth in the installed renewable energy capacity. The new coal plant will replace an older one with carbon footprints of 1,000 gm/kWh, and will have 15-25% lesser carbon footprints with respect to the older power station. In the second scenario, if we renovate an old power station for biomass co-firing, we minimize the investment made and maximize the benefits achieved. For example, an older plant with CO_2 emissions of 1,000 g/kWh, through 50% co-firing, can effectively bring down its specific CO_2 emissions to 600 g/kWh, which is 10-20% lesser than the specific CO_2 emissions of a supercritical or ultra-supercritical plant. With that, units can also achieve significant reduction in their SO_2, NOx and even PM emissions levels without a lot of additional investment. SO_2 and NOx emissions reduction will be based on the proportion of biomass co-firing, existing coal quality and emissions. A power plant utilizing coal with a sulphur content of around 0.4% can even meet sulphur emissions norms through leapfrogging co-firing percentage from 10 to 40-60 and, hence, avoid investing in FGD. Similarly, NOx emissions can also be reduced in proportion with biomass co-firing. In Maharashtra, UP and Madhya Pradesh, some of the older units are able to meet applicable NOx emissions standard of 600 mg/Nm^3; through biomass co-firing they would be able to achieve additional reduction in NOx emissions levels based on co-firing percentages.

FEASIBILITY OF BIOMASS CO-FIRING

The three North-western states of India–Punjab, Haryana and Uttar Pradesh—immensely contribute to the agricultural production of the country. But unfortunately, in recent times, the three states have had to bear the stigma of excessive stubble burning. Some of the power plants located in these states can opt for higher percentage of biomass co-firing at their older power stations. These states can easily meet co-firing needs of their older plants by utilizing the available surplus agro-residue. As per the National Electricity Plan of 2018, around 10.8 GW capacity was schedule to retire in these states by 2027. Out of this, 5.3 GW falls in the Central sector and 5.5 GW in the state sector. About 0.7 GW capacity is located in Delhi and has already been retired. This includes the Rajghat power station (2 × 67.5 MW) and Badarpur power station (2 × 95 MW and 2 × 210 MW). Rajghat power stations land is planned to be utilized for a solar park whereas NTPC Badarpur, spread over 884 acre, will be converted into an eco-park. In Haryana, Unit 5 (210 MW) at the Panipat power plant is schedule to retire. This operational life of this unit, along with other units that are 17-20 years old, can be extended through biomass co-firing. In Punjab, 1.7 GW of capacity is schedule to retire. Out of this capacity, GND Bathinda (4 × 110 MW) has been retired in 2018. The plant was under consideration for biomass co-firing, but recently a decision has been taken that the plant will be dismantled and the land will be sold (Anon, 2020b). At PSPCL Ropar (6 × 210 MW), two units (1 and 2) have already been retired, others are schedule to retire by 2022. This plant has a unique opportunity to shift to biomass co-firing. Doing so will avoid huge investment in new units, and also save the investment otherwise required for FGD installation and operation. Thus, these plants can continue to supply cheaper electricity with reduced CO_2, SO_2 and NOx emissions. In Uttar Pradesh, 8.2 GW of capacity is schedule to retire by 2027. At Obra thermal power plant, units 1, 2 and 8 of 40 MW, 50 MW and 94 MW respectively have already been retired. At Panki, Units 3 and 4, of 105 MW each, have been retired. Theoretically, Uttar Pradesh can generate 3-4 GW of power based on surplus agro-residue availability. Power plants in the state have an opportunity to become a benchmark for other states when it comes to the utilization of agro-residue.

RECOMMENDATIONS

1. *A beginning must be made:* India lost the opportunity of converting GND Bathinda to a co-firing or all-out biomass plant. A beginning in a few plants will provide immense experience and confidence to the sector to address concerns associated with biomass utilization at thermal power plants.
2. *Start with low co-firing ratios and gradually increase them while upgrading the facilities:* Once we have sufficient experience of 5-10% co-firing, older plants can gradually be moved to higher co-firing ratios, optimizing costs and benefits based on biomass quantity, quality and plant technology.
3. *Decide which plants to cover:* It is essential to make a list of old plants that can operate with biomass co-firing based on efficiency and safety parameters, and assessment of biomass and space availability so that higher co-firing ratios can be implemented with minimum investment. CEA should take a lead in identifying such plants. Identified plants may be considered on a trail or research and development basis for a couple of years. A team of experts may be formed to coordinate between various experimenting plants and share experiences to avoid repetition of mistakes.
4. *Separate, marginally relaxed environmental norms may be specified for co-firing plants:* In Maharashtra, Madhya Pradesh and Uttar Pradesh, older coal-based power plants are able to meet PM and NOx standards. However, to meet SO_2 standards, they need to invest in FGD technology. In fact, this is becoming an additional factor to expedite the retirement of older plants which do not have space for FGD installation. We recommend that old plants that can be operated safely and with good efficiency, can be chosen for biomass co-firing at higher ratios. This will automatically reduce SO_2 emissions and may make these plants complaint with SO_2 emissions norms. Simultaneously, keeping in consideration the various other environmental and social benefits of biomass co-firing, the SO_2 norms for these units can be marginally relaxed so that the investment which would be needed to install FGD can be utilized for installation of storage, transportation and safety facilities for higher biomass co-firing ratios.
5. *Promote torrified pellets:* Torrified biomass pellets are regarded as one of the most efficient biofuel manufacturing processes. Torrification can bring the properties of agro-residue closer to coal properties, making biomass co-firing at higher ratios

economical feasible. Further, a wide variety of biomass can be torrified, i.e. municipal waste, sewage sludge, and agro-residue. Thus, MoP, MoEF&CC and other concerned agencies should promote torrified pellet manufacturing.

CONCLUSION

Utilization of agro-residue is an opportunity which India has neglected for decades. Being an agrarian country, every year, millions of tonnes of agro-reside are generated, but a significant quantity is wasted on the fields, stubble burning being one of the horrendous forms of this wastage. A country where around 50% population is engaged in farming cannot afford to ignore this resource. Agro-residue co-firing in older power station can be a panacea for governments multiple problems.

1. *Improving farmers income:* The government has set itself an ambitious goal of doubling farmers income by 2022. Sale of agro-residue for pellet manufacturing can contribute to achieving this goal.
2. *Generating rural employment:* Pellets and briquette manufacturing, storage, handling and transportation can chip in the generation of employment at the local level.
3. *Easing financial burden on the government:* The future of coal is uncertain. Governments and private investors are suspicious about new investment in coal plants due to growing concern about pollution and climate change. Thus, by investing a miniscule amount in old power station, significant investment in new coal power plants can be avoided. If old power stations can be run with reduced CO_2 emissions, it is a win-win all around. The fixed cost from such plants would already have been recovered. The financial health of discoms will also improve. The money saved from this can be invested in renewable energy or cleaner technologies.
4. *Reducing GHG emissions with minimal investment:* Biomass co-firing is a cost-effective approach to reduce CO_2 emissions from thermal power plants.

REFERENCES

Anon (2019a). Expression on Interest for A Research Study on Mass Production of Manure/ Fertilizer from Agricultural Bio-Mass, NITI Aayog, New Delhi

Anon (2019b). Crop Burning Responsible for 19% of Delhi's Air Pollution, Finds SAFAR, Hindustan Times, 22 October 2019. Available at https:// www.hindustantimes.com/ cities/crop-burning-responsible-for-19- of-delhi-s-air-pollution/story-Ezp8P9fnl FYWjTlBzmohFM.html, as accessed on 23 September 2020

Anon (2019c). Biomass Utilization at Coal-Fired Power Plant: A Choice for Environment and Economy CEA-JCOAL Workshop, November 2019.

Anon (2020a). Current Status, Ministry of New and Renewable Energy, Government of India. Available at https://mnre.gov.in/bio-energy/current-status, as accessed on 3 August 2020.

Anon (2020b). Govt. to Sell Bathinda Thermal Plant Land, Indian Express 23 June 2020. Available at https://indianexpress.com/article/cities/chandigarh/govt-to-sell-bathinda-thermal-plant-land-6472146/, as accessed on 23 September 2020

Dayton (2002). A Summary of NOx Emissions Reduction from Biomass Cofiring, National Renewable Energy Laboratory.

Jaap Koppejan (2019). Rep. Task 32 Biomass Combustion and Cofiring Triennium 2016-18, IEA Bioenergy. Available at https://doi.org/https:// www.ieabioenergy.com/wp-content/uploads/2019/11/IEA-Bioenergy_ Task-32-Triennium-2016-2018-1.pdf., as accessed on 23 September 2020

Leah Burrows (2018). Agricultural Fires Can Double Delhi Pollution during Peak Burning Season, Harvard John A. Paulson School of Engineering and Applied Sciences, 30 March 2018. Available at https://www.seas.harvard.edu/news/2018/03/agricultural-fires-can-double-delhipollution-during-peak-burning-season, as accessed on 23 September 2020

Moonmoon Hiloidhari, Dhiman Das, and D.C. Baruah (2014). Bioenergy Potential from Crop Residue Biomass in India, Renewable and Sustainable Energy Reviews, 32: 504-512.

Niveta Jain, Vinay Kumar Sehgal, Sanjay Singh and Nirmala Kaushik (2018). Estimation of Surplus Crop Residue in India for Biofuel Production, Technology Information, Forecasting and Assessment Council (TIFAC), New Delhi.

Niveta Jain, Vinay Kumar Sehgal, Sanjay Singh and Nirmala Kaushik (2018). Estimation of Surplus Crop Residue in India for Biofuel Production, Technology Information, Forecasting and Assessment Council (TIFAC), New Delhi.

Pratik Parija (2019). Delhi Pollution: Toxic Air in Delhi Fuelled by Rice Fields That India Doesnt Need, the Economic Times, 12 November 12, 2019. Available at https://economictimes.indiatimes.com/news/ economy/agriculture/toxic-air-in-delhi-fueled-by-rice-fields-that-indiadoesnt-need/articleshow/72016990.cms, as accessed on 23 September 2020

Rohan Fernando (2012). Cofiring High Ratios of Biomass with Coal, IEA Clean Coal Centre, 300, 194.

Siddharth Singh (2018). The Great Smog of India, Penguin Random House India Private Limited.

Sushruth Sunder (2018). India Economic Survey 2018: Farmers Gain as Agriculture Mechanisation Speeds up, but More R&D Needed, the Financial Express, 29 January 2018. Available at https://www. financialexpress.com/budget/india-economic-survey-2018-for-farmersagriculture-gdp-msp/1034266/, as accessed on 23 September 2020.

Index

❖ ❖ ❖ ❖ ❖ ❖